IF EVER TWO WERE ONE

The first [letter] ... darling,
written as ship starts for Crawfordsville, Indiana, Feb. 2, 1857, and
handed to me by Jennie Loring on
the same day.

[Copied Jan. 25, 1894.]

[Copied Feb. 3, 1894.]

(Received Mar. 17, 1857.)

A Private Diary of
Love Eternal

IF EVER TWO WERE ONE

KEPT BY

FRANCIS ELLINGWOOD ABBOT

1855–1903

Edited by Brian A. Sullivan

ReganBooks
An Imprint of HarperCollinsPublishers

Portrait of Frank Abbot, 1859; view of Hollis Hall; pages from diary of Frank Abbot courtesy of the Harvard University Archives.

Portrait of Katie Abbot, 1870; view of Fayal, Azores; view of Katie Abbot's empty chair, courtesy of Harvard Divinity School Special Collections.

Portraits of Frank Abbot, 1857–1903; all other images courtesy of Abbot descendants.

HarperCollins books may be purchased for educational, business, or sales promotional use. For information please write: Special Markets Department, HarperCollins Publishers Inc., 10 East 53rd Street, New York, NY 10022.

FIRST EDITION

Designed by Cassandra J. Pappas

Printed on acid-free paper

Library of Congress Cataloging-in-Publication Data has been applied for.

ISBN 0-06-056411-3

04 05 06 07 08 WBC/QW 10 9 8 7 6 5 4 3 2 1

To the untold love stories in
attics and archives everywhere

The Scroll

. . . Dear traveller by my side,
Dear sharer of my joys and hopes and fears,
My sorrows, burdens, dangers, toils, and tears,
Companion true and tried,
My comforter divine, my crown, my pride,
Sweet lifelong bride!
Through Time's long avenue of years,
How bright, how beautiful, how glorified
Thy Shining Path appears—
Footprints of living light that still abide,
And pave the past with stars!
Heaven's mark on thy brow!
Heaven's peace transcendent made thee without peers!
Angel of home wast thou!

FRANCIS ELLINGWOOD ABBOT, 1899

Contents

July 1, 1883. — This leaf is from the wreath of leaves laid on the coffin of my grandfather Larcom, and preserved by Mother under glass, in a black walnut frame. At the funeral of my dear Mother, June 28, 1883, by request of Emmie and Edwin, I carried this wreath to the cemetery at Beverly where we laid the precious dust, and placed it on her casket just before it was lowered into the grave; but previously I had taken this leaf, and Willie another, as a last memorial. For over twenty-one years Mother cherished fondly this memorial of her father; I lay it reverently here as a memorial of her.

Foreword

In a bundle of nineteenth-century letters in an archive at Harvard University—still tied with crimson ribbon—there is a passage, written in 1858 by twenty-one-year-old Frank Abbot to his fiancée, eighteen-year-old Katie Loring, in a lost language of love:

> Today a mere boy or girl, tomorrow a husband and wife, then two graves, lying side by side, I trust. One of us must in all human probability go first to that unknown land; but if we act toward each other as lovingly and as faithfully as we now both mean to do, that dreadful separation shall be robbed of its bitterest sting. Hope shall spring from the ashes of earthly happiness, and cheer the lonely heart of the one still destined to toil and suffer below.

Nearly fifty years later, Frank's prophesy came true. Before dawn on Friday, October 23, 1903, his heart—the one that was destined to "toil" below—stopped. Sometime after dusk the night before, the sixty-six-year-old poet and philosopher made a final pilgrimage to the Beverly, Massachusetts, burial place of Katie, his wife of thirty-four years. He placed a bouquet of flowers at her headstone, which was inscribed "She made home happy, and was all the world to her own," drank poison, and died. It was the tenth anniversary of Katie's death.

The official inquest into Frank's death noted that "several letters were found on his person giving his reasons for suicide and the same effects found at his residence at Cambridge."* In his book-lined study, Frank had pasted a duplicate of his farewell note onto a page of his diary. But the written evidence of the workings of Frank's heart did not end there: lovingly preserved were volume after volume of diaries, ledgers of poems, and hundreds of letters documenting a lifetime of his love for Katie. With extraordinary intensity, he recorded their youthful courtship in the Concord, Massachusetts, of Ralph Waldo Emerson and Henry David Thoreau, the triumphs and sorrows of their decades-long marriage, their separations caused by economic circumstances, the heartrending death of Katie in 1893, and in his final years, his unceasing yearning to rejoin her. Frank's inked passion reminds us of the eternal aspects of the human condition: if we live, we must love; and, eventually, we will lose what we love. On that topic, Frank once wrote "Sooner or later every soul must encounter grief, in some of its myriad shapes. All life is checkered with light and shades, success and failure, gain and loss, pain and pleasure, fear and hope, bliss and woe."†

After his death, as Frank had specified, he was laid to rest at the foot of Katie's grave, with this inscription on his marble memorial: "Love was the Light, Philosophy the Guide of his life."

There could be no more fitting epitaph for Francis Ellingwood Abbot, about whom a friend wrote "his mission was not so much to reform as to recast man and society, melting them first in the consuming furnace of his thought and love."‡ Born in Boston on November 6, 1836, to the educator Joseph Hale Abbot and the diarist Fanny Ellingwood Abbot, Frank entered Harvard College in 1855. In his journal, Frank recorded the rowdy life of a Harvard student in the nineteenth century—full of hazing and conviviality. In the fall of his freshman year, Frank wrote "It seems that all this 'fun' is of very low order, and if amusement cannot be found without destroying the property, and disturbing the quiet of others, the work of civilization is not yet complete."

*Medical Examiner's returns, Essex County, Massachusetts. Massachusetts State Archives.

†Sermon: "Bereavement," December 16, 1865. Abbot papers, Harvard University Archives.

‡Eulogy by George Chaney. *Christian Register,* 1903, p. 1359.

On January 17, 1857, however, the young man's life, and his diary, changed forever when he wrote:

> I went to a party at Mrs. Dana's, ten days ago, and was introduced to Miss Kate Loring, a most charming and lovely girl . . . I danced with her twice or three times, and found her very pleasant and well-informed, and very lady-like. I thought of her all night—instead of going to sleep. If there ever was a fool, his name was Frank Abbot.

Blissful weeks of companionship followed, and by month's end Frank and Katie were engaged to be married. Born on October 18, 1839, to David and Susan Frost Loring, Katie was described as a "fine scholar" with large gray eyes who was "always loving and sympathetic."* In her Concord youth, she was apparently a "great pet" of Ralph Waldo Emerson, whose daughters Edith and Ellen were her friends. David Loring was heard to have said "I don't believe Mr. Emerson knows whether you belong to him or me."

Only weeks after they met, Frank and Katie encountered the first of a series of unwanted distances that would take place throughout their courtship and marriage. Luckily for us, these separations generated both detailed diary entries as well as heartfelt correspondence overflowing with delicious nuances and gentle flirtation. Although the letters do not enjoy a perfect one-to-one correlation in number and content (Frank appears to have written more letters than reticent Katie, and their letters often crossed in the post), the exchanges are wonderfully indicative of the lost eloquence of Victorian courtship. The letters of Frank and Katie are a testament that the records of human emotion, no matter the age in which they were produced, are forever compelling.

In the decades that followed Frank and Katie's marriage in 1859, he experienced careers as a Unitarian minister, an advocate for "Free Religion" (a doctrine free of historical tradition and authority), a tutor to Harvard students, and a writer on philosophical topics. In these pursuits, Frank did not find sustained success. In life with Katie, however, he found

*Memoir of Susan Loring, 1898. Abbot papers, Andover-Harvard Theological Library, Special Collections.

strength and stability, and on February 9, 1894, several months after he had lost her, he confided to his diary that "her soul was the violet of my home."

As the century came to a close, in sorrow and longing, Frank sought "every trace of her angel-flight through this world" and reaped a nostalgic harvest of commemorative artifacts that represented Katie. Pasted on the blank end pages of his College Journal was a lock of her youthful hair, prairie flowers she had picked in 1859, lilies of the valley from her funeral casket in 1893, and a tiny piece of pine from an 1857 woodpile stacked in the parlor where they courted. No object was too humble to have profound significance to him.

Still, for a man who recorded so much of the love that he once knew, Frank lamented that he had not done enough. In 1901 he wrote "O that I could say in words what I knew her to be! If I could only say it, in verse or prose, all the world would weep for her."

But Frank did say it in words—through diaries, letters, and verse. During an 1895 pilgrimage to Concord, a place "once so luminous with love," he wrote "The Living Flower," a poem that celebrated his union with Katie.

> For who that love can ever forget
> The hour when first their kisses met,
> The hour when first, no more alone,
> Two souls became forever one?
> For him, in love alone was bliss—
> For him, there was no love but this!
> So love made two forever one!

From youth to old age, Frank Abbot was the archivist of his heart, and there are clues of the intentions he had for his chronicle of Katie—a testament that begins with a warning and ends with a sanction. In 1855 Frank began his college diary: "If this volume should fall into the hands of any one to whom I have not myself entrusted it, I beg him at once to lay it down, and, if he cannot return it, to destroy it entirely . . ."

In 1899, however, as Frank approached old age, it seems that he hoped for an audience after all. In a faded envelope among his papers, nestled with a review of the publication of the love letters of Robert

Browning and Elizabeth Barrett Browning by "E.S.F" (who called the work "a beacon-light to all true lovers of all time"), is a note in Frank's hand: "I unreservedly approve the judgment of E.S.F. on this subject, and wish it to govern the action of my own children in publishing the letters of their parents and my own poems. The world can never outgrow the need of every such story of wedded love."*

In the spirit of Frank Abbot's consent, offered here is that story of wedded love. Is this antique love story relevant today? When is a love story not relevant?

On June 6, 1894, Frank asked his diary "Who knows what is going on in the human heart?" We do, because of the gift that Frank left for us in his study on that autumn day. In love and woe, his words defy mortality. Love may have been Frank's light, but recording that love was his mission. In 1898 he wrote "Nobody will ever care for these lines—they have done their work for me." Those lines survive, and Frank Abbot would like to tell us his story.

*Boston Evening Transcript, July 31, 1899.

still he found it not. At length he found a beautiful little garden, and the gardener let him into it. Here he saw three lovely flowers growing side by side; and he knew the middle one was the living _flower_. And he longed to pluck it, and place it in his breast, and cherish it dearer than all beside; but he had not asked the gardener. And now the young man wants to know _if it will do any good_ to ask the gardener — can he then have the flower?

I repeated my dream, with my head buried in my hands; and after I got through, I waited for an answer in the most agonizing suspense. At last she said, very softly, and very sweetly, —

"I HOPE SO!"

I felt my face twitch and my whole frame quiver with uncontrollable emotion, as I looked up, and, gazing into her eyes, said huskily —

"Do you mean that, Katie?"

"Yes, I do," said she, returning my gaze.

I caught her hand, and covered it with kisses; sprang up, and kissed the dear little mouth turned up to mine; and sinking on my knees with my head on her

PART I

"*This journal is meant to be a faithful mirror of my heart . . .*"

A

PRIVATE DIARY:

kept by

Francis Ellingwood Abbot,

from

August 30, 1855,

to

—⫶—⟩—(·⊙·)—⟨—⫶—

"A Private Diary"

"Know Thyself"

August 30, 1855

If this volume should fall into the hands of any one to whom I have not myself entrusted it, I beg him at once to lay it down, and, if he cannot return it, to destroy it entirely; for in these pages I mean to write thoughts and feelings which no one but myself should know. My object is self-improvement; and I think one means to this end will be the faithful transcript of my thoughts and emotions, my hopes and fears, my sorrows and my joys.

On the 17th of last month, I was admitted to Harvard College free of conditions, and today I begin the first term of my freshman year, and, at the same time, a new era in my life. From this day I cease to be a burden upon my father, because he is unable to give me a college education, and therefore I intend to carry myself through the four years of my studies on borrowed money. From this day, then, I am practically my own master, and henceforth I must rely on my own efforts for support and existence in this money-getting world.

Here then I am last, where I am no longer under the watchful supervision of my parents, and where I am to act for myself, and use my own judgement in many matters which seldom are referred to the decision of a mere boy. It will be a most useful school in some respects, as giving me self-reliance, and habits of prudence and economy which must be learned sometime. But the idea of being in debt will cause much uneasiness, and will weigh upon me a good deal. Truly, I have proved my desire for an education to be sincere, in thus incurring a debt of more than a thousand dollars to begin life with, which will require a year or two, or even three, to pay. It is a desire which I felt when I was too young to know what it really meant to "go to college." But, I now know the full value of the phrase, and would ten times make the sacrifice rather than forego my education.

September 23, 1855

I find college life very pleasant so far, and although there are some disagreeable things connected with living in college buildings, I should prefer to room here, if I were to choose again. The sophomores still keep up

Hollis Hall, Harvard University, where Frank Abbot lived, 1855.

the barbarous custom of "hazing," which renders the life of a freshman full of anxiety for his furniture, and everything else belonging to him. They have thrown brickbats and watermelon rinds into my room, and put my mattress on the floor, piled the chairs in the middle of the room, tossed my books round, locked my door and carried away the key, and then, to crown the whole, took my trunk which goes to Beverly by express every week containing my dirty clothes, and carried it up to the highest story of the building, where they hid it; and of course I was in great trouble when the express man came for it, but owing to the good nature of the man, at length I found it. Besides all this, they have thrown water on me several times. They have done much worse, however, to Billy Swan and others in my class. They entered his room in his absence, and tumbled everything together in the middle of the floor; reversed the places of his wash-basin and chamber-vessel, pouring into the former red and black ink, and dipping a good pair of pantaloons into the latter, rendering them unfit for use. It seems that all this "fun" is of very low order, and if amusement cannot be found without destroying the property, and disturbing the quiet of others, the work of civilization is not yet complete.

September 27, 1855

. . . Just now a sophomore put a cracker filled with some bad-smelling stuff into my key-hole, and it popped in, but I luckily put it out immediately; nevertheless the smell thereof offendth my nostrils. These are the delights of "College Life."

October 3, 1855

Before I began to study tonight, I called on Shurtleff and Cilley, and there I smoked a cigar, and played a game of cards. I think it is foolish and wrong for me to smoke, since my parents would not approve it, and I cannot afford to spend much money in tobacco; but I like it, and it is pleasant to smoke if others around are doing the same thing. I know that it is a lack of moral courage to be unwilling to deny myself, but I suffer conscience to speak in vain in this matter, as I do in so many others.

"This journal is meant to be a faithful mirror of my heart . . ."

5

There! Those d——d sophomores just popped through my keyhole another "infernal machine" in the shape of a quill filled with powder, but luckily it did not go off, but only fizzed and filled the room with the delicious perfume of burnt quill. A few minutes afterwards, one of the scoundrels climbed up, and pushed open my shutters violently, and then sneaked off. I should like to have his nose opposite my fist.

October 7, 1855

I have not had time until now to write an account of the supper given by the Freshmen of the Anonyma Society to the sophomores (who then leave it,) every year. When it was time to go, it rained very hard, and was as dark as pitch, so that it was favorable to our expedition after the meeting, which was against the college laws. John Gray called for me, and at half past seven we sallied forth in the Tartarean darkness en route to the Hunneman engine house in Church Street. We found the "fifteen" assembled in the lower part of the building, and the sophomores had already collected overhead. After waiting a few moments, we went up in a body, and were received with "deafening applause" by the sophs. At last order established, and Lee [son of Robert E. Lee], the President of the Society, introduced Pond, the orator of the evening. His speech was very good in its ideas, but not well expressed, and it was not appropriate to the occasion. Then, Gordon, the poet of the evening, was introduced to the meeting and of all the poetry I ever read and heard, his was preeminently the sappiest. Besides it was preposterously long, and most relieved did I feel when he concluded. Then Lee read the names of the newly-chosen members one by one, and we were obliged to get up and make a speech in acknowledgement of the honor conferred upon us in being elected to this most august association; and then, after making obeisance to a horrid grinning old idol stuck up on the President's desk, we signed our names to the constitution. My speech was as follows, as nearly as a I can recollect it:

"Gentlemen; you'd scarce expect one of my age to speak in public on the stage; and as there is a popular prejudice that when a man has nothing to say, he had better hold his tongue, I will content myself, (and you too, gentlemen,) with thanking you for the honor you have done me by electing me a member of your society, and promising to do my best to be a worthy member."

When Duncan made his salutation to the old bust, he threw his arms affectionately round his neck, kissed the hideous old hob-goblin on the cheek, to the greatest amusement of the company; and afterwards every one did the same except Cutting. Gray kissed him on both cheeks. The officers, after the election of their successors, delivered up the insignia of their respective offices, and there we prepared to start on our spree. We went up in squads of half dozen to the omnibus stable near the Arsenal, where we re-assembled, and having filled three "ominibi," drove to Fresh Pond, to some hotel I know nothing about and there we safely got out, and piled in together in a room which one of the sophomores averred to be the ladies' sitting-room. After waiting for a long time, we at last marched up stairs, and took our seats at a couple of tables laden with good things. Gray sat at my right, and there at the end of the table, at Gray's side, sat the redoubtable Duncan, vice-president of the Society. Opposite to me were Lowell and Phillips, Ned Blagden's cousin. We did full justice to the supper, and ate of goose, duck, chicken, scalloped oysters, with the customary "fixins," and for dessert had pies, oranges, grapes, peaches, ice cream, etc., and cigars, of which I smoked one. But before we had finished eating, the waiters brought on bottles of champagne and, I believe, of sherry and other wines. I was very much surprised to see Duncan steadily refuse to drink anything but water, although, being vice-president, he was repeatedly pledged. Lee came up to me before he got tight, and told me he recognized me from my resemblance to my brother Henry, whom he had seen at West Point, as his father is superintendent of the Academy. Gray and I had agreed not to drink at the supper, but he changed his mind, and took a little, and this made me want to very much, but I had the courage not to. There were few fellows who did not drink; Duncan; Phillips, Ricketson, and myself, are all I can recollect who did not drink some. Bradford drank without limit, and yet did not get half so much fuddled as many who drank a good deal less. As time wore on, we got jollier and jollier, and sang songs appropriate to the occasion, joining in chorus and having a rousing good time. But by and by it began to be disgusting, although infinitely amusing, and very interesting to me, who had never seen a "frolic" before.

"This journal is meant to be a faithful mirror of my heart . . ."

———

7

Hauteville got stupidly drunk, and sat simpering with a most meaning-less expression, calling out, "I want to fight! I want to fight!" "By G——d!" "Gentlemen!" screamed Bradford, who was only rendered more lively and excited by wine, "Hauteville wants to fight! To fight, gen-tlemen!" and he pointed to the weak, silly face of the poor fellow, who only simpered more.

"Gentlemen!" cried some one at the bottom of our table, "A toast: The class of '58! May they always beat their enemies as they beat us on the foot-ball ground!"

"Hurrah! Hurrah!! Hurrah!!!" rang thro' the hall, and Lee got up, and roared,

"And may the class of '59 always fight as they fought on the foot-ball ground!"

Again the loud and hearty cheers rang and re-echoed through the whole length of the room.

"Lee! a song! a song!" cried twenty voices at once, and Lee got up and said:

"Gentlemen, I only know one song, and that is very smutty."

"Let's have it! Let's have it!" answered they, so Lee gave it; he had not belied it in calling it "smutty." Thus they kept it up, until Gray spoke to me, and asked me if I did not want to go home. I told him yes, and we went down stairs. Here we found others were going, and that an om-nibus would start presently; pretty soon Lee came down, swearing at every step, and told all those who were going, to stand on his right.

"You going? And you? G——d——you, what do you want to go for? One, two, eight, sixteen—sixteen can go. Here bring up your omnibus." And he stood out in the rain, giving everyone a push with his mighty fist, perfectly good natured all the time, and then slammed the door to, and roared to the driver to go along. Goodwin was there, ferociously tight, and Murdoch, affectionately tight.

October 11, 1855

Yesterday I went to Greek recitation at 12 o'clock, leaving my door un-locked, because I had not yet had another lock put on, and the large door-key is unwieldy. While I was gone, sophs got in, tumbled my mat-tresses and bedclothes together in the middle of the room, piled all my chairs together in a heap, put my boots carefully on my pillows, stole my door-key, and my closet key after locking the door. I was quite wrathy, and looking round, discovered that half the slats of my bed were missing, so that, if not found, I could not use my bed until new ones were made. However, with the help of Billy's key, I opened my closet and there were the slats safe and sound.

October 14, 1855

A letter from Henry [Frank's brother] reached Beverly a little while ago, when we had no expectation of receiving one. Susie [Everett] also had one. Henry is now living outdoors, on his railroad survey from San Francisco to Vancouver. He enjoys it very much, he says. I wonder if he will be married when he comes home. My dear journal! I wish I could be sure no eye but mine will ever see these pages! Then would I write here things which I long to say, and which it will almost burst my heart to conceal; but so many accidents may occur by which this little book may pass from my hands, that I hardly dare to write my inmost feelings.

October 20, 1855

Professor Chase gave us a cut last Monday, at which I greatly rejoiced, because I went to Beverly after evening prayers to spend Tuesday, the first Exhibition this year, and had no lesson to learn for Wednesday morning. I had been looking forward to going home with great eagerness, and all day long I felt as nervous as I could be. At last the hour came, and off I packed for the omnibus, meaning to catch the 6 o'clock train; but the 'bus went so slow that I got out at Chambers Street, and by dint of running, arrived just in time. When I got to Beverly depot, I heard Stanley's whistle, who had come down to see me home safe, and to give me his mighty protection. They were all very glad to see me, and we passed a very pleasant evening. Edwin read one of Galt's novels for about an hour.

"This journal is meant to be a faithful mirror of my heart . . ."

Before I went to bed, I stole in Emmie's room, and we had one of our old chats in the dark. I went to bed about a quarter to eleven, and lay thinking over old times . . . I was awakened by hearing little Willie's voice in the next room, making Mother repeat "Jack and Jill," and other "melodies" . . .

October 27, 1855

This afternoon I walked through Vine Street by the Everetts' old house. Everything seemed nearly the same, and I felt a choking in my throat as I thought of the happy hours I used to spend there. There was the garden,

Frank Abbot, circa 1850.

just as it was when I helped Susie transplant her flowers, and where she and I used to pick cherries, and have our frolics together. There was her little back-room, where we sat together, my arm round her neck, and my heart was happy as mortal can be; and where I roguishly locked her and Frank Vaughn in the little closet, and kept them there till they begged to be let out. Then there was the parlor where I used to hear Susie play the piano, and, I knew not why, the tears started to my eyes at the sound of her dear voice. There, too, was the place, and it all rushed back with overpowering force, where stood the little sofa on which we sat in the dim twilight hours with my head resting on her bosom, and her arm thrown gently round my neck. How like a paradise did it seem then, and oh! how doubly now! Dear, dear Susie! If you knew the depth of the love I ever felt for you, and the more than brotherly tenderness I would gladly lavish on you, would you but suffer me. But no! It cannot be. My boyish dreams did indeed build bright castles in the air, whose brightness was all from you, and paint sweet pictures, of love without alloy.

November 6, 1855

Here I am at my table, twenty minutes past nine o'clock in the evening, the evening of my nineteenth birthday. Before I go to bed, I mean to write out my opinion of my own character, as honestly and truthfully as I can, which I shall seal and not open until my next birthday. I mean to do the same then, and see if I have improved. God grant I may!

1 8 5 6

January 1, 1856

For a few days past, there has been a splendid spectacle out-doors; it rained hard, and froze during the night, so that in the morning the sun lit up the trees as if they were robed in diamonds. I never saw so magnificent a pageant; the trees were perfectly covered, and the weather was so cold that the ice remained for several days without melting, glittering and flashing most graciously.

March 9, 1856

I did not write at all in my vacation, and spent nearly a fortnight, doing nothing of consequence, except reading considerable of Gibbon's *Rome*. I had intended to play guitar a great deal, but I was too indolent to learn anything new, and contented myself with thrumming over the few tunes I had already learned.

In the afternoon, Henry called at my room. He has come home to spend three or four weeks, and is going to be married immediately. His wedding day will be like that of my own funeral.

March 25, 1856

I went home again last Sunday, and we all went to church together; and this time we all sat in the same pew. Henry, on Sunday morning, while I was shaving, asked me to give up smoking as a favor to him, and I could not refuse him. It has grown a very hard thing to do, and if I do not break off now, I doubt if I ever shall. I am very fond of it, and already it is very hard not to take a cigar when it is offered me and it will soon be harder. However, I mean to give it up, since I have promised to do so. I told him I would tell him if I ever took it up again.

"This journal is meant to be a faithful mirror of my heart . . ."

April 12, 1856

On Wednesday, the second of April, 1856, Henry Larcom Abbot and Susie [Mary Susan Everett], in the presence of their assembled friends, plighted their mutual love, to continue till the hand of death shall separate them. Oh God! Wilt thou watch and guard them; wilt thou ever be to them a friend and father and will thou lead them through the journey of life in peace and happiness!

All the family, from Grandfather to Willie, were present in the wedding, to which none but relations were invited. Dr. Walker excused me from recitations, and was himself present. At about 12 o'clock the bride and bridegroom came down stairs, and Dr. Newell married them; then Dr. Walker made a prayer. About an hour afterwards, the guests dispersed; and we went in and dined with Cousin Susan. Soon after dinner we saw the appointed signal at Mrs. Everett's window, and we went over to see them till they started for Washington. It was sad enough for us who were left behind. At quarter four they set out, and I watched the retiring carriage with a heart desolate indeed. Before Susie left, she gave to mother for me, without my knowing it, the flower she wore in her hair; but I asked her for a flower from the little basket which hung over her head in the bay-window. Emmie gave it to me after she was gone.

What right have I to indulge such feelings as I do indulge? Yet this journal is meant to be a faithful mirror of my heart, and I know that these feelings form a too important part of my life to be omitted here. Therefore I will write them down though each word cuts like a keen dagger.

When I came back to my room, I could no longer control the emotions which till then I had pent up in my breast. I groaned, I tore my hair, I threw myself on my face in a paroxysm of agony which I hope to God it may not be my lot to go through again. Up to this day, it seemed a dream; I could not make it real to myself that I must lose forever my more than idolized Susie, who has been the subject of my reveries and fancies since I can remember. But after I was alone with my own soul, after she had gone, really gone, then it seemed as if the sun had been blotted from the heavens. Everything is so desolate, so dreary! This concealment is dreadful; it is terrible to be obliged to have a secret like this which I cannot tell to anyone, not even to Mother; to seem as though there were no hidden cause of uneasiness, when I am in despair.

[Penned in the margin is the following later entry.]

I shall never forget that day. Mother told me I looked pale and sick, which I attributed to sitting up late. She knew I always had a peculiar friendship for Susie, and was not surprised there when, unable to check myself wholly any longer, my eyes filled with tears and my lips quivered; but she recalled me to self-control by a look of gentle warning not to damp Henry's happiness by grief at losing my old friend. So I restrained my feelings by an effort which almost broke my heart. But in the solitude of my own room, I gave full vent to my anguish that afternoon. The agony of years seemed compressed into each moment, and I learned what grief was.

September 7, 1856

CAMBRIDGE, HARVARD UNIVERSITY, HOLLIS HALL 18

Here I am, once more settled in college at the commencement of my sophomore year. A bad head-ache prevented me from arranging the furniture in my room that night, but Cilley gave me a bed. It required some days to get in order. Monday night we had the annual football match, and here I am very much chagrined to say that the freshman beat us in one of the first three games. Many of our fellows thought they had pushed the ball home, and were taken by surprise when it was run up the other side of the field and sent "home."

October 11, 1856

Henry and Susie are going home tomorrow morning. They have stayed here four or five weeks, and Henry is summoned home again. Before I bade Susie good bye, I reminded her of her old promise that she would give me one of her curls, and claimed fulfillment of it. She evaded it, and seemed unwilling to give it. God grant me she does not suspect anything! She has seemed for some time back, ever since her engagement, more distant and reserved, and I fear she has divined my secret with the intuition of a true woman. How I have guarded my every word, look,

"This journal is meant to be a faithful mirror of my heart . . ."

13

and gesture, to avoid detection and how I have suffered in doing it, God only knows. Oh Susie, Susie! How I yearn and yearn and yearn, and am paid back with my own yearning.

November 5–6, 1856

It is a quarter to twelve, and I am waiting for the stroke of the midnight bell which will usher in the twenty-first year my life. Yes, in a few minutes I shall be twenty years old. And let me pause at the threshold of a new year, and think over the events of the last.

On the 6th of November last year, I wrote a description of my character as truthfully as I could, sealed it, and have not opened it till now. I am going to break the seal as soon as the bell strikes and see whether or not I have improved as I prayed I might. —I have broken it, and wait for the bell—there is the bell—

I have read it—the first reading of the first chapter of the Sermon on the Mount—and no increase in goodness! Nay, even a loss. It seems my aspirations are feebler than they were. Still wandering astray. God help me!

[In December 1856 during the winter vacation, Frank took a teaching position in Concord, Massachusetts. After his arrival, he wrote to his father, Joseph Hale Abbot.]

CONCORD, MASSACHUSETTS

December 24, 1856

Dear Father,

When I came to Concord, I did not expect to be able to go to Boston at all, but I find that my school, or rather academy, as it is called here, gives me very little trouble in the matter of government. The scholars are all more well-behaved than is usual in the country; some of them from a considerable distance . . . Two of Mr. [Ralph Waldo] Emerson's children attend the school, and they are the most interesting pupils I have . . . I board at Mrs. Thoreau's, who is the mother of Henry Thoreau, somewhat known for his writings. She is a very motherly kind of person, and he is very entertaining to converse with. Last night I called on Mr. Emerson with Mr. Sanborn, and was very much pleased with his manners. He is a perfect gentleman and received me very cordially. He had evidently heard of me before probably through his children, and invited me to call again. Mrs. Emerson I did not see, but all his children were at home, and they were quite entertaining. It seems a very genial home and they are all very cordial.

I am rather sad that the poet [William Ellery] Channing is not staying in Concord now; for I had some curiosity to see him. Mr. [Amos Bronson] Alcott, also, I should have been glad to meet, but he has been living away from Concord some years, and there is no likelihood of his crossing my path.

The first week I was here, Belinda Randall was staying at Miss Elizabeth Hoar's, and I was invited there to tea to meet her. By mistake I went to Rockwood Hoar's house, and was received with perfect politeness. I sat there waiting for my entertainers to appear, and did not discover my error till supper-time. But I did not lose my self-possession at all, and Miss Hoar told me afterwards that I had made more friends than I was aware of . . .

Yours affectionately, Frank

December 25, 1856

Here I am in the good town of Concord keeping "academy"; but I will describe my situation at some time when I feel more inclined to. At present, I wish to record a conversation between Henry David Thoreau, Mr. Ricketson, and myself.

MR. RICKETSON: We went to Baker Farm yesterday through all the snow, Mr. Abbot; perhaps you recollect the description of Baker Farm in *Walden*.

MR. ABBOT (greatly confused and overwhelmed with a sense of his own ignorance): I regret to say that I have never met the book, although I have been desirous to see it.

MR. RICKETSON: What! Never read *Walden*! Dear me, let me show you this passage: (quotes) "My way led through Pleasant Meadow, an adjunct to the Baker Farm, that retreat of which a poet has since sung, beginning,—

> 'Thy entry is a pleasant field.
> Which some mossy fruit trees yield
> Partly to a ruddy brook,

"This journal is meant to be a faithful mirror of my heart . . ."

———

15

By gliding musquash undertook
And mercurial trout
Darting about'

MR. ABBOT: (mentally ejaculating): Heaven help us!

MR. RICKETSON: Those are fine lines, but our friend Channing rather disregards grammar—"undertook"—bad, very bad.

MR. THOREAU: The grammar is no objection, poets are not hampered like other men. It is not mere rhyme and grammar that make poetry; a machine might be made to turn out poetry of that kind very easily, but it would not be poetry.

MR. RICKETSON: Why not? I think it would.

MR. THOREAU: What! Would it be poetry?

MR. RICKETSON: Yes, poetry is like architecture, you have to build in certain ways, and it makes no difference whether the machine does it intelligently, or whether the poet does it by following his metres and feet.

MR. THOREAU: But—

MR. RICKETSON (interrupting): I see you do not like my argument— ha!ha!

MR. ABBOT (aside): No wonder he doesn't.

MR. RICKETSON:—but I understand you, yes, I understand you. But grammar is necessary.

MR. THOREAU: Channing writes ideas, and disregards all such trammels. Poets must be original.

MR. ABBOT: (aside) Channing is original in his grammar, at least.

MR. THOREAU: They must not try old, hackneyed measures, they must leave the old jingle and invent their own rhythm.

MR. ABBOT: Do you mean to say that every poet must invent new metres?

MR. THOREAU: Yes. Unless he does, we are reminded of some other verses, and the charm of originality is lost. Wordsworth in his 'Laodamia,' and 'Ode to Immortality,' and even Campbell, in his battle odes, adopt their peculiar measures, and thereby avoid the monotonous jingle of other poets.

MR. ABBOT: Why, you value the casket at the expense of the jewel that it contains. Poetry does not depend upon the length of the lines, nor the different intervals at which the rhymes occur; the essence of poetry is, that beautiful ideas should be beautifully expressed.

MR. THOREAU: You seem to consider rhythm arbitrarily.

MR. ABBOT: Certainly, to a degree it is arbitrary. The poet can select his metre as he pleases: if his work is well done, it will seem to us best adapted to the measure in which it is written, whereas he might have used another, and still have been equally successful. I think Milton made a mistake in writing *Paradise Lost* wholly in the same stately style; a long poem needs variety, and Scott well understood this.

MR. THOREAU: I must still differ; a poet must be not only original in his ideas but also his rhythm; otherwise he is only an imitator, and cannot lay claim to the name of a true poet. There is endless variety in rhythm; and there is no need that one poet should slavishly follow the track of another.

MR. RICKETSON (evidently bewildered in his understanding faculties): Well, I suppose that is the way you philosophers think; but you breathe a higher air than our feeble lungs can endure.

MR. ABBOT (aside, with great inward disgust, and dissent from the last remark): Fiddle-stick's end! Mutual admiration! Thoreau, Thoreau! That man of facts and metaphysics! Stick to thy facts and metaphysics.

Evening. I have spent a quiet day, alone, reading and writing. Among other things I wrote to Mr. [William Cullen] Bryant, the poet, and expressed the pleasure I have always derived from his poems.

December 28, 1856

It is a beautiful Sabbath morning as I look out my window, I see the bright light of the sun streaming over the snow-clad hills, arraying all nature in a robe of beauty. How calm and tranquil everything seems! Is it imagination only that there is a peculiar repose in the woods and hills on Sabbath?

The river is bound fast in its wintry fetters, and I can trace its path by the grayish-blue ice that hides its stream. Beyond rise the dark-brown, naked woods, and between are the meadows, not yet so deeply wrapped in their snowy mantle as to prevent the faded grass from peeping through. And there is a little clump of evergreens, the memorial of the

"This journal is meant to be a faithful mirror of my heart . . ."

fair summer, when all was green and lovely. Why is not the winter as charming as the summer? To me it imparts as keen a pleasure as the soft green grass and delicate flowers of its younger sister. Nature is always beautiful, the cold, and bleak hills of January, the fresh young blossoms of May and June, the dark, glossy green of August, and the magnificent pageantry of October. I love and admire them all. And may the day never come when their beauties fail to awaken the glow of pleasure in my bosom.

1857

January 7, 1857

I am teaching school. Salary, $45.00 per month; length of term, 15 weeks; branches taught by myself, Latin, Greek, Geometry, Shakespeare, Plutarch, Composition, Declamation. I board at Mr. John Thoreau's, known to fame only as father of Henry D. Thoreau. Enjoy it pretty well, work easy. There! So much for my whereabouts. I am not going to write every little confounded particular of my daily life in this book; I shall keep this as a record of what really is my life. I intend to disregard the shell of the nut and stick to the kernel; that is, if I can reach the kernel. Possibly, after the shell is broken, the kernel may be withered up. Who knows? Not I.

I spent New Year's Day at Cambridge . . . and I sat up to welcome 1857. The tutors were making asses of themselves by watching that poor old Rebellion Tree; we were enjoying ourselves indoors at their expense. A few moments before 12 o'clock, Jack How proposed that we should all keep silence until 1857. We agreed to. Just at the moment I began to cough the same old cough that was once so familiar to me, and I have been coughing ever since. If I was superstitious, I should be alarmed; as it is, my imagination is unduly excited, and though I ought to know better, torments me with the strangest fancies. As these whims are a part of my experience, I don't see why I should not write some of them down.

I got through the year 1856, [and] as it ended, I began to cough the old consumptive wheezing I had once, I am perfectly aware that this is ridiculous, and should not have noticed the coincidence if my mind had not been filled with thoughts of death lately. I never feared death, and do not know or understand that shrinking from it which so many profess. Pain has always seemed to me an infinitely more dreadful object to contemplate. But I do not wish to die till I have fulfilled my destiny; I feel as if I should one day become a poet, and do not like [to] die before that time. I love too strongly to be willing to part from these I love, and I know well, that there are some who would grieve for me, unworthy as I am. . . . I am taking all sorts of old women's remedies at the suggestion of the good folks of the [Thoreau] house; but of course they cannot injure me, or I would not touch one of them.

January 17, 1857

Well, old boy! Your cough still hangs on, and it has gained me much kindness among the good folks of the place. I went to a party at Mrs. Dana's, ten days ago, and was introduced to Miss Kate Loring, a most charming and lovely girl; she seemed to feel so much compassion for me, alone and sick, among perfect strangers, that I was really very much touched by it. I danced with her twice or three times, and found her very pleasant and well-informed, and very lady-like. I thought of her all night—instead of going to sleep. If there ever was a fool, his name was Frank Abbot.

Last Sunday evening, January 16, Mrs. Dana met me at the booksellers, she asked me to stay to tea. When I met Miss Katie, she gave me such a warm pressure of the hand that I trembled all over with pleasure. I then found that she was not going to the lecture, and Mrs. Dana told me my cough ought not to let me go; she wanted me to stay and keep her and Katie company. I was only too glad to stay.

Katie is apparently seventeen or eighteen, small and slightly made, and to me very beautiful; rather pale, with hazel eyes and that peculiar kind of light hair, that I would not know whether to call light or dark. She seemed so gentle and refined, so pure and amiable, that I felt an involuntary reverence towards her, if not a tender feeling. Katie is in my head the whole while, and I cannot bear to think of never seeing her again. I hope it is not vanity when I think she feels a peculiar interest in

"This journal is meant to be a faithful mirror of my heart . . ."

me. She is certainly a sweet and lovely girl, but I am not in love with her yet. I ought not to meet her, I suppose, but I cannot help seeking opportunities to do it; she is going out West with her father soon, but not to live; she will live nearer Boston than Concord is, when her father gets settled. It is very foolish, but I cannot keep my thoughts away from her, she is so beautiful. Probably it is only a temporary liking; but if I were to be with her a great deal, it would soon be something more. If I thought she could ever get to love me, I think I would be satisfied with her love. I would write poetry and get fame and money, and should delight to lay my laurels at her feet. My air-castles are always of domestic happiness; an attached and idolized partner, smiling children, and a happy fireside. That sweet face haunts me, I write about it now because I am thinking about it now; if the next time I take up my pen, I am thinking of something else, then I shall build no more air-castles like this. But I mean this diary to be merely a record of just these fancies and hopes, these cares and sorrows, that, when I am an old man (if I ever am one) these pages may bring back the days of youth, when every feeling partakes of the nature of excess, and every impulse is violent.

Katie Loring, 1857.

I used to disbelieve in that sanguine fire of youth which we read in books, but I am no longer a skeptic. The past two or three months have altered my whole character; freedom from the weight which crushed my very soul, has made me as I was meant to be, impetuous, hopeful, and foolish. Youth is brief and sorrow dogs us always; I'll please my imagination if I can please neither my intellect, nor my heart, nor my conscience. I will love my friends, I will forget everything in the vortex of the affections, and if ever the day of reckoning comes, as come it will, then will be the time to despair. I am not a Christian, but I know it too well; I am not a wise man, I know that better; I am not a good man, I know that best of all. So while the sun shines, I will forget the night—which is hurrying on so fast, and—oh I wish I had died when I was an innocent child.

Kate, Kate, Kate! My silly head will let nothing else in. Dear Kate! I cannot help it; "Tis better to have loved and lost, Than never to have loved at all!" Oh did I ever look into those beautiful eyes, and fancy I could read there either pity or regard? If I am again to suffer all the frightful pangs of unsuccessful love, may my cough prove fatal! Whatever happens to me, may happiness be your lot, sweet, gentle, Katie! I would I might forget you, or else win your love. How happy that would make me! Oh what a fool, what a fool, what a fool!

11:00 o'clock, P.M.

I am just returned from Mrs. Dana's, where I have spent the most delightful evening I can recollect. Sweet Katie Loring was there, and I drank delicious poison the whole evening. They got me to read aloud, and consequently the time flew fast to me; the book was Bryant's poems—oh may that prove a good omen! I know she likes me, perhaps she loves me, or may love me; she is not rich, thank God, so that we are equal there. Her father was well off, but has lost his property, and now, at the age of sixty, has to begin life anew. Oh that were I out of College! The fever is gaining, and I know not whether it will be cured or not.

January 19, 1857

I do not know that I am really in love; certainly I am strongly attached, and it is possible I mistake one of my ardent friendships for a tendered feeling. But I can not think of anything or anybody five minutes, without seeing that sweet face before me; I cannot help contriving plans to win her. To think of losing her forever! Oh it is too much to bear. How I hope her father will not stay out West! He has relations in Indiana, and it is possible that he may. If he does, shall I not have to despair? Dear, sweet, lovely, Katie! You could never find one who would understand you better, or love you more truly; you are so quiet and gentle that few would suspect how much is hidden from view. But those dear eyes set me wild with hope and longing, oh must I secure your love. God help me, or shall I be crushed indeed. I never thought to meet another girl so refined and gentle as Susie, but I have, and I must love. At any rate, I no longer

"This journal is meant to be a faithful mirror of my heart . . ."

———

love Susie as I ought not, and do love Katie as I may without sin. Oh my Father! Take pity on me now.

11:00 P.M. Sunday

Yesterday Katie invited me to sit in her father's pew in church. This morning therefore I went in good season, although the thermometer was −14° Fahrenheit. Only Susie Loring came to church, although I had hoped to meet Katie. The church was very cold, and after escorting Susie home, I made pretence of warming my feet to call on Mrs. Dana. As I hoped, she would not hear of me going home, and I saw Katie in her room, I was not hard to be persuaded. I found the reason she had not been to church was, that she had dropped a soapstone upon her foot, and was severely hurt. The poor girl suffered terribly with it, but smiled as sweetly as ever, and did not utter a word of complaining. My heart ached so to see her pain that I felt almost faint; but she concealed it as well as she could; and when I could not help expressing my pity in my face, she would smile upon me so sweetly that my heart beat thump, thump against my breast. She evidently likes me, but does not suspect, I think, how much I like her.

I offered to read aloud to her, and she accepted my offer with pleasure; I read Milton: the 'Lycidas,' 'Hymn of the Nativity' (omitting, of course, in one place) and some of the other shorter pieces. I found her well-acquainted with him, and she could repeat whole passages; her taste is exquisite. Mrs. Dana would not let me go to church, it was so cold, nor home to supper; I compromised by not eating supper at all. But before this, poor Katie had gone up stairs, unable to bear the pain longer; and I offered again to read to her, after her foot was dressed. So when the rest went to supper, I was delighted to be told by Jenny Loring that Katie would like to have me come and read to her. So up I went, and during the evening read the *Deserted Village, Traveller, Morte D'Arthur* and "May-Queen" of Tennyson, extracts from Bryant, Longfellow, etc., etc.; and all the while she lay on the sofa, as pale and as beautiful as a statue. Her hair had fallen down about her shoulders, and there never was a lovelier girl than she in God's world.

Now and then she would repeat some exquisite thing or other, and she displayed admirable taste. Her favorites were the same as mine, and her favorite pieces were mine; nor did I mention them first. Was there ever a voice so musical or clear? Oh I love her dearly.

When I left her room, I stopped at Mrs. Dana's, and she was so kind and sympathizing that in the fullness of my heart I could not but tell her my secret. She was not surprised, but said that she suspected it before; that she was no match-maker, and when she invited me to her room, she had no suspicion of such an attachment springing up, but had perceived it. She said so many kind things that I felt very grateful to her; I left her at about half past ten, and walked home in a violent snow-storm, the wind roaring fiercely round me, and the cold being intense. The die is cast, I cannot live without the darling girl. Is not it ungenerous to repay her pity and regard with this love of mine? And still her eyes seem to express a very strong degree of regard, and may not God turn this into love?

Quarter to 12 o'clock. I have just come back from Mrs. Dana's. Last night did not go to bed till between 1 and 2 o'clock. The storm was fearful all night, the wind roared furiously round the house, and the snow formed in huge drifts, so that this morning very few of my scholars were present. All day the same, sweet suffering face was before my eyes, and I so yearned to be with its sweet, suffering owner. And I sat and thought the matter over, and I do truly believe that I love Katie well enough to choose her for my life-long partner. After supper, waded through the drifts, for the storm still continued, [to Katie's]. Poor thing! She was really sick with the pain, and my own heart felt a pang every time she winced. She was lying on a couch in Mrs. Dana's room, and her two sisters were there too. After I had read as much as I thought she would like to hear of John's book, she seemed to suffer so much that I did not offer to read more. I say seemed, for she did not utter a word of complaint the whole evening. Whenever she was free from pain, she was smiling as gaily as the rest, and would not allow her own suffering to dampen the mirth of others. Now I felt my heart beat within me! At last her father came in, and told her it was time for her to go to bed, and she went off up stairs as well as she could, but not without bidding me a pleasant good-bye.

"This journal is meant to be a faithful mirror of my heart . . ."

When she had gone, I had quite a talk with Mrs. Dana, and she spoke to me as she would her own son; I feel very grateful to her. She told me that it was necessary for Katie's health that she go out West; and if so, may she go as soon as possible! There is no danger of her staying there forever, thank Heaven, but only for a short time. Before she goes, I must and will speak to her father, and ask his permission to love his daughter. I will tell him frankly I am poor, but have an honest heart and willing hands, and that I love his daughter more than all the world beside; that I am energetic by nature, and with such a prize in view as Katie's love, would move heaven and earth. I will tell him—why, who could not be eloquent then? And he must, he will let me have her, for how can I live without her?

When I came home, Mrs. Dana led me to the door, and as soon as she closed it almost, I fell upon my knees in the snow, and looking up at Katie's window, then perfectly dark, cried with a heart sincere and true, as I believe, "Oh God! May she be happy, what ever happens to me! If she will be happy with me, oh God, may she marry me; but if not, oh my Father, let her not marry even if it tears my heart to pieces!" And the beautiful stars looked down on me, and I felt calmer. More than once before I reached home did that prayer go up from my breast. God bless her, oh God bless her!

January 20, 1857

11¼ o'clock. Another evening of delight. After school in the afternoon, I went straight to Mrs. Dana's, and was very glad to find Katie's foot better. When the rest went to supper, I was left alone with Kate, and I would have given worlds to be able to tell her how I loved her; but of course I did nothing of the sort. The time we were alone, in the dim twilight, with the red sunset sky glowing through the window, all seemed too short to me.

January 22, 1857

Last night I spent as usual with Mrs. Dana and my darling girl. Oh how I love her! After I got back, instead of writing her, I wrote eight pages to

Mother, in answer to a most touching letter from her; in it I gave her a short history of my love. I wait an answer eagerly.

Tonight I went right after school and found Katie and [her sister] Susie alone. We had a delightful talk in the twilight together, and more from the heart than ever before; of course not of love. Mrs. Dana got me to give her my manuscript book of poems to show them to Katie, and as I went in, I saw the book open before her. I can scarcely write, my hand trembles so; surely there is no doubt in my own mind now, that I love her as a wife should be loved.

This evening I read the first two cantos of *Childe Harold*, and under pretence of being nearer the light, Katie moved from her seat in the corner, and placed herself on the couch nearer the table, close to me. Her foot does not trouble her so much, and she looked so lovely that I was half mad with love. I know she loves me, but whether it is more than sisterly love, I do not know. God grant it may be!

After I got through reading, we sat laughing and chatting together, Jennie playfully pulling down Katie's hair, and it fell beautifully around her shoulders.

There! I am better now; I could not write any longer, I had to walk up and down the room. I have never been so moved before, I never loved Susie half so vehemently as I see it now. I loved her with all a boy's affection, but this is man's one love, I know. Great God in Heaven! Take pity on me, and spare the agony of losing my loved one!

As Katie's beautiful hair at random lay upon her shoulder, I ventured to request a lock of it, and half in sport, half in earnest, called for a pair of scissors.

"Do you want some?" asked Jennie, turning to me smiling.

"Yes," I said, very quickly, as the possibility of a lock flashed over me. Katie laughed.

"Do you really want a piece?" again asked Jennie, taking a pair of scissors.

"Yes, indeed, I do," I replied with my heart in my mouth; and perhaps in my face, for Katie gave me such a smile, and glance of her heavenly eyes, that I felt bewildered with love and tenderness. Oh that meaning eye of hers! Surely she loves me, for she made but a feint of resistance, and looked at me so tenderly and lovingly. I am all on fire; the lock of hair that Jennie cut for me, is now before me; and I have kissed it

"This journal is meant to be a faithful mirror of my heart . . ."

———

25

You have my whole heart now and forever. Katie.

(11th the gift of a gold watch chain, on our
Silver Wedding.)

Dear Frank, – That the links of this chai
prove as strong and lasting as the links of the
chain that has bound us together so long, is th
of your loving wife and children.
Aug. 3, 1884.

From the casket in the study bay.
October 26, 1893.

My sister Emily brought the
of the valley, and my daughter
laid them beside the dear stil
The violets I laid myself on t
der bosom that had never ce
before to throb with love for
These perishing memorials
imperishable love are placed
on the thirty-seventh annive
of the day when we first con
that love to each other,
January 25, 1894.

Kaleidoscope.

A lovely girlish head,
   With falling tresses fair
Over the shoulders spread,
And wondrous eyes that said,
"I love you!" All is fled!
   Alone with a lock of hair!

A sweet wife's honored head –
   Oh, sweet beyond compare! –
And happy eyes that shed
Heaven's light on me, and said
"I love you!" All is fled!
   Alone with a lock of hair

A mother's dying head,
   In grief and voiceless pray
Bowed on my heart of lead,
And holy eyes that said,
"I love you!" All is fled!
   Alone with a lock of hair

March 13, 1894.

Katie Long's Hair,
cut for me by Jennie,

and clutched it to my heart again and again since I came home. Oh the agony of loving!

January 24, 1857

Last night I read the last two cantos of *Childe Harold*, except the last twenty stanzas of the fourth. After I went there, immediately after school, I was left alone with Katie for some time, and had a delightful conversation. I was talking of college life, and said that there was really that romance and cordial feeling which is spoken of sometimes as merely imaginary.

"Yes," said she, "I suppose it really exists for some; but perhaps it is not so for everybody. Probably it depends wholly on the character of the student."

"Certainly," I answered, "it is possible to walk blind in the Garden of Eden."

"But those are happy who learn to open their eyes," said she, gently.

"Happy, indeed," said I, thinking of my dear friend Will.

There was a basket of [wood] chips lying by the stove, and in continuation of a joke we had had together before, I asked her if I should not pick her out a nice clean chip for a spoon.

"No," said she, "I hate chips."

"Notwithstanding, we find a great many in good society," I replied, laughing.

"It is best we should," she answered, "for then we learn to prize the ebony by comparison."

"True," said I, "yet we weary of seeing the pine too often; we cannot love the chips."

"The chips are not to be pitied," she said, gravely, "they do not know what happiness is; they cannot appreciate the ebony."

"Yet they are not so much to be pitied," said I, "as those who can appreciate the ebony, yet find only the pine."

"That is not quite the case," answered she, "there is some ebony everywhere."

"Yes, but we are not fully satisfied with only a little, we must find more than a little ebony before we can forget the pine."

"This journal is meant to be a faithful mirror of my heart . . ."

"Do you not love to lie under the pines in summer, and hear the wind moaning above your head?" asked she.

"Very much," I answered, "but it is because it makes me remember the distant sea."

"Then the pine has its use, has it not?" said she, with a pleasant smile.

"Yes, truly," answered I, "but though we lie under the pines, we think not of them. But of the ebony which we have not."

"Then we should not despise the pines," said she, sweetly, "since they teach us to prize the ebony at its true value."

Was not she in the right, and I in the wrong?

"Don't you love to build air-castles," asked she after a pause.

"Yes, dearly," I answered.

"Are they pleasant ones?"

"Sometimes, they are very pleasant."

"Were they pleasant?"

"Very pleasant," said I, so warmly that she looked up in surprise.

"I hope I do not disturb them; I should be sorry to dissipate such agreeable dreams."

"Indeed you do not," said I, sincerely.

"Don't you think they are the happiest who can build such air-castles?"

"They are both the happiest and most miserable."

"My day-dreams never make me miserable," said she.

"I am glad of it; but it is not well to build the same castle in the air too often; we get to regard it as if built on sure foundations, and grieve to see it melt away into nothing."

Just then the tea-bell rang; and as I do not take any supper, I told her not to stay there with me, but to go to the table. She laughed.

"I will leave you to build some more castles then." And she left the room.

Sure enough, I fell into a reverie, with my elbows on my knees and my head on my hands; and this was my dream:

A young man once walked by a lovely river, and looked on the beautiful scene with pleasure; but was not happy. His guardian spirit met him, and asked him why he was sad; but the gloomy man only sighed. His flowers were dead (so he thought).

"Go seek the living flower," said the angel; "when you find it, then will you be happy." And the spirit vanished from his sight.

So the young man girded up his loins, and went forth to seek the living flower. And he wandered far and wide, roamed through many a garden, and searched many a secret forest glade; but he found it not. Once he deemed he had it, but before he could pluck it, it melted into thin air. At last he spied three lovely flowers growing side by side in a small garden, and the gardener let him into his garden. Soon he knew that one of the flowers was the living flower, and his heart throbbed within him; but he lingered by the flowers, and delayed to ask the gardener if he might pluck the one he coveted. But at last— A light hand was laid upon my shoulder, and I suddenly started, and looked round. There in the dusky twilight stood Katie. She laughed.

"Well sir, you obeyed me, I see; and you lost yourself in your own castle. Did not you hear me come in?"

"No, I was musing too deeply. You must have come softly."

"Not at all; I made a good deal of noise. Perhaps you do not thank me for knocking down your airy mansion."

"Perhaps it was best it should be knocked down, after all. I did not know I was so absent minded."

"Nor I either," said she, laughing merrily, "you must be a true day-dreamer."

"Not so; for I am never content with my day-dreams; if they do not become more than day-dreams, I am not happy. And my day-dreams are all the same kind."

"So are everybody's, I suppose; mine are."

"Some of them have faded, and some of them have become founded on a rock; I ought not to complain."

"Do you think your present air-castle will fade or flourish?"

"It does not depend on me to tell; but I hope—and fear."

"Well, I wish you success," said she, with another merry laugh.

So ended our colloquy; for just then in came Susie, and for the time being we put an end to our long allegorical conversation, of which I have been able to record but a small part.

"This journal is meant to be a faithful mirror of my heart . . ."

———

9½ o'clock P.M.

I can now write more of that same allegorical strain which I have written above. I went right after dinner, and found Katie alone, but soon Susie came in and we conversed on indifferent topics. At last she went to put more wood into the stove, and I of course went to do it for her; but she sat down on the floor before the stove, and amused herself with letting the draught draw in little bits of pine wood, while I sat down near.

"What attraction can that hot fire have for those little chips?" said she, at last.

"The same that a burning candle has for a moth, perhaps," I answered, smiling.

The pine chip, Katie Loring's gift
to Frank Abbot, 1857.

"But the moth need not fly into the flame."

"The candle cannot help shining bright and beautiful, neither can the poor moths help being dazzled by it."

There was a short pause, and then she said—

"We could not kindle the fire without the chips; there is another use of the pine."

"True; the pine kindles easily, burns readily, and consumes quickly; but the ebony burns with a stronger, more lasting flame."

She picked up a little bit of pine, and handed it to me with an unutterable expression in those soul-like eyes of hers.

"I will give you this pine chip; if I had the ebony, I would give you that."

With a thrill in my every nerve, I received her little gift, and only said—

"The ebony does not know it is ebony, and mistakes itself for pine; but those who see the two, do not make that error."

"The varnished pine can look so like ebony that it is often mistaken for it."

"Not by those who seek the ebony sincerely and wisely. There is no glow in the west tonight, as there was last evening at this time; why should there not always be a beautiful sunset?"

"Because we should cease to love it, if it came too often."

"But this should not be so; the good man never tires of goodness—why should the lover of beauty ever tire of beauty?" I asked.

"We cannot say why, but do we not feel it to be the case?"

"I am afraid I must admit it; but it is because we shut our eyes, and do not look at the loveliness around us."

"It might be worse if we had beauty round us always; then we might never open our eyes. Is it not better to see, although seldom, than to be forever blind?"

"Yes, truly."

"Mrs. Dana said that a boy and girl play together best when alone; is not this rather sober play?" (Susie had left the room some time before.)

"Yes, it is; but to me, at least, it is very pleasant play."

"What a splendid time this is to day-dream! Was your dream yesterday which I drove away, very pleasant?"

"Indeed it was; but it was not driven away by your coming. Sometime I will tell it to you."

"I hope it will be soon," she said very softly and gently.

"It shall be soon," answered I, warmly.

"If it is so very agreeable, I wish it success with all my heart."

"You cannot wish it success so warmly as I do. But there goes the bell, and I will not keep you."

"Well, I will go; but I hope you will finish your day-dream while I am away." So saying she left me.

When she was gone, I threw myself on my knees beside the couch which she has occupied so long, and prayed God sincerely and eagerly to grant me this crowning happiness of my life. And I had not risen from the attitude of my prayer before she returned; she saw me in the act of rising. At once she knew what I had been doing, and said very low and gently.

"I am sorry I came in so soon."

"Nay, I am very glad; I was only striving to make my air-castle a real castle."

"Whatever it is, I think it must prosper," she said, almost inaudibly.

For a long time we sat without speaking; but presently in came the rest, and before long we set to reading. I finished *Childe Harold*, and read elsewhere in Byron. But I left at quarter to nine, as Mr. Loring is unwilling

"This journal is meant to be a faithful mirror of my heart . . ."

31

to have the girls sit up after then. So saying, "Good night—to each and all light-slumbers and a happy heart!"

I left them. But I never leave the house without kneeling in the snow, and invoking a blessing on my dear, dear girl.

January 25, 1857

Sunday, noon. I went to church today, and while there, determined to delay no longer asking the most important question I shall ever ask on earth. But I must first speak to Mr. Loring, and as he does not go to church, I shall try to take a walk with him alone, and break my mind to him. Oh how I feel! If he should reject my suit, forbid me the society of her who is dearer than life, and thus take away my only happiness, how can I live! In this all-important step, I must not go alone, unaided; I will wrestle with God, plead with him, and ask his blessing, before I seek the permission of any human being—

Hear the prayer of thine unworthy child, and grant him this boon which he so ardently yearns for! Holy God! Make my supplication sincere—may my dearest one be blessed whether I have her love or not! But oh! May it be mine to make her happy! And if thou entrustest this priceless jewel to my hand, may I have strength to keep it safe and pure as when thou gavest it to me!

The time is slowly approaching; with what hope and terror do I count the moments! Before I write in this volume again, I suppose my doom will be sealed; and then I shall share either the happiness of Heaven, or the unutterable woe of Hell. Suspense is worse than all; let me read a chapter in the Bible, which I have neglected too long. I have read the Sermon on the Mount; and now, dear journal, I will close your pages, until I have either to write my unspeakable joy or immeasurable grief.

Sunday evening. He has helped me, and may I be truly grateful for his mercy, so little deserved!

I went to Mrs. Dana's about three o'clock, and found Katie on the sofa, and Mrs. Dana on the bed taking care of little Mary, or "Bay" as they call her. Feeling so moved as I did, I was not entertaining company; but after some trivial remarks, I took a little volume from my pocket, called *Bryant's Poems,* on the fly leaf of which I had written, "Miss Katie F. Loring, January 25, 1857. Gold and silver have I none, but such as I have, give to thee."

"Katie, I am going to ask a favor of you," said I.

"What is it?"

"Will you please accept this book from me? It is the poems of a poet whom I love very dearly."

She thanked me, and looked up in my face; but I could not trust myself to meet her glance, and looked down.

During the afternoon we were a good deal interrupted, but at last on some pretext or other Mrs. Dana carried off the baby somewhere else, and left us alone, with a true woman's kindness. For a long time we sat silent; at length I took up a catalogue of the Episcopal Clergy, which lay near, and turned over the leaves in an aimless manner.

"What queer names we find in these lists!"

"Yes, very."

"Henry W. Duchachel! How many do catch it? A great many chase it, but few catch it."

"Yes."

A pause, in which I still continued nervously turning the leaves.

"What am I doing this for? The book is not [at] all interesting to me."

"Perhaps to keep your fingers busy."

"I suppose it is for that; I won't do it any longer." And I threw the book into Bay's crib.

"Are you putting some things in there for me to take out?" said Katie, laughing.

"I believe so," I answered, and, laughing myself, tossed it on the bed.

Another long pause, in which I took up Bryant and turned his leaves over.

"There is scarcely a line in Bryant that does not call up some association in my mind. I first learned to love him through Mother. She read and explained 'Thanatopsis' to me when very young. He is connected in some way with almost all the happiness I have ever had, and now with—" I did not finish, but hurried to say—"I am sorry this copy is a little shopworn; I have to get it by proxy, and could not help it."

Another long pause, which at last in desperation I broke by asking if she had not felt a great desire to see a diamond when she was very

33

young. (I was meaning all along to ask Mr. Loring's permission to speak to Katie about what was nearest my heart, before I spoke to her herself. But the tax on my self-control was becoming fearful.)

"I do not know that I did when very young."

"I did, from reading the *Arabian Nights*. But perhaps I could not have told a diamond from a piece of glass, if I had seen one."

"Then the glass would have given us as much pleasure as the diamond."

"Yes. But after seeing the diamond, I cannot go back to the glass. Possibly Gray's lines would be applicable here—

—where ignorance is bliss,
Tis folly to be wise."

"Ignorance is bliss, sometimes," Katie replied.

"Yet I would not be ignorant for all that. I was never sorry that Adam and Eve ate the apples."

"No, because all is for the best."

Just then a little boy brought in a dish of parched corn, sent by the keeper of the house, I believe. I handed some to Katie, and took one or two myself, for the purpose of having something to do.

"Are these sprinkled with pepper?" said she.

"I do not know; there is salt on them. Nothing can do without flavor, not even Life."

"Life always has some flavor or other, good or bad."

"But only the right kind can make it of my worth."

Here another long pause occurred. Katie went to the table, and examined the books; I sat by the stove. At last I could brook suspense no longer.

"Katie!" I said.

"What?" she answered, very low.

"Do you wish me to tell you my day-dream now, that you wanted to hear?"

"Yes, very much."

"Will you please take this chair by the stove, then?"

She complied.

"Here it is. A young man once walked by a beautiful river, and he loved the river and the forest and the fields and the flowers, very much. But he was unhappy because the flowers all died. At last his guardian angel told him to seek the living flower, and then he would be happy. So he still he found it not. At length he found a beautiful little garden, and the gardener let him into it. Here he saw three lovely flowers growing side by side; and he knew the middle one was the living flower. And he longed to pluck it, and place it in his breast, and cherish it dearer than all beside; but he had not asked the gardener. And now the young man wants to know if it will do any good to ask the gardener — can he then have the flower?"

I repeated my dream, with my head buried in my hands; and after I got through, I waited for an answer in the most agonizing suspense. At last she said, very softly, and very sweetly, —

"I HOPE SO!"

I felt my face twitch and my whole frame quiver with uncontrollable emotion, as I looked up, and, gazing into her eyes, said huskily —

"Do you mean that, Katie?"

"Yes, I do," said she, returning my gaze.

I caught her hand, and covered it with kisses; sprang up, and kissed the dear little mouth turned up to mine; and sinking on my knees with my head on her lap, while she threw her arm around it, —

"O God! I thank thee! O God, I thank thee!" was all I could gasp out.

went, and sought far and wide, and found it not. He roamed through many a garden and many a hidden forest glade; but still he found it not. At length he found a beautiful little garden, and the gardener let him into it. Here he saw three lovely flowers growing side by side; and he knew the middle one was the living flower. And he longed to pluck it, and place it at his breast, and cherish it dearer than all beside; but he had not asked the gardener. And now the young man wants to know if it will do any good to ask the gardener—can he have the flower?"

I repeated my dream, with my head buried in my hands; and after I got through, I waited for an answer in the most agonizing suspense. At last she said, very softly, and very sweetly—

"I HOPE SO!"

I felt my face twitch and my whole frame quiver with uncontrollable emotion, as I looked up, and, gazing into her eyes, said huskily,—

"Do you mean that, Katie?"

"Yes, I do," said she, returning my gaze.

I caught her hand, and covered it with kisses; sprang up, and kissed the dear little mouth turned up to mine; and sinking on my knees with my head on her lap, while she threw her arm around it,

"O God! I thank thee! O God, I thank thee!" was all I could gasp out.

As soon as I could recover myself a little, I drew my chair up to hers, sat down by her side, laid her darling head on my shoulder, put my arm around her waist, while her little hands grasped mine so tightly over her bosom, and imprinted kiss after kiss on her forehead. And that, I know, in the eyes of God, was a pure and holy sight.

"Why do you tremble so?" said she.

"Because I cannot help it; you are dearer than all the world beside. Dearest Katie!"

"Dear Frank!"

"I can hardly believe it is not all a dream; yet I know my air-castle is not a real castle."

"Yes, I hope it is real."

"And now that little hand is mine; and the heart, too."

"Indeed it is, and both hands, and all the heart."

But I cannot write half what we said, all I know is, that the angels in heaven cannot be more happy than I was and am; for I was as happy as I could be, and they are no more.

The tea-bell found us still in each other's embrace, and I reluc-tantly let my newfound treasure go. And after supper, I asked Mr. Lor-ing if I might accompany him on his walk; he consented. He escorted his little grandson, David Loring, to Mrs. Ripley's; and after staying there a short time, we came out together. I was too impatient to delay long.

"Mr. Loring," said I, "I may as well come to the point first as last. I am going to ask of you the greatest gift one man can ask of another— the gift of your daughter Katie."

"This is rather sudden, Mr. Abbot," he replied; "your acquaintance-ship is very brief. I must have time to consider."

"I know it is, very; but I know my own heart very thoroughly; I told her this afternoon how I loved her, and she answered with her own love."

"You are both too young to form an engagement. She is only seven-teen; a most affectionate little thing, and very well cultivated for her years."

"That she is," said I enthusiastically, "I know well the value of the gift I ask. I am poor, Mr. Loring, without one cent in the world; but I am industrious and economical, and will work my fingers to the bone for such a prize. I am perfectly willing to answer any inquiries about my cir-cumstances and family, for you have a right to inquire; and I am sure that I have nothing to be ashamed of in them except my youth and inex-perience."

"Yes, but those must be taken into consideration. However, I have no objections to the continuance of your intercourse as heretofore." So say-ing, he turned aside to call on the Gourgases, and I made for Mrs. Dana's.

I found Susie there, but kind Mrs. Dana, who knew where I had been, and for what purpose, proposed to Susie to go and call on Mrs. Emerson. But I could not wholly restrain my desire to let Katie know the result of my interview, so I scrawled on a bit of paper, the words

"This journal is meant to be a faithful mirror of my heart . . ."

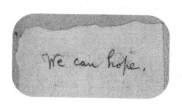

and passed it to her. When the two were gone, I told her the main points of my conversation with her father; and she said she had told her mother, who had made no objections, but said it must not be considered an actual engagement.

"We can afford to wait, Katie darling," said I, "for I do not fear the test of time. They say marriages are made in Heaven, and I believe this one was. Only think, Katie, this love will be lifelong! And it will not end with life, but will last through eternity." And we gazed into each other's eyes with emotions we could not speak. I bowed my head over her two hands and felt a rapture of bliss that would atone for ages of woe and pain.

"What God has joined together, let no man put asunder," I said slowly as I raised my head. "I shall keep no secret from you, Katie; I want to be loved for nothing I do not possess, and I will not deceive you. I have loved before, and ardently, too; but I know now that that was but the boy's affection, while this is the man's one love. I cannot love again as I love now, and never shall."

Few were the words we spoke, but deeply did we feel during those precious moments of solitary intercourse. At last Mrs. Dana returned, and my darling had to leave me for the night. When she had gone, I told Mrs. Dana the events of the day, and she rejoiced with me. I shall never forget her good offices, never.

And now, I am loved as I have yearned to be loved, loved as warmly and strongly as I desire. God has given me a jewel of great price, and it rests with me to make dear Katie happy or unhappy. May my heavenly Father make me faithful to the trust, and may I never in thought, word, or deed, cause pain to that gentle, loving heart. God bless her, oh God bless her!

Concord, January 25, 1857

Love

Struggling heart, O struggle now no longer!
Yield thee up, and drink the draught of love;
Let the chain be closer drawn and stronger—
Time and Death its links shall ne'er remove!

Yes! I'll head the strange, mysterious yearning
Which uncomprehended fills my soul;
Love's pure fires, with heavenly radiance burning,

Like the whirlwind o'er my spirit roll!
Heaven above is not those fires reproving—
Be they ne'er by erring man reproved!
O the blissful agony of loving,
O the speechless joy of being loved!

Concord, January 1857

Dearest Mother,

. . . When you get this, you will understand me when I say that I am happy as any mortal can be on this earth. If not, I must explain. And I beg you to lay aside all anxiety on my account. My cough is gone, and I have recovered from that morbid state in which I have been so long, thanks to an angel whom God has sent me. When I say this, you know me well enough to understand that God can bestow no greater happiness on me,—that now the cloud which has darkened my heavens for so long has wholly passed away, and that the sun shines at last undimmed and bright. Darling Mother, I cannot write more; I feel so strongly that words are but mockery. But I know that it will give you joy to know of mine, and therefore I have told you before I have told any other. You must not speak about this to any one yet; wait till I give you leave to do so. Last Sunday I asked the most important question which I can ever ask here below, and I found that my hope was well-grounded. Sweet Katie Loring is my plighted bride in the eyes of God, although her parents say it must not be yet considered an engagement; but they make no objections. She loves me as passionately as I love her, and you know that, in saying this, I say that most I can say. You will not wonder at the suddenness of this attachment, though others will; you know that my friendships have been as sudden, and you know that also death only will end them. And so will it be now—except that I believe death itself will not end either those friendships or this love. Write soon, and send your blessing to me, and to her who is dearer to me than my own self. I will tell you more about this matter when I next write, but now goodbye, and give me your blessing.

Your loving child, Frank E. Abbot

"This journal is meant to be a faithful mirror of my heart . . ."

Beverly, January 1857

Dear Frank,

I have read and re-read your letter which came only today . . . Do not fear that I shall give you "timid counsels." I am not a particularly timid woman, and do not fancy that you will see evidence of it in anything I am about to say. You are precocious in some things, in sentiment, in feeling, in the development of affections peculiarly. But you have really little knowledge of the world, and, as I fear, little self-control—both which requisitions are desirable to possess, and are also attainable by every person of common sense. If, on good grounds, you are fully persuaded of the value of this new object of pursuit, first of all inquire if you be worthy to follow it. This comprehends many things which, at your age and with your temperament, "your philosophy has not dreamed of." Be sure that you examine and understand yourself, before you seek in any way to involve the happiness of a gentle, loving woman. Seek not to bind yourself or another by any rash engagements for, if you have conceived an inspired, a true regard which is to be lifelong— true love always is life-long—you may leave it free; it will stand the test of time. At 20 and 17, you cannot know your own hearts. The indestructible flame may have been kindled; if so, it will continue to burn. No true man and true woman will ever marry where they do not love; both will bide time and trial, and only such as can ought ever to marry. Cultivate each other's acquaintance as much as propriety admits—leave affection to thrive in its own way. If you rashly propose, you will defeat your object with sensitive parents—with a sensible maiden. You give an attractive picture to my fancy—God grant it may be the true one to hang in your "chamber of imagery." Remember, if you have desires like this, how important it is to you to improve your stores of useful knowledge. Try to imitate your elder brothers in making yourself fit to occupy a useful station in life. You know the misery which a want of worldly wisdom may produce on the relations of life. Do not suffer yourself to think or talk wildly. Be a man. And a wise man "will not despise the counsel of his mother." I long more than ever to see you. Write again very soon, and do not for a moment misunderstand your own dear Mother

[Frank later added to the foot of letter: "O wisest of mothers! Too wise for your giddy, impulsive, headstrong boy! And yet he was in the right, and you knew it at last."]

January 27, 1857

Instead of writing last night after coming home, I sat and thought over the strange events of the last few days. I was too happy to write. But I wish to preserve the memory of all I can, of this the happiest period of my life.

Immediately after school, I went to see my Katie, and found her alone in Mrs. Dana's room, waiting for me. Her confiding, tender, pure caress set me all in a tremor of love, and we sat side by side on the lounge for a long time, silent, but feeling the bliss of mutual affection. She laid her dear head against mine, and pressed my hand between hers, while I quivered like an aspen. Truly, we are sometimes most eloquent when we say the least. I said a thousand things to her during the brief time of our intercourse, which she answered by a warmer pressure of the hand, or a long, intoxicating kiss. Heaven bless her! Before her maiden purity and love, I feel an involuntary reverence, an emotion which is almost awe. I am compelled to respect myself because I have inspired such surpassing and devoted love in so lovely and heavenly a girl; yet I feel more deeply in my own unworthiness to possess such a treasure.

"Katie," said I, "in the hour of happiness, let us not forget Him who gave it!" And I whispered a prayer to the loving Author of our bliss. "I do not ask any pledge of eternal love for I have no fears; you will not find me a jealous or suspicious husband. But it is very pleasant to hear words of love, notwithstanding; for there are some truths which we never weary of hearing, although we know them well."

My answer was a kiss so sweet and rapturous that I felt almost delirious with affection. Soon she had to leave to go to tea, but she soon returned. She sat before the stove watching the bright wood fire dance and flicker in the twilight; and I took my seat beside her.

"How brightly the fire burns! Some fires burn very brightly, but soon die away; but some fires are more lasting. There was a fire in ancient Rome, which burnt year after year, and never went out; but then that fire was kindled by the sun. And no fire, that is not kindled there, will burn long."

A meaning glance of her eyes told me I was understood.

"What are you going to do when you leave college?" asked she at last.

"I do not know yet. I shall have a debt to pay when I get out, and shall devote myself to that first; honor must come first. And then I shall do whatever enables me to give my dearest Katie a home the soonest. I believe what God sent me into the world for, was to write poetry; it is a high and mighty gift, and I almost fear to think I possess it; but one star differeth from another star in glory, and I may be a lesser star. I will never prostitute it to unworthy uses, and shall never regard it as a means

"This journal is meant to be a faithful mirror of my heart . . ."

41

to get money; if I did, I should be no worthy poet. Thus you see I have two objects in life; I might say, I hope I have a third object, higher than either, but I dare not say it. I fear I do not regard that aim so dear as either of the others; I hope I shall."

Presently came in Mrs. Dana, Jennie, Susie, and soon after Edith Emerson; and I then finished reading the "Lay of the Last Minstrel." The time flew by pleasantly; and by and by it came time for the other girls to go. But Kate lingered, and Mrs. Dana left the room on some pretence. Then I leaned forward, and kissed Kate again.

"Do you repent of what you have done, dearest?" I said, very low.

"No, indeed!" was the passionate answer, and she flung her arms around my neck, and kissed my cheek. I folded her to my heart.

"If you find you have mistaken your own feelings, you must tell me so." But the only reply was—the same that I had before.

But I must go, and Mrs. Dana soon came back. Katie went to the door with me, and I sallied out into the dark night with her pure kiss still fresh on my lips. Oh what boundless joy!

Concord, January 29, 1857

Dear Mother,

I received your letter yesterday, and it made me feel sad, because I feel you do not yet understand me fully. You must not think that a few letters can give you that knowledge of my real present life, which can only be gained by long and intimate intercourse. Depend upon it, in these matters I know myself better than my dear mother knows me. You dread the suddenness of this attachment. But God has given me an intuition, an instinctive feeling, which he grants to few men, and which has never led me wrong. And this told me long before now that Katie was my appointed bride. Do not despise this prescience—it is the voice of God. I am impulsive and passionate enough, heaven knows; but in this I have not listened to the voice of passion and impulse. I have taken this all-important step in the fear of God, having first asked his guidance. I have consulted only my own conscience and my Creator, and I fully believe I am right.

But there is another thing, which I must speak about. You asked me if I am worthy of Katie, and without hesitation I answer no, except in the fervor and fidelity of my love. No true man ever did feel worthy of his wife, if he really loved her. Every man is conscious that he is far below the goodness and purity of a true woman; but he is not therefore wrong in marrying her. No, the happiness of a wife is much better insured by her husband's knowing this unworthiness and trying to remove it, than by his feeling himself perfect and fully as good as she. I have not much knowledge of the world as you say; but there is a knowledge higher than that, and I have yielded in this instance to that untaught knowledge. If you are still distrustful, it will only grieve me; I cannot be shaken in thinking I have pursued the wisest and manliest course. I was rash, I admit; but rashness is sometimes the highest wisdom, as the result proves to my mind.

Katie is going to Indiana next Monday, and had I let her go without declaring my hopes, how could I even have had another chance? For she will not return until after I leave Concord.

If I can, I will come home a week from next Saturday. I shall write again before that time, and hope to hear from you soon. Send me that coveted blessing, and tell me you no longer fear that I have done unwisely. You will find my Katie everything you could wish, when you know her; our opportunities of intimacy have been remarkably favorable; and I regard her with a feeling of awe, almost as I would an angel of God. Her mind is the most vigorous and well informed I have ever met in a girl; her heart I need say nothing of now; her habits are essentially practical and housewifely. No affection, no extravagance, no ill-temper,—nothing but kind and gentle and endearing ways about her . . . But it is almost two o'clock, and I must stop.

Your loving child, Frank

January 29, 1857

Last night I had to correct a batch of compositions, and could not write in my journal, but I spent the evening as usual. Tonight I got out of school earlier than common, and had a delightful hour's converse with Katie. She took up a book of gardening which lay on the table, and turned over the leaves slowly.

"What is your favorite flower?" said I.

"I do not know, I love them all."

"I think you once said you were very fond of the crocus."

"Yes, perhaps I like that the best; but which is your pet flower?"

"Mine? The living flower!"

"Dear Frank!"

"The majority of mankind, when they have found a beautiful blos-

"This journal is meant to be a faithful mirror of my heart . . ."

———

43

som, pluck it, admire it, then throw it away; but when I have found one, I transplant it into my heart, and it takes root and grows there: it will flourish as long as its soil lasts, I know."

She only nestled closer to my side. Heaven bless her!

"Do you think the fire will last?" asked Katie.

"Yes, until the poor old stove is worn out, and then we shall not need the fire here. It will go back to the Sun, whence it came and then, I believe, it will glow brighter than ever."

But I can only give disjointed scraps of our conversations, and those, of course, imperfectly, but I like to preserve as much as I can of them, for when my dearest girl is gone (and she goes to Indiana next Monday), they bring back to me each look and tone that I love so dearly. It would be too much bliss for us to be always together.

Mrs. [Ralph Waldo] Emerson had invited me to tea to meet Signor Gajani, who was to lecture at the Lyceum; and I could not find a decent excuse to decline. So I had to leave the sweet society of her who is all the world to me, and go to the Emersons. Mr. Emerson is away in the West, lecturing, and I did not see him, therefore. I had a pleasant time enough, but stole away as soon as possible, and returned to Mrs. Dana's. Here I found Mrs. Loring, Katie's mother, and was greeted by her most cordially; this pleased me, for it confirmed my hope that my addresses to Katie did not displease her parents. I read, at Mrs. D's request, from the *Gold Legend,* and stayed till half past ten, passing a most delightful evening. Katie showed me to the door, and her maidenly yet warm caress seemed to me a charm against every evil and danger, where from within or without. It almost makes me awestruck to gaze into her eyes, such truth, and purity, and goodness, and undying love are there.

Surely there is nothing on earth so holy as a gentle, true, loving woman.

January 30, 1857

"Do you like to keep school?" said Katie, this afternoon.

"Yes, pretty well; but I am too sensitive for a teacher. I care too much for the good-will of my scholars, and feel too deeply a slight neglect, to be happy in such an occupation. I dislike both to rule and be ruled, for I am a true republican."

"The more you try to win their good-will, the better you will succeed."

"But I am too unequal in my temperament. I hardly know which is the better: to joy along contentedly without great grief or great happiness, or to experience all the alternations which must be the fate of a more mercurial disposition."

"You said once you would rather have great grief and great happiness than the other kind of character."

"I think I should not change my temperament; few would. We get used to it. But I doubt if it is the happier one to possess. It is easier to travel on a level plain than among the mountains."

"No, the monotony is worse than the extra fatigue."

"Yet the dwellers on the plain love it more than the hills."

"So do the mountaineers love their mountains, with a still stronger affection."

"Certainly they know what it is to be near the glorious heavens; which those below do not."

I left her (shall I say it?) with a heavy heart, for our approaching separation weighs on my mind. So it is: our happiness here is of brief duration. For every blissful hour, we have ten wretched ones. But I will suffer myself to fall into no unmanly repining. Heaven bless my darling!

January 31, 1857

After dinner I went again, of course, to Mrs. Dana's, and found Katie alone, busily sewing on some work for her journey. I sat down near her, and watched the active little fingers as they sped to and fro; and occupied myself in ransacking her work-basket, a thing, by the way, which I have done before.

"Did you ever climb a high mountain?" said I.

"No, never."

"It is very interesting to watch the change in the vegetation as we ascend. At first the trees are very large and tall, and continue so for more that half the way up; but finally they grow less and less, and dwindle down to mere stunted evergreens, which are very hardy and strong. But soon even those change to a thick growth of short trees, wholly dead, without foliage or bark, nothing but mere stakes. These are very hard to

"This journal is meant to be a faithful mirror of my heart . . ."

get through, as they are stubborn and stout, branching off sidewise, and forming a kind of network over the ground. Then come the naked rocks, dreary and desolate; but even on the very top, I found beautiful flowers, or moss rather, which grow only in Greenland, and Iceland, and on very high mountains. They must derive their nourishment from the clouds, as there is not much in the bare rocks on which they bloom. I could not help thinking at the time that it was an emblem of life; even in the most desolate and dreary periods of existence, we always find some flowers to console us."

"Yes, and when we least expect it. Do you know, Mother says that we can correspond when I am gone?"

"I am very glad, very glad indeed. And your letters will be the flowers on top of the mountain."

"I hope you have not got to the top yet; have you?"

"No, I shall not get to the top until next Monday."

"Have you finished your work?"

"Yes."

"Let me take my own seat at your side then."

She blushed, and laid her head on my shoulder. We said nothing for a long time. At last I whispered in a low voice, "When I keep my guitar strung all the while, some of the strings snap. Perhaps that is the reason why we two are separated; I cannot bear so much happiness all the time. But when the guitar is strung again, what beautiful music it will make!"

"Beautiful indeed! But I must put some more wood in the fire. Poetry and prose together. I know; but I can't help it."

So saying she went to the stove, and after we had replenished the fire, I drew a chair up near the stove, and sat down on it; but she sat on the floor, with her head on my knee.

"That's not your place, Katie; you must sit in my lap."

"Nay, I would rather look up than look down."

"But it must not be; if there must be kneeling, let me do it, for heaven's sake."

"No, no; let me stay here. It is my proper place."

"Oh Katie! I am not worthy to loose the latchet of your shoe, and how can that be your place?"

She only answered by pressing my hand between hers. I leaned forward and rested my head on hers. At length she said,

"What is it makes me tremble so? I am quivering all over."

"You said once you could not help it."

"I cannot; but I cannot see the connection between the cause and the effect . . . it is not the only mysterious thing about love. There is that scroll [on the iron stove] still, unwritten on yet; if you were to write the inscription, what would it be?" She paused. "You may be the scribe. What would you write?"

"I? I don't know; yes, I do, though, I would write, God bless my darling!

She seized my hand and kissed it passionately, while I strove to raise her from the floor.

"Katie! Dearest! You shall not sit at my knee—come to my heart, for that is your place, and ever shall be!"

And she rose, and sat in my lap, throwing her arms around my neck, and burying her face on my shoulder. And I—I was in a delirium, almost, of rapturous love. She kissed my forehead.

"Rhoda Ann Melvin would say I was very naughty to kiss you," said she, blushing and smiling at the same time.

"So she would; but Heaven would not echo her words, I know."

Just then a knock at the door startled us, and Katie went to it. It was Mr. Loring.

"What! Alone?" said he; then observing me, he added, "Oh! How do you do, Mr. Abbot?" and withdrew. Katie came back blushing, looking more lovely than ever.

"I am not quite alone, am I?" said she, taking her former seat in my lap, and lay her cheek against mine.

"No, I trust not. It would be much more romantic if your parents forbade our love; but I am very willing to dispense with that part of the romance, aren't you?"

"Yes, I am very willing."

Again there was a long pause, each of us being occupied with our own thoughts. At last I said,

"Do you see how the hot air near the stoves makes everything oscillate, as we look through it? Do you suppose that is the effect of all fire, to distort all other objects?"

"I think not. We cannot see cold air at all, we can only see hot air."

"Yes, but we see hot only when it distorts everything else. But the fire

"This journal is meant to be a faithful mirror of my heart . . ."

47

of love is not so; love is not blind, as the ancients painted him, but very clear-sighted. When he is blind, then he is not immortal."

Very soon after supper, Mrs. D. and the two girls came in and we had quite a lively chat for some time. At last I said to Katie.

"You seem to be tired; you look pale and exhausted."

"I am tired, somewhat."

"Well, I shall go home, then, and you shall go to bed."

With these words, I bade them all good-night, and came home.

February 1, 1857

The last day of seeing Katie! I have just come from Mrs. Dana's, and with Katie's tears scarcely dry on my cheek, and her warm kiss yet lingering on my lips, I sit down to write a record of our last day of sweet companionship, the last for a long time, I fear. May she be blessed below and above, may no sorrow ever crush her tender heart, and may no wind of care or suffering visit her too harshly! God bless her, God bless her!

I went to church this morning, but heard very little of the sermon. Immediately after the services were concluded, I went to Mrs. Dana's, and she kindly called Katie to come down stairs, while she left the room. How precious every moment of the time seemed! I forswore both dinner and supper, because it would take too long to go back to Mrs. Thoreau's for them, and I did not wish to go to the table where I should have to meet the prying eyes of Mrs. Clarke and Rhoda Ann. I stayed in Mrs. Dana's room, therefore, while Katie went to the table.

I will not try to describe this afternoon and evening. Once I took a bit of paper and scrawled the following lines impromptu—

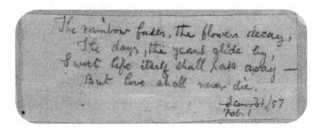

I threw the scrap of paper into her lap, and after reading it, she placed it in her bosom, next to the dear little heart that throbs so warmly for my unworthy self. She took a cushion, and sat at my knee, resting her head on it, and would not let me raise her.

"Nay, dearest, if you will kneel, let us kneel together." And we did kneel, side by side, and with sincere heart, I hope, I whispered a prayer to the all-seeing Father for help and guidance through this world of sin and sorrow . . .

"Call me darling once more!"

"Darling! Ay, that I will—darling, darling, darling girl—darling a thousand times—darling now and darling forever! Tell me once more you love me, darling, darling, Katie!"

"Oh! So much!"

"Darling, darling, darling!"

"God be with you, and bless you, dear Frank!"

"And with you, darling Katie."

"Dear Frank!"

"Farewell, darling, farewell!"

"Good-bye!"

And the door closed, and I stood alone in the cold, dark night. But it was colder and darker in my heart than it was round me. God help me!

Longing, February, 1857
The wintry winds around me blow
With wild and melancholy moan;
My midnight lamp is burning low,
Yet I am not alone:
Thy parting words my bosom thrill,
I feel that thou art with me still.

My yearning heart beats thick and fast;
But though the present dark may be,
Sweet Memory points me to the past,
Made beautiful by thee;
While Hope, my anguish to remove,
Illumes the future with thy love.

"This journal is meant to be a faithful mirror of my heart . . ."

———

49

(Extract from Katie's letter at Crawfordsville, Indiana, March 1, 1857.)

"You ask me when I first _suspected_ that I loved you. I will tell you when I first _k_
that I loved you. Do you remember the night we sat by the stove, playing with
hips, and I gave you one and told you that, when I found the ebony, I wou
ive it to you? I knew then that I loved you as I could never love another, _o_
" knew, too, that you would think me that piece of ebony. God grant that
may prove _true_ ebony! Perhaps you think it strange that, knowing what I d
" should have told you so. But I could not help it — something seemed to _t_
_me_, '_tell him so_,' and I could not resist it. "

(See p. 132.) _____ [Copied Jan. 25, 1894.]

(See p. 132.)

(Extract from her letter at Beverly, Jan. 11, 1858.)

" I was afraid that you sometimes thought me rather bold, particularly that night when
ave you that piece of chips, but I could not help saying what I did. What have you done wit
that piece of chip? I know you kept it for some time."

[Copied Feb. 8, 1894.]

(Extract from my letter at Cambridge, Jan. 12, 1858.)

" You say you feared I should think you bold, when you gave me that little slip of wood. If I had loved you less
should have thought you so. But I had read your heart well enough to know that you would not show your feelings
hey were very strong. If you had been a coquette, you would never have done it; if I had been flirting with you, I _h_
not have been pleased with it. You were too honest to do such a thing for effect; and I was too deeply earnest t
our love to pout at my own success. It certainly was a strange thing; but, as Kingsley says in 'Two Years a_
it is the strange things that keep the world alive? At first I was too diffident to believe you meant all you
mean; but, after I got home, I saw you could mean nothing else. You have that little bit of worthless pine to th_
that I did not keep silence when to have kept silence might have changed the destiny of both of us. A_
you imagine I could lose it? Do you pretend to wonder if I have it still? You know as well as I do that it
cherished among a few tokens of my real life, of no value in themselves, but speaking whole volumes to me, wher_
ook at them. Only think, Mignonette, one year has gone already! How quick in passing will the rest seem, when they a_
assed! Today a mere boy and girl, tomorrow a husband and wife, then two graves, lying side by side, I trust. Oh _o_
my own, own darling, may that dark curtain of death, which must sooner or later fall on us both, when it rises, open _o_
_he_ view of some happy realm where grief and fear are strangers, and where truth and love shall dwell together forever!
_of_ us must in all human probability go first to that unknown land; but if we act towards each other as lovingly and
ally as we now both mean to do, that dreadful separation shall be robbed of its bitterest sting. I hope at all _ifting f_
ashes of earthly happiness, and cheer
the lonely heart of the one still
destined to toil and suffer below.
earest let us never have to
eproach ourselves with harsh
ords towards one another, for
they bring untold suffering
oth to the speaker and the
spoken to." [Copied, March
2, 1894.]

The first letter from my darling,
written as she was starting for Crawfordsville, Indiana, Feb. 2, 1857, and
handed to me by Jennie Loring on
the same day.

Dear Frank; please direct your letters to the care of
Jacob Linn. The reason why I sent you off so
early was because I did not want you to see Mrs. Lane
again. I could not forget what she said to you.
Katie

_Dear Frank, you must be satisfied with this without
a letter this time. I hope it will say to you as much
as any of my letters have, and tell you how much I love
you. Your own Katie._

(Received Mar. 17, 1857.)

PART II

"I have found my hopes
of happiness with you . . ."

Found in the MS. book
of poems I gave her on
her birthday, Oct. 18, 1857.

From Maine at Concord, June 22, 1858.

Sumac

Found Sept. 24, 1894.

From Susie's garden,
given to me by her
in the spring of 1855.

Abutilon.

From the little basket in the
bay-window
April 2nd, 1856

A flower once grew beside my garden wall,
Which I scarce noticed till one day it died;
And as I mused o'er its untimely fall,
A loving friend my secret tears espied —
"Why weep'st thou for the flower?" "'Twas Hope!"
it said, and sighed,

Apr. 20, 1856.

From the cherry-tree in front
of Susie's old home.
May, 1856.

The rainbow fades, the flowers decay,
The days, the years glide by,
Sweet life itself shall pass away —
But love shall never die.

We can hope.

[Jan. 25, 1857].

Jan. 24,
1857.

Saxifrage

Jan. 30/57
Feb. 1

Treasured up by darling all through her innocent life

Concord, February 2, 1857

My darling Katie,

    Although it is rather late, I know I should not sleep if I went to bed, and I might as well think to you, as think of you; therefore I am going to write you my first letter on the very day of your departure. I did not go to the train depot to take one more look at my dearest of earthly treasures, because I would not have my last recollections of it profaned by any such scene of bustle and confusion as would have been unavoidable; I preferred to cherish the memory of our last interview, so sweet to me in the remembrance, unmixed with the more earthly sights and sounds which must have met the eye and ear.

    I was unhappy all day, and suffered fully the pain of parting from you; but this afternoon I received a letter from a classmate, who loves, and dares not hope. He too is separated by hundreds of miles from the one who is more precious than all the world beside; and has no sweet assurance of her love. As I read his manly, noble words, my conscience smote me that I should be so selfish as to grieve for a mere temporary parting, while he repined not at a fate so much severer than mine. I thought of your gentle words of affection, and your pure caresses; and I said to myself,

    "I will be more worthy of my Katie than to selfishly wish her back when it is best for her to go."

So, I hope, and look forward to our next meeting, and will strive faithfully to check every selfish thought and wish; surely love will swallow up grief.

My ideal was high and rare; but I feel you are as much higher than my ideal, as my ideal is higher than the rest of your sex. But do not think that my love is therefore blind, and is doomed to a bitter awakening; far from it. I never was hoodwinked by my affection; I am not making a goddess, not a perfect angel of you; but I find so much to love and reverence that I wonder how I ever dared to gaze into those eyes of yours, and not sink mine in shame and awe to the dust. If you had ever shocked my taste or my sense of the gentle and lovely, depend upon it, I should not have loved as I do love; I am very sensitive, and see such trifling indications of character as few men notice, in the light of the most absolute revelations of inward life. Do not fear that I am deceiving myself with a paragon of excellence never met on earth, as they say men will do; I know you will disdain what I attribute to you, but in this I know you better than you know yourself. And it is right that it should be so; the ebony does not know itself to be ebony, but modestly thinks it is only pine.

Ah my darling girl! It is worth while living to learn the value of love; it is worth while to spend years of anguish and craving, to know the rapture, the immeasurable joy of loving and being loved again. If I can feel your warm kiss on my cheek now, and can almost fancy you are at my side again; how eagerly I shall count the moments until our happy reunion! I am not fearful of your forgetting me; no, I feel that I can never waver in my love for you, and I will not do you the injustice to esteem you less than I esteem myself, who am not worthy to kiss your hand, if moral worth be the standard; but who, if faithful, passionate, and pure affection be the standard, shall without misgiving, claim you one day as my bride, nor feel that I am unworthy of such a priceless gift as your love.

Tuesday morning. I wrote the first sheet last night, and as the letter can't go out till this afternoon, I am going to put in another sheet this morning. Yesterday, I had six letters, one from home, containing twenty pages! Mother had not received my last letter, and is still anxious about my love for you; but when I see her, which I hope to be next Saturday, be sure she will not then be troubled. My darling Katie, I could be eloquent indeed when talking of you to my own mother. Do not fear that she will be anxious long; it is only for her love for me that makes her uneasy till she feels assured I have not made a fatal error in thus rashly, as she thinks, taking the most important step in my life. How I wish that we need not keep it a secret! But patience is a heavenly virtue, they say, and we shall have a chance to cultivate it, shall we not?

Perhaps this will reach Crawfordsville before you do, and in that case, I doubt not it will be a little surprise to you. Jennie came to the school-house yesterday after leaving you at the depot; and occasioned the girls in "the lobby" to open their eyes in amazement, she said, by asking for me. As I had not yet come, she still further astonished them by saying she would go and meet me, which she did, just as I entered the gate. I was very glad to get your little note, and have read it since I received it—well, not more than fifty times. I am ashamed to send my miserable chirography to you, who write such very neat and pretty hand. I began, intending to be very nice in my penmanship, but, alas for any good resolution! It has shared the fate of many a predecessor. I invariably deteriorate towards the end of a letter, and generally begin to do so after writing the date and name of the town; and thus never fail to arrive at a pitch of illegibility "seldom equaled and never excelled." However, I rather think you would prefer to have a letter from your own Frank, even if it is badly written, to not having it all. Am I not vain to flatter myself with such a hope!

Mrs. Dana told me last night, that when she was at Mrs. Emerson's Sunday night, Mrs. E. asked her "if Mr. Abbot was attached to Katie Loring?" Mrs. D. replied she thought no young man could help it, seeing her so often as I had done. "I am very glad to hear it," said Mrs. Emerson, "how happy for them if this cold, hard winter has borne such a beautiful flower of love and happiness!" I think you will feel with me that this was no gossiping curiosity on Mrs. Emerson's part. And has not this cold winter borne fruit of love and happiness?

Let this content you, though it will not and cannot content me, to know that I love you with my whole heart and my whole strength and my whole mind and my whole soul. You do not require any declarations of my love to convince you that it really and truly exists; no indeed! But there are some truths we are never tired of hearing, how often so ever repeated; and it is so pleasant to read words of affection written by those dearer than life to our own hearts. But it is time to stop; and I must be content with signing myself ever and truly,

Your own Frank

Concord, February 4, 1857

Ever darling Katie,

How long the days seem now, when I can anticipate no delightful meeting with you at their close! . . . How I yearn to clasp you once more to my heart! While I sit waiting for the others to eat supper, I cannot help straining my ear to catch that sound of your foot, as you come to see me and sit by me in the dim twilight. The chips, the stove with its blank scroll, the little corner of the sofa where you used to sit, all bring back to me those rapturous moments of love and happiness, which we

"I have found my hopes of happiness with you . . ."

———

55

passed together so recently. Every day I grow more and more firmly attached to your gentle little self, and more and more fully convinced that this is to be the one great love of my life. I have sat all the evening looking at your two pictures, and it was almost impossible to lay them down. To think that you, you whom I regard so much purer and truer and nobler than myself, can bless me with such a warm and passionate affection, is almost more than I dare believe. Yet I cling to that sweet belief more eagerly than to life, and would sooner forfeit all hope of life and other happiness, rather than your love. Tell me again you love me; I know you do, but let me read it again and again, for I can never tire of contemplating my own bliss. Eagerly do I anticipate the time when we shall indeed be one, as now we are one in spirit. Yet how long that time is distant! We cannot tell what accidents, beyond the power of love to prevent, may shatter our frail castles in the air; fear must still mingle with our hope. But notwithstanding, so long as we preserve our mutual confidence and mutual love, we need not feel unhappy; if we do not find the fruition of our hopes here below, I believe there is a land where loving hearts shall never more be parted. Let us so live that there we may meet where no tears shall dim our eyes forever, where is nothing but love and peace through the endless ages of eternity.

Dearest and loveliest Katie! Never for one moment doubt the truth and constancy of your loving, Frank.

Crawfordsville, February, 8, 1857

Dear Frank,

I received your letter this morning. I was surprised at hearing from you so soon. I supposed I should get a letter from you sometime this week but did not expect it so quickly. I reached here Friday night about five o'clock. The Doctor's saying that we must not travel at night did no good, for we traveled from necessity not choice. At Albany we could not get but one room in the whole city, and that opened the barroom and above the furnace by which they heated the whole house and was so hot we could not sleep in it, although Mother and I went to bed. I slept till half past ten when I woke up and found Mother and Father bending over me to see if I was still breathing. Father wanted to know if we could dress ourselves and get ready to start for Buffalo, in ten minutes, so we traveled the first night, the second we stopped at Buffalo, and the third, we traveled again.

There now, I think I have given you a long account of my troubles on the way and now for the pleasant things. Monday night we spent at the United States Hotel in Boston, and I sat by the bright coal fire in the twilight, building castles in which your own dear self figures pretty largely. I had a dream that night to which I must tell you for they say that what you dream the first time you sleep in a strange place always come true. I thought we (you and I that is) were sitting in a little parlor of our own and you had you arm around me and my head was on your shoulder. I hope that dream will come true and I know you will too. I can not thank you enough for my Bryant Poems, I don't know what I should have done without it those long days we were riding in the cars.

I am going to tell you something I read the other day because I think it agrees with your ideas on the same subject—this is it: woman was not taken from man's head, that she might overtake him; nor from his feet; to be trampled on; nor from under his arm that he might protect her; but from near his heart that he might love her. Dear Frank, you say you do not think I am an angel, I know you don't but I think you think I am better than I am, I would rather have you think I am worse than I am.

Does Mrs. Thoreau continue as benign as ever? And do you think Concord gossips are satisfied that there is nothing between you and me? I want you to get acquainted with the Concord girls for some day you will be brought into close connections with them, for when we are married (how strange that looks and sounds) you will be a member of our club. I am sorry your mother thinks you have chosen rashly! I hope she may one day change her mind. I do not think she would think so if she knew how much I love you, till that I will try to be to you all you need and deserve I should be.

Dear Frank, cousin Edwin told me I should be homesick in a week. I do think I shall be homesick but I want to see you so much, I know I can't see you but I could see a likeness of you if you would send me one.

Katie

Concord, February 9, 1857

Dearest Katie,

. . . I can hardly dare to believe that I indeed possess the priceless treasure of your love; not that I doubt your true and faithful heart, but because I feel my own shortcomings so keenly that it seems almost impossible that heaven should have coupled the violet and thistle. If Heaven has made such a union, then it must be for the end that the thistle may be changed to the violet, by reverently assimilating itself to

"I have found my hopes of happiness with you . . ."

———

57

its companion. Do not think this language of exaggeration; it is the sober, honest conviction of my heart.

As I told you I should do, I went home Saturday, and informed the rest of the family of what had befallen one of its members. Jennie very kindly lent me the two photographs of your dear little self, and I took great pleasure in showing them to Mother and Emily. Neither of [the] latter knew exactly what to do, as we are not formally engaged; but I asked them to send each a word of welcome to one who might eventually be drawn so near to them. What they have written, you will find in the same enclosure with this sheet; and I hope that their words of appreciation will please you; certainly they are sincere. Mother is fully satisfied, as I knew she would be when I came to see her about you, in which she said the very kindred and most affectionate things about you (and every word was gospel truth). So that now I know of no cloud to darken our horizon, if we keep it clear as far as we are concerned; and how could a cloud ever arise between us?

I had my hair cut when in Boston, and I saved a lock of it for you. I do not know whether women care for such things; men do, for they value such little mementoes more highly than I can tell you. If it gives you any pleasure to have it, I am well satisfied; if not, I shall not therefore conclude you do not any longer love me, but let such trifles go at their true value.

I am looking forward eagerly to the period when I shall leave Concord for Cambridge. It was you only who made this town pleasant to me, and now I am only restless and impatient at the drudgery of school recessing. Three weeks more! I am beginning to expect my first letter from you now, and you can guess how eager I am to receive it. I have heard indirectly from Jennie that you bore the journey well, but I long to hear from you yourself.

God bless you! Frank

"Mother's Blessing"

Beverly, February 1857

Sweet Katie,

I have listened with all a mother's deepest interest to the story of Frank's young love, but have now only time to send you her blessing for having made her beloved child so happy by reciprocating his pure and innocent affection. That what has been begun may be continued on Earth and perfected in Heaven, and that the best blessings of God may ever rest on you both, is the fervent prayer of one who, though she has only seen your image, already loves you.

Frank's Mother

"Katie's Response"

Crawfordsville, February 1857

Dear Mrs. Abbot,

I cannot tell you how happy your little note made me. Frank told me one day that you thought that he had chosen rashly and hastily, and I feared you still might think so. I hope that he has not, and I shall strive very earnestly to make myself worthy of his love, and to be to him all that a true wife should be.

Yours affectionately, Katie

Crawfordsville, February 12, 1857

My own dear Frank,

You may thank my pride for this letter or rather for getting it so soon. I'll tell you why; there was a dance here tonight and I did not get my invitation till seven o'clock this evening and I would not accept it. I thought if they wanted me to go they could have asked me before; so here I am all alone in the house. Give my love to Mrs. Dana and tell her I shall always love her if for no other reason than her kindness to you and me. She says you say you are sorry I have carried your heart so far from you, I cannot give it back but I will keep it very carefully for the sake of the one who gave it me.

Dear Frank, I must tell that those eyes of yours are very tell-tale eyes—they told me you loved me long before you told me so. That night when I waked you out of that day-dream was the first time I suspected it, but when I looked into your eyes they said so plainly "I love you" that I almost expected to hear your lips say so. I know you love me but I want to hear you say it and to feel your warm kisses on my cheek. I don't know what I shall do about your letters, if they don't come often I find the days

"I have found my hopes of happiness with you . . ."

———

59

so long till I can expect one and if I get one I want to go home and see you so much. Aunt and Cousin Nellie tease me about your letters, but both together they are not so bad as either Father or Uncle, they bring home my letters and show them to me and then put them in their pockets and will not let me have them for a long while and when I do get them father tries to get them from me so that he may read them.

You wanted that I should write and tell you that I loved you. I do love you. I want to tell you how much . . . The folks have just got home and I must say good bye to you, dear Frank.

Your own Katie

P.S. They are telling me about the dance but I don't believe they enjoyed themselves any more than I have writing to my own Frank.

Crawfordsville, February 15, 1857

Dear Frank,

. . . Heaven never joined the thistle and the violet and never will; you are not so rough and thorny as the thistle, neither am I so meek and lovely as the violet. I was very, very glad to receive your Mother's note—it is what I have wished for so much . . .

I am glad you sent me that lock of hair. I shall value it very highly, as I should anything you sent me. Oh, Frank I have wanted to see you so much. Last Friday evening I felt so lonely that I went off by myself and cried; now don't laugh at me and think I am dreadfully foolish; women's tears come more easily than men's and I could not help it. I cannot watch the beautiful sunsets here, for they do not have any; I have not seen a bright star since I left home either at morning or at night. The weather is so warm there that the honeysuckle on the porch has begun to send out green leaves, and it seems more like the last of April or the first day of May than the middle of February. All last night it thundered and lightened, and today it rains so hard that it is impossible to go out to church, and even if it did not rain the mud would be so deep you couldn't move one foot after the other; you don't know what mud is there at home; here the horses go above their knees into it.

May God's blessing rest upon you, dear Frank, and help you to obtain the mastery over your passions.

Your own darling, Katie

Concord, February 16, 1857

Dear Katie,

    Although I have written to you three times already, dear, dear, Katie, and have as yet received no answer, I do not think you will be displeased at my writing again. It is two weeks today since you left Concord, and to me it seems two full months; I have watched the Post, oh how eagerly! And cannot help feeling a little heart-sick as I turn away unsuccessful mail after mail. Never, hardly for a single instant during the whole day, is your dear face absent from my mind; I think the most jealous mistress that ever lived would not require a more sleepless memory of her love, and I rejoice to believe that jealousy does not enter into our love on either side. "Perhaps love casteth out fear." Judged by this standard, my love is perfect; nothing will ever shake my faith in your truth and constancy till I hear your own lips tell me I am no longer loved. Yet there is a feeling, akin to doubt, though infinitely removed from it, which I cannot banish from my mind; I cannot describe it better than by calling it an intense realization of the uncertainty of happiness below. I feel like one who stands on the brink of a precipice, and sees, a thousand feet down, the angry waves lash its base, curling and foaming over the jagged rocks, while he clasps in his hand a jewel of inestimable value: let him clutch it ever so closely, he cannot but have an overpowering apprehension that his fingers will relax their grasp, even against their will, and consign their precious charge to the wild whirl of the waters below. This shadowy dread is hard to contend against; so long as I cannot clasp you to my heart, it seems that ten thousand things may happen, any one of which would dash from my lips the newly-raised cup of joy.

    . . . Whenever I think of you (and when do I not?) I long to lavish blessings and terms of affection upon you, but they look so cold and unmeaning when written that it shames me to do it. Yet in my inmost heart you could find nothing but just such thoughts and feelings; I dare not write them, lest they seem wild and extravagant, but not all the English language would satisfy me, if I did. Madame de Stael, in an oft-quoted passage, says, that love is an episode in the life of man, while it is the history of woman's existence. That this is true in most cases, cannot be denied; but like all such general statements, it has its exceptions, and such am I. If the affections could be blotted out from the chart of my real life, nothing would remain but a barren waste. Love is the only motive power with me; I have very little ambition for myself, not enough to make me work; I have a consciousness of intellectual power, and this mere consciousness of possession would satisfy me, if no other motive urged me but that of personal advantage . . .

"I have found my hopes of happiness with you . . ."

———

If, after the weary years of waiting which are in store for us, it will be our blessed lot to be joined together in the holiest of earthy ties, it will be my wish that you should be the chosen companion of my studies and pursuits; and I hope that during this period we shall fit ourselves to be true companions, darling. I do not want my wife to share only my hours of idleness and recreation; I want her to participate in the serious business of life also. To this end, we must assimilate still more of our tastes and preferences, already so similar; we must learn to love the same things; if we would enjoy the highest delights of loving. There must be perfect confidence, perfect love, perfect sympathy; and if this becomes as I hope and pray it will become, we need not then fear that time will take away our happiness. Every year will but add to it; and then death itself will be but a temporary separation, only a little longer than that which now causes us so many yearnings.

You know that I love poetry more than anything else, except love itself; and I feel peculiarly desirous that you should be my companion here, for poetry is my vocation, my chosen calling, the calling for which God sent me to this earth, as I devoutly believe. Read all the poetry you can, think it over, criticize it, do not fear to form independent opinions upon it; already your taste is more cultivated and true than any other lady's I ever met; and I shall want your help in the great business of my life, which is poetry. If I live, I shall publish; and you must be my critic, my helper, my sympathizer, and my incentive to exertion.

Do not think from all this that I am going to be a poor author; authorship will not be my occupation. No, I will not ask you to share my home, before I can offer you a comfortable one. I am not the fool of romance, nor do I think that the true poet is necessarily a shiftless, eccentric, wayward blunderer through this world: he can no more dispense with common sense than the merchant or the broker, and I think the reason why modern poets fail so utterly is, because they ignore that most uncommon quality. Moreover, he will not succeed who prostitutes this divinest gift to purposes of money-getting; if a poet has anything to say or sing which will do good or increase the love of the beautiful among men, let him say and sing it with that motive before him; or else—let him be silent. I will never publish poems for the sake of the dirty dollars they may bring me; I will be worthy of my trade. It does not follow, however, that a poet must refuse to derive profit from the children of his brain; far from it. He must only in his own heart not barter the love of the beautiful for the love of gold. He may sell for money—he must not write for money.

* * *

February 17. I wrote so far last night; and had not time to finish the sheet, for it was approximately the "small hours" of the morning. Jennie had your two photographs copied and gave the copies to me. They have given me the keenest pleasure; every night before I go to bed, I refresh my weary soul with looking at them, and anticipating the time when I can see the dear original. Your face is always before me . . .

Just as soon as I return [to] Cambridge (which will be in two weeks) I will have my daguerreotype taken, and send it to you; but up here I could not get a good one taken. If you can get a good one of yourself, do get it; I hope you will not be prevented from doing it because I have the photographs. I want a picture of my other self to carry round with me wherever I go, and I cannot do this with the photographs.

If you do have any intimation of where your home will be when you return, please let me know; of course it is of the highest interest to me. May it be near Cambridge, is my devout wish. If it is within a reasonable distance from old Harvard's protecting walls, you will go often to see me; especially on Saturdays, when I shall have most leisure. Sometimes I close my eyes and then I seem to feel your head on my shoulder, and it makes me tremble as I used to, when it was really there.

Everything increases my love for you. Even distance and time are not unkindly teachers; they show us our own hearts more plainly, and convince us that we were not mistaken. Your quotation, as you thought it would, pleases me very much, it is true. I have often had disputes with some of my college friends about the true relation between man and wife; they all insist on the text—"Wifes, obey your husband." But I understand it very differently. In love, as in friendship, there must be equality: I want no obedience. What I do want is, that my wife should have entire confidence in me; that she should respect my judgement, and that she should not have to yield to it against her will. I never will be a tyrant to anyone; I will neither rule or be ruled, if I can help it, and I call that the true love of liberty. One of the old English poets says truly—

"I have found my hopes of happiness with you . . ."

———

63

> *"If I have freedom in my love,*
> *And in my soul are free,*
> *Angels that dwell in heaven above*
> *Have not had such liberty."*

Therefore what I mean is, that I want my partner's will to be the same as mine, for then there can be either obedience or command. I would never pledge my faith to one who I thought would require commands to please me; and I should not be able to keep my truth if I did so. You see what you are to expect: how do you like the prospect, dear Katie?

My darling girl! You must not think I over rate you. I am not deceived; love is clear-sighted. I have seen more of life than you have, both on account of my age, and because I have mingled more with men and women than you have; by which I do not mean to boast of worldly wisdom, but only to tell you that I have studied character from my earliest days. In all this period (not long, I know, compared with others, but still long compared with your years) I never met anyone whom I could love as I love you. And you must not quarrel with my reverencing you, for the highest love is always mingled with reverence; no man who loves truly, will ever love where he cannot look up. The day that bids me no reverence for my Katie, will bid me no longer love her. O pity the man, especially the young man, who looks at woman as no higher, purer, better than himself; I would not have such a man love my sister for all the wealth of the Indies.

Frank

Concord, February 18, 1857

Dearest Katie,

One reason why I hate to have you so far off is, that we have no chance of knowing each other better; we must learn each other's character's fully, if we expect to be happy with one another, and this knowledge can only be acquired by long and familiar intercourse. Now there is one little remark in your first letter, which gave me great pleasure, because it helped me to determine one point about which I am very anxious to be sure I am right; you tell me you wish that I should "become acquainted with Concord girls." You wonder what I see in that simple remark which can help me to understand your character; and it is because you would never dream of the interpretation I put on it, that gives it its value. In the sentence you tell me more satisfactorily how you love me, than in all the rest of the letter; it shows confidence in me, and perfect absence of jealousy. When there is jealousy, I always think it argues that the party jealous feels unsure of him or herself; for "perfect love casteth out fear." I am so far from being jealous myself, that if it is possible for you to meet one who will make you happier with his love that I can with mine, I pray God (sincerely, I hope) that you may forget me, and be joined with him. Selfishness is the death of love; if I felt otherwise, I should not love you, so well as I loved myself; I should be seeking my own happiness rather than yours, and should deserve to lose you. When you wrote that sentence, I know you did not have any idea of the importance I should attach to it, and that is why it is important. I always judge more from such little indications than from greater things, concerning the character of those around me. And from this little thing, my own dear girl, I see that you love me as I would be loved, trustingly and sincerely.

If you want to get letters from me often, you know how to do it; I will answer all yours to me immediately. I like to write to you, and hope it is not tiresome to you to write to me. If it is, do not write; keep it a pleasure. I love you, darling, more than I can express in feeble words; I am always thinking of you, and counting the moments until your return. I am very glad that you may come home soon; it is an age since you left me, already. I long to look into those dear, dear eyes, and have one more sweet kiss from my Katie's lips. But if we have honey all the time; it palls; so I suppose I must be content.

Perhaps you will say, "If the honey palls, what shall we do when we are married? Shall we grow tired of each other?" I answer, no: because we shall have something besides the honey. If we had only kisses for each other, they would pall after a while; that is why so many couples tire of each other after the honeymoon. But we will have something else beside; we will study together, read together, do good together, and grow good together; then the honey will never lose its sweetness, but will always give us the same delight. If we only try to make each other better as well as happier, we may be sure our love will never die; and our happiness will be the more intense, the better we become. This is why I love you so dearly, because I hope that loving you is loving goodness at the same time. Shall I not then say our love is for eternity?

But I must stop. If I should write all the day long, I could not express my love; but you like to hear words of affection, as I do; and therefore dearest Katie, I tell you again, I love you as I never dreamed I could love, I love you more than all the world together, I love you more than I love myself, more than I love my own soul. May I never be loved less than I love, is my prayer; and may you never cease to prize my love more than anything else.

Goodbye, dear, dear Katie, Frank

Concord, February 21, 1857

My dear, darling Katie,

Here I am alone in my room, Saturday morning, thinking of you . . . Every moment spent away from you appears like a blank in the pages of my life; the present fades from my sight, for Memory points me back to the past, to those happy hours of your society that I enjoyed so keenly, while Hope points me forwards to the future, where I see a whole lifetime of such hours. Dear, dear Katie! When will that time come? We must wait long years before we can find your day-dream realized; but why do I say your day-dream? Am I not always dreaming of that "little parlor of our own," with my arm round you, and your dear head on my shoulder? Those eyes of yours haunt me . . . I yearn to look into them again, and read the same tale of love that I once saw there.

While I am writing now, your two photographs are before me, and the lock of your hair that Jennie gave lies between them. Will it make you vain if I tell you I think you are beautiful? There is something in your eye I never saw in any other's, something which first made my heart beat when I looked at you. I would rather not have everybody admiring my own dear girl; not that I am jealous, but I should hate to have the world have anything to do with what it cannot understand nor appreciate. You have told me now when you first suspected that you loved me. I feel thankful that my homeliness saves me from the fear of your being first attracted to me by that kind of love which is all to so many young ladies; I mean, that school-girl admiration of a handsome man. I do not believe it possible for even your love to deceive you into thinking any such absurd thing about me, nor do I wish you should entertain any such ideas. I would rather feel I am loved in spite of my plainness, than feel your imagination has made you regard me other than I am: not even your saying so would make me consider myself anything but homely. But luckily I do not care if I am; I should not like to be repulsive, but I am not at all desirous to be thought handsome. And nothing gives me so great faith in the sincerity of your love for me, as the consciousness that your romance has not dazzled your judgment; that you knew all the while I was poor and ugly and yet loved me notwithstanding. It would give me no pleasure to find you thought me handsome; but I should like to have you think my face expressive of love, honesty, and common sense. I have not much vanity, but a good deal of pride, and only feel humiliated instead of gratified, at being praised for what I do not possess. If you thought me handsome, I should fear you did not understand me in more important matters; and nothing is so hard to bear as to be misunderstood by those we love.

I found my hopes of happiness with you on no slight foundation: I think that you can share my inner life, that which is alone life to me, my thoughts, my imaginations, my hopes, my fears, my joys, my griefs, my love. Yes, my own darling, I hope and pray that our love is of that enduring kind which is not driven away by misfortune, not lessened by time, not terrified by the gray hairs and tottering steps of old age, not destroyed by death. If either of us feels that our love cannot stand these tests, it will be kindness, not cruelty, to tell the other so: let us pause before it is too late, *before we take the solemn vows of marriage upon us, and humbly and sincerely ex-amine our own hearts. There is no greater source of bliss, unspeakable, heavenly bliss, than a true and well-chosen one.*

My own Katie, my pure, gentle, loving Katie! We are not boy and girl; although our years are few, we are man and woman in thoughts and feelings. One great reason why I feel so sure that I have taken a step of which I shall never repent, is, that my love for you wakens holy desires with me; it stimulates me to seek goodness, and to fit myself to be your companion in heaven as well as on earth. Therefore, even if it should be my lot to lose you now, never to see you again in this world, I would not wish I have never seen and loved you; I would still feel, in the midst of anguish and despair, that—

> *"Tis better to have loved and lost,*
> *Than never to have loved at all!"*

How I wish you could look into my heart, and see how truly and ardently I love you! And yet, you can tell how much I love you by looking into your own dear little heart and seeing how much you love me; for I will not do you the injustice of think-ing that you love me less than I love you. But you cannot learn what a tumultuous, wild, passionate thing my love is, for you are not a man, and cannot understand the intense vehemence of a man's attachment. Woman's love is no less strong and abid-ing, but from her nature it must be more quiet and gentle; it cannot have that impetu-osity characteristic of man's love. But do not fear that I shall ever cease to love the true and the beautiful, so long shall I love my darling girl.

It is only four weeks since I first learned that you, dear, darling Katie, blessed me with your love. As it grew the same time, with the setting sun lighting up the west, I sat down before the stove, my head on my hands as then, I lived over again that happy hour. Once more I heard those sweet words, "I hope so!", once more I seemed to taste the transports of that first, hallowed kiss. Only one short week from that hour, so dear to me, so sacredly cherished in its remembrance, we were called upon to part for the first time. What happiness was mine in that fleeting week! What agony at its close! All I want is, that you should remember me, and love me as before, not that you should have a moment's grief on my account.

I do not dare think of the consequences if I should lose your love; it almost maddens me even to think of it, and how could I endure the reality? Remember my earthly happiness is wholly in your power—oh guard it well . . . I could not, would not live deprived of your love. Every fiber of my heart is twined round yours, and

"I have found my hopes of happiness with you . . ."

———

67

nothing but annihilation shall ever separate them; love is life, and they two cannot be separated.

Concord gossips are still busy, of course, but they are off track. The story now is that I am paying attentions to Susie, as I continue my evening visits at Mrs. Dana's as usual. Perhaps it is better to have it so; folks of common sense will not give credence to a tale so evidently absurd as that there is anything between myself and a mere child like Susie. Susie generally meets me at the Office, and it makes me almost choke with laughter to see the curious glances and wondering looks of the good people assembled. I find myself devising plans of reading and studying together after your return (blessed word!), if you live within a practicable distance. Just imagine it with me; we are sitting side by side at a snug little table in a room by ourselves (for your mother and sisters have very considerately found occupation elsewhere), studying German, we will say, for instance; I will hold the lexicon, and look out the words. Pretty soon you want to look over the book too; our heads accidentally touch, and then of course, we take a little recess, which we occupy in kissing. After we have got through this little play-by-play, we resume our studies; we must be careful not to take too many recesses, however. Or perhaps you will be reading and correcting my last poem. I hope it will be realized some day or other: if not sooner, at least in that "little parlor of our own." When you write, tell me what you think of this castle in the air, darling.

When you write again, please direct to Cambridge, Box 87. I shall soon be in the arms of Alma Mater again. But wherever I go, I shall still carry in my breast the image of your sweet face and loving eyes, and they will be like an amulet to save me from harm. How different this term will be from the last! Then my heart was still yearning to find the living flower destined to make me blest; now my search is ended, for I have found my flower, and I am blest.

Good-bye from your loving Frank

Crawfordsville, February 25, 1857

Dear Frank,

. . . You will never hear me say that I love another better than you, for I can never love anyone else as I love you, yet much as I love you, I would never marry you if I did not think I could share your cares and sorrows as well as your joys and pleasures. I do not quite agree with you in your ideas of the relation between husband and wife; for I think it should be "Wives, obey your husbands." I do not mean the blind obedience we require from a child, not that which requires com-

mands, but a kind of obedience which I can not explain to you, but which I hope one day to show to you.

I cannot tell you on paper why I love you, but the next we are together I will tell you if I can wait as long as that before you know. I think you are mistaken when you say "that we have no chance of knowing each other better because we are so far apart." I think that I at least know you better now than when I left home.

The last thing I should think of in the world, would be to be jealous of you Frank, you told me you loved me, and I believed you and shall always believe it. I would not love you if I thought you had told me what was false. When I get tired of receiving your letters and of answering them I will send you word but I can tell you it will not be very soon.

Katie

Crawfordsville, March 1st, 1857

Dear Frank,

. . . You ask me when I first suspected that I loved you. I will tell you when I first knew that I loved you; Do you remember the night we sat be the stove playing with the chips; and I gave you one and told you that when I found the ebony I would give it you? I knew that I loved you as I could never love another; and I knew too, that you would think me that piece of ebony; God grant me that I may prove true ebony! Perhaps you think it strange that knowing what I did I should have told you so, but I could not help it, something seemed to say "tell him so" and I could not resist it. I think your air-castle very pleasant indeed. I hope it may be realized before long and it will be if I can do anything towards it.

I am afraid you will be disappointed twice at not getting my daguerreotype. The day after I sent the letter saying I [would] send it, it commenced to rain and rained all the rest of the week till Saturday.

Katie

"I have found my hopes of happiness with you . . ."

Cambridge, March 6, 1857

Dear Katie,

I read and re-read your letters, and I know them almost by heart. While I write now, the setting sun streams into my college room, and there is scarcely a cloud in the sky; everything is bathed in yellow sun-light. Nobody is in the room; a bright coal fire is burning by my side, and the flame dances as merrily as it used to in Mrs. Dana's room. How I wish you were sitting in my lap, with your dear, dear head resting on mine, both of us looking at the beautiful fire, and listening to the wind, which is roaring and whistling out-doors pleasantly. I do not want you to return, if you are getting well and strong in Indiana; but I shall feel sorry if you get no benefit from our separation. But the sunset sky grows cold and dark; I must face the biting March wind, and trudge to my boardinghouse. Good-night my darling.

March 8, 1857

My own dear Katie! You did well to rebuke my words of passion—"I love you better than my own soul." Thank you, my precious girl, for your answer to my wild and wicked words; I shall never forget it. I would not wish you to love me better than your soul, and I will remember what you say.

In the happiest moment of my life, when you said to me those sweet words "I hope so—," this unmoved part of me seemed to say, "Is this joy?" while I, the whole I, answered, "Yes!" and my trembling frame attested the truth of the response. Is all this strange and unintelligible to you? I do not wonder; it is so to me, and only shows me how vain and foolish it is for a man to say he understands his own character thoroughly. The lesson I draw from this examination of myself can be comprised in a few words—

"Be modest and charitable, and despise not the weakest of your fellow-men."

The rest I leave to God, "who doeth all things well."

My dear girl, my promised wife, may the choicest blessings of Heaven fall upon your head!

Good-bye, darling, Frank

Crawfordsville, March 13, 1857

My own Frank,

How I long to see you once more. I wish I could tell you when we expected to come home but Father will not say and there is no way of finding out whether we shall stay one week or six longer, I hope it will be only one. I received your ambrotype last Tuesday and I was sadly disappointed when I opened it, for it does not look at all like you; I do not think ambrotypes are ever so good as daguerreotypes. Do not think because I say that, that I was not pleased with it, I like it very much, not the picture but your taking the trouble to have one sent to me . . .

I had a letter from Sue the other day and she tells me that Mr. Emerson says *that you were a most faithful teacher and a better Greek scholar than Mr. Sanborn, and I like to hear such things of you particularly from Mr. Emerson for he seldom says anything of the kind.*

Dear Frank, I often find myself building air-castles about the place we shall live in when we go home, it is always near Cambridge where I can see you often. I so hope it will be, but whether I'm far from there or near I know you will always love me, even if we cannot see each other . . .

Sunset is the pleasantest and the saddest time of the day to me; saddest because that is the time I used to wait for your coming, and now I think how very long it may be before I can wait for you again; the pleasantest for it is the only time of the day that I can sit idly and dream of you and build air-castles of the time when I shall see you again.

I do not think we learn to know each other better when apart than when we are together. Since I left you I have learned that when you feel deeply you make use of stronger expressions than you intend to. When you told me that you "could not and would not live deprived of my love," you did not mean I should believe that you would take the life God gave you; if I told you that I loved another better than you . . .

God bless you and keep you always, Katie

Cambridge, March 15, 1857

Dear Katie,

You will not complain, I am sure, my own darling Katie, because I anticipate the letter I expect from you tomorrow morning, and write to you tonight. I am as busy as you can conceive, but I find time enough to think of you, and love you, and long for your return; I must be busy indeed, not to be able to do that. Yes, Katie, I feel that my love for you grows deeper and stronger every day, and I know that I can never love another as I love you. If affection can make you happy, I think you will be so; I cannot conceive of greater love than mine for you. Nor is it like the tides of the sea, which keep on rising higher and higher, but presently sink away again; it is like a deep river, rather, which at first is only a noisy, babbling brook, but as it becomes deeper and wider, flows on in silence, swift and strong. Words are weak, very weak; I cannot say what I could, dearest; you must interpret my words with the meaning which your own heart will suggest. All I can say is—I love you, I love you—may God bless my love and make it the means of your happiness. Dear, dear Katie.

My good classmates have seen fit to elect me the Odist for the Class Supper, which comes off tomorrow night. My Ode is not yet written wholly. I am conscious that I shall one day accomplish something worthy of men's notice, something which I hope will do good, and add to the realm of poetry. And you, dear girl, have consented to be a poet's bride, and to share his lot; you shall not share his heart, for that is wholly yours. You have said, though not in words, that you value love and sincerity higher than gold and lands; and I have believed you. Heaven grant you may never repent of your choice!

Evening. I have finished my ode, and I feel quite glad to have it off my mind. I cannot help looking forward with eager anticipation to that time when I do not have to work in solitude; when you will sit by my side while I write, and re-inspire my flagging zeal by your encouraging smile and approval. May I not hope that time will come? I count the days till I can once more claim a sweet kiss from the lips that said, "I hope so!"

But there is the midnight bell—I sit alone in my room and must seek my bed. May dreams of you refresh the sleep of your own,

Frank

Cambridge, March 17, 1857

Dear Katie,

I feel very tired tonight, dear Katie, for I have only had one hour's sleep in the last forty hours; but I am going to finish my letter that I may send it to you tomorrow morning. Our "Sophomore Class Supper" came off last evening most successfully, to the great glory of the immortal "Class of '59." It was dark and rainy when we set out, about sixty of us, in a couple of omnibuses crammed as full as they could be, bound for Lexington House. We reached our destination about 10 o'clock, and after waiting an hour or so, we marched into the supper room. I was disappointed in not being able to sit by Will Huntington; but was placed by the side of the President of the evening, in my capacity of Odist, and had no choice. Perhaps you would like to hear the particulars of a college "Supper," and I will try to describe it.

The supper was served up in great style; a bill of fare and copy of the Ode lay by each plate, and waiters were as attentive and polite as so many Frenchmen. After discussing the more solid part of the banquet, the wine was brought on, and circulated freely; nothing was heard but laughing and joking throughout the room. I did not drink at all myself, not because I felt any danger of drinking too much, but because I had "sworn off" with a classmate who I feared would indulge to excess if he drank at all; when the "Class of '59" was proposed, I would have liked to drink one bumper, but did not. However, I consoled myself with the cigars. When the dessert was brought in, the President called upon the class to sing the Ode; they all arose, and sang it to the national air of Cambridge "Fair Harvard."

After they had got through they called upon the "Odist," with uproarious clapping, which I will not deny gave me pleasure to hear. I made a short speech, (are you laughing, Katie?) and then they heard various speeches and songs from other members of the class. Toasts were proposed, and among others "Lovely Woman," which I did not drink even in water; your dear face was before me all the while, and I could not drink to your health at such a time. But in the course of the evening, one of my intimate friends came to me with a couple of glasses of wine and whispered to me,

"Frank, drink to my Fanny, and I will drink to your Katie."

"I cannot," I answered, "I do not drink this term at all."

"Very well," he replied, "just put the glass to your lips without tasting it then."

"So be it," said I, and grasping his hand, I raised the goblet to my lips, while he did the same. That was not ribaldry, my own darling. Poor fellow! He is not happy like me, and the tears stood in his eyes as we pressed each other's hands; perhaps my own were not wholly dry, but if so, I am not ashamed of it.

But I cannot decide to describe to you the latter part of the evening; such scenes are not for the eye nor the ears of a young and innocent girl. It made my heart-ache, as it always does, to see noble-hearted generous young men voluntarily resign the crowning glory of manhood and reason; yet I could not avoid the sight. It is too often the case that the most amiable and warm-hearted fellows yield to excess; but I most assuredly will cast no stones. Everybody has his own peculiar temptations; and it is no goodness of mine that my feelings are not the same as theirs. Still it is a sad, a very sad spectacle, to see young men to whom I am warmly attached make themselves lower than the brutes that perish.

We did not get home till nearly four o'clock in the morning. I did not take off my clothes, but took an hour's rest on my bed with my shawl thrown over me. I felt pretty worn out this morning; but you cannot guess how much better I felt when I took from the Post Office your little daguerreotype. It drove away a headache which was coming on, and I feel perfectly well with the exception of fatigue. I cannot stop now to write more; I can only say that I thank you so much for your beautiful little present, which I shall value more than I can tell.

Frank

"I have found my hopes of happiness with you . . ."

———

73

Cambridge, March 21, 1857

Dearest Katie,

I was overjoyed this morning to get a sweet letter from you, when I had given up all hopes of hearing from you this week . . . I am sorry my ambrotype is not satisfactory; my classmates who saw it, said it was pretty good, and I thought it was too good-looking for the original altogether. But when you get home, I will try and see if we cannot have better luck at a second trial. I wish I could say I was fully satisfied with yours, to console you for your disappointment; but truth compels me to say that my delight is confined to the case, and does not extend to the inside. It is awfully wicked to prize the casket above the jewel, isn't it? But do not think I was not very much pleased with your present; it gave me proof of your love, and that dear face of yours is too deeply daguerreotyped on my heart ever to be effaced. How I wish I could see it now! My own darling!

I am very glad Mr. Emerson was pleased with my instruction of his children; I certainly tried to be a faithful teacher, and I own it is very pleasant to find I succeeded. One reason I want to know where you are going to live is, that I shall try to get a school in the same town for the next winter, in order to be with you as much as possible. If I cannot get over there, I do not think I shall teach this year, but I cannot tell yet.

You say you were glad I did not think you very unreasonable to find fault with "those words of mine." Of course I could not think your gentle reproof unreasonable, when I felt it to be so well deserved; instead of being offended, I thank you for it, and hope you will always be my guide when you see me go astray. You will always find me very patient under your rebuke, if I feel it to be merited, and know it to be prompted by the true love of my darling.

But I am going to give you another look into my heart, even if when you take your eyes away again, you esteem me less than you do now; only love me as dearly as now, and I shall have strength to be sincere with you. I do indeed wish you to know me as I am; it is necessary for your happiness, and if on further knowledge, you find me less than your loving heart believed, then tell me so, and God will give me courage to act only the manly part. And I will not dissemble my apprehension that you have overrated me in more points than one; but time will show you the truth, I hope. Now listen.

You think that when I said "I would not live deprived of your love," I said what I did not mean. It is true I did not mean to make a threat, or avow an intention to "take the life that God gave me"; but I did mean to say that if you ceased to love me, I believed I should be unable to endure life. However much it shocks you, dearest Katie, and however much cause it gives you to doubt of your wisdom in accepting me as the one friend for life, still I must go on: I dare not be silent on a point so closely involving your happiness. You, with your gentle nature, have no conception of the volcano I carry in my breast; you cannot understand the violence of the passion which I know to be only slumbering there. I tell you that if it had not been for the fear of breaking my mother's heart, years ago I should have committed suicide. Do not shudder—I must tell you. I have no constitutional fear of death, as such, whatever; I am subject to mental depression, which when augmented by despair, as it once was, made me utterly reckless of right and wrong.

I once made up my mind, three or four years ago, to take poison; I asked for prussic acid at an apothecary's, and if he had not refused it, suspecting some mischief, I should have taken it. I have more than once stood on the side of the bridge at Beverly, intending to throw myself off, when I was only prevented by the sudden thought of my mother's grief. Thank God, the strength of my affection counterbalanced the strength of my despair. Now when I wrote those words, I only gave a hurried glance at what I believed would be the consequences if I were to lose your love. Every fibre of my heart is twined around yours; and if you were to take it away, I know you would carry away alas my reason, my conscience, my all.

Death I never dreaded, pain, whether bodily or mental, always; and if stung to desperation, I feel there is that in me capable of any crime whatsoever. If kept under, and ruled with an iron hand, this something will give me all that is valuable in my character; if not, it will work my utter ruin. I love you better than my life, because I feel that in loving you, I am loving gentleness, goodness, God, and my own soul. You can tame this demon by your influence, if you will; the reason why I sought my "living flower" so eagerly was, because I knew it would be the flower of my life indeed, if ever found. And now I believe I have found it; and I feel greater confidence that with God's help I can rule my own spirit, than I ever felt before.

No wonder you did not suspect all this, for how could you? Think over what I have written, Katie darling, and interrogate your own heart closely, if you be indeed willing to run the risk—to give yourself to me, being what I am. Then tell me once more of the result—God grant that it may be favorable.

So God bless you, and good bye from one who will love you always.

Frank

"I have found my hopes of happiness with you . . ."

———

Crawfordsville, March 28th, 1857

Dear Frank,

Your letter surprised and startled me, it was what I should never have suspected of you. I can only say that when you tell me such things they make me fear not for my own happiness but for yours. It makes me love you more if that were possible to feel that you need me so much.

God bless you now and always, Katie

Cambridge, March 31, 1857

My dear Katie,

Your letter reached me this morning . . . this morning after reading your letter, I sat nearly an hour indulging my fancy. I am afraid you were the cause of my not shining very brilliantly in the chemistry recitation.

I should think you were "taking care of yourself" with a vengeance, when you took your first walk almost two months after being in Crawfordsville. I wonder how you contrive to live without more exercise in the open air. If you are determined to make me useful in the sewing line, I shall take my revenge by acting the part of a doctor, and making you take long walks while I darn the stockings at home. How should you like that? If you take walks, I fear the stockings will go undarned, for I shall not be able to stay behind when you go out . . . I like to think of my after life as devoted to love, and not to fame, for which I am not at all eager. Domestic happiness is my chief desire on earth, and that I can never have without my darling Katie. Our love is not of the kind that will grow cold and dead under the chills of old age. The snows of winter protect the roots of the flowers, and do not destroy them; so the snows of time will only shield the flower of love until they bloom once more in a realm where there is no more snow and winter.

Do not fear that I "love you too well;" if you fear that already, I am afraid you will never be satisfied, for I only love you more and more as the days wear on. Love cannot stand still; it must either grow or perish, and I know you would rather have it grow, would you not? But the bell just struck mid-night and I must say good-night to my own darling.

Frank

April 5, 1857

For nearly two months I have not written a line in my journal, because my inner life has not been connected much with the every-day incidents through which I have passed. My dreams have all been of Katie; not for a moment has my love for the sweetest, dearest, best of God's children flagged, or been forgotten.

April 21, 1857

At last the weary period of waiting is brought to a close—Katie has returned.

Friday evening I received a note from Mrs. Dana, informing me that the Lorings were expected Friday or Saturday, and inviting me to spend Saturday and Sunday at Concord. I got it just as I was going to hear Mrs. Kemble read "Much Ado about Nothing," and I am afraid I could not be a fair judge of her performance. I took the first train the next morning for Concord, thereby cutting Prof. Felton's recitation in Romaic; all the way I was schooling myself for disappointment, for I could not believe that happiness and I were to shake hands again so soon. But on approaching the house, I saw somebody sitting at the window, who left it as I drew nearer; and no sooner did I enter the door than I heard a light step on the stairs, and Katie's dear lips were pressed to mine. My God! I could scarcely believe my own senses—I seemed to be in a dream. But it was a dream from which I have not yet awakened.

She showed me upstairs, and introduced me to her sister Sarah, whom I had not seen before. They all received me with the greatest cordiality, and the moments flew by unheeded. Katie was quite pale, owing to the fatigue of the long journey, but in my eyes was lovely indeed; if gentleness and innocence and love are not beautiful, then there is no beauty. That afternoon and evening we spent in each other's company, alone; Mrs. Dana contrived to leave us in her room, with a true woman's kindness, and I at least was not ungrateful for it.

Katie went to her old seat before the stove; I drew my chair beside her, and tried to raise her to hold her in my lap, but she looked up in my

"I have found my hopes of happiness with you . . ."

face with a sweet smile, and gently shook her head; then laid her cheek on my knee.

"There is one thing you do not understand yet, Katie."

"What is that?"

"That there must be equality in love; I am not a tyrant, neither are you a slave."

"But the fire will burn better if the draft is down low," she replied, pointing to the stove.

"Then sit on my lap to please me; I hope your place will be next to my heart, and not at my feet."

She complied, and buried her head on my shoulder, while I trembled like an aspen. I could hardly speak for very joy; was ever a mortal so blest as I? There are times when silence is the greatest eloquence, and her soul-like eyes, that seemed to read my very thoughts, spoke more than words. I gazed into their pure depths till I almost forgot my own existence; for a time I was conscious of nothing but an intensity of passionate love that swallowed up all other thoughts and emotions as the ocean swallows up the rain-drops. Her warm and tender caresses thrilled me to the soul; yet her maiden modesty, her delicacy, her guilelessness, made me feel almost an awe, as if in the presence of an angel of God.

I told her more particularly than I ever did before, the story of my love for Mary Susan Everett; and when I had finished, I asked her if she loved me any the less, that I had loved before. If there is truth on earth, then her eyes spoke truth as she looked on me; there was love measureless, unspeakable, heavenly.

Oh God! What have I done to deserve such happiness?

"Have you ever suffered much, Katie?"

"No, not much; I think I have, though."

"From sickness?"

"Yes, somewhat, although I was never confined to my bed with a long sickness; I have had to suffer a good deal of pain. But I did not mean that."

"What was the cause, darling? Can you tell me?"

She hesitated.

"Was it from the same cause that I suffered from? Do not tell me unless you wish to."

"No, not exactly: but I so longed to find somebody who would love me as much as I wanted; and now I have found that somebody," she added, blushing, and laying her dear little cheek against mine.

I could only clasp her to my heart, and promise I would be her friend indeed; one who would love her better than all the world beside, and one whose love would not cease with life.

"My own sweet girl! We will go side by side through this world, and I hope we shall not be parted in another; if we do not go up together most surely we shall not go together at all."

And I pushed back the hair from her forehead, and turned her face up to mine; what a tale I read there! Meek, trusting, confiding, undying love—what more need there be?

Sunday we went to church both forenoon and afternoon. I saw quite a number of my old scholars, and shook hands with all I could. Storrow Higginson, one of my best and pleasantest pupils, said to me—"O, I wish you were coming back tomorrow, Mr. Abbot!" But I did not see them long.

We were alone about two hours Sunday evening, and had a very pleasant conversation, though nothing that I can write here very well. She laughed at me a little for kissing her so much, yet with strange inconsistency did not withdraw her cheek! She said if I kissed her so much, I should get tired of it; to which I replied I would try and see. So I did try—and I saw, plainly enough, that the more I kissed, the more I wanted to; it seemed to intoxicate me, almost, with the excess of happiness.

But it is growing late, and I must stop. I left early Monday morning, and am now looking forward to my next visit with more than a little impatience. My first thought in the morning and my last thought at night is, "God bless my darling Katie."

April 29, 1857

My darling is not well and strong. When I saw her, she was very pale; she looked so frail and delicate that a nameless apprehension sprung up in my breast which I stifled; and must stifle or I shall die. I told her, if I lost her, I should lose my all, my everything; and so it is.

I know I should not bear up against a loss whose very shadow fills me with dismay; which I cannot look in the face. My God! I could not live

"I have found my hopes of happiness with you . . ."

without her, and drag on through weary, weary years—no, it would be too much for me to endure. I shall not think of it, unless I wish to run mad. I yearn to be with her all the time; there is an aching sense of something wanting from morning till night, a passionate desire to be with her and forget in her dear company the thousand cares and vexations that harass and agitate my spirit.

Cambridge, May 4, 1857

My darling Katie,

I just went to my drawer to get a new pen, and what do you think I saw in my pen box? A little piece of slippery elm which you gave me only a few days after I first saw you; I kept it, for I knew very soon how much I loved you, but I never hoped then to have you love me. Now that you have promised to be my wife, to share good and bad fortune with me, till death do us part; as truly and sincerely, I believe, as I now repeat my promise to love you for better, for worse, for richer, for poorer—to love you, and you only as long as I live.

I love you dearer and dearer, and I cannot help believing that our love will always thus increase. We are very young to have taken this all important step; it is impossible that we should perceive the awful import of our words when we promise in the eyes of God and man to cleave to each other for life as husband and wife, to leave father and mother and be all in all in each other. I almost shudder to think of my daring to incur such a fearful responsibility at my boyish years; to think that henceforth your happiness involves the peace of two immortal souls . . .

Frank

May 8, 1857

This past week I have been very happy, for last Saturday I got a letter from Katie saying that her mother is willing now that our engagement be made known. Accordingly I have been congratulated by my classmates repeatedly, with the greatest kindness and cordiality, and it seems so strange to think I am engaged! To think that a young, innocent, trusting girl is willing to declare to the world that she loves me more than all beside me. I hope to God that there will be a perfect confidence between Katie and me; I cannot be happy unless there is an absolute, unreserved blending of soul with soul. It is the deepest want of the human heart next to that want of God's love and help; and I fear that is not to be found even in the closest friendships. Man and woman were meant to be all they can be, to each other; if they find it impossible to attain this one-ness of heart and purpose, I cannot conceive of a drearier lot than the wedded state, a more dreadful hell than that which was designed to be a heaven. With fear and trembling did I make up my mind that I had found the one woman who could alone be my heart-wife; and with prayer and unspeakable yearnings did I venture to ask that one woman the most momentous question I can ever ask of any mortal being. Now we stand up together side by side, and say to the world—"We promise to be to each other the one companion who shall share our real existence, and to open our hearts fully to each other as far as we may with the im-perfect medium of human expression: and may God help us to do so." I almost shrink in dismay at the vastness of the responsibility we take upon our shoulders at our early years; but I trust that our Father will assist us in performing the sacred duties of our new relationship.

May 12, 1857

Saturday morning, after waiting very impatiently until eleven o'clock, I took the cars at Porter's for Concord. Katie had written to me that she would meet me at the depot to show me the way to "the cottage" which they have rented for six months. So I was not surprised to see her when I got out of the cars, but I was most egregiously surprised to find that she had come up in the same train with me from Boston. She had seen me get into the cars, but could not signal me at all. I was very kindly re-ceived by all the family, but I was very sorry to find Katie had a bad headache; she bore it without the least complaining, however, and smiled as pleasantly as she could all the while.

"I have found my hopes of happiness with you . . ."

———

81

Just as the clock struck eight, I recollected an agreement I had made with a classmate, and leaning forward, whispered to Katie, "One of my classmates whom I like very much, is in Boston at this very minute with a young lady whom he likes very much; and we made a compact to think and speak of each other exactly at eight tonight."

She laughed. "Do you like him very much?"

"Yes, a great deal. He is almost as bad off as I am."

"Is he indeed! I wonder if the young lady is as bad off as I am!"

"I am afraid she is. But she has had better luck than you have. Do you pity her very much?"

"Well, no—not a great deal."

"How hard-hearted!"

"Do you think so?"

"Perhaps she does not need to be pitied."

"I don't believe she does."

"Nor I either."

One by one the others dropped off and left us alone.

We sat looking out of the window side by side before supper, and talked a long while.

"How black the sky looks in the west. It is going to rain," she said, after a pause.

"The storms will come, sooner or later."

"I know it, but if we are together, we shall not mind them, shall we?"

"O Katie! By and by a storm will come that we cannot withstand. Pray God that storm may be long delayed! And when it comes, may it come upon both together!"

She clung closer to me, and pressed my hand almost convulsively. Meanwhile the sky was all overcast with black lowering thunder clouds, and we could hear the rain-drops fall heavily one by one against the window panes, while the lightning flashed every now and then, followed by distant peals of thunder. The wind rose, and blew round the little cottage with a wild wailing sound, which awoke in my heart that same nameless apprehension that I have mentioned before. As I looked on her delicate, frail little figure, for a moment I was filled with a shuddering fear that I did my best to stifle. We sat watching the clouds in silence, till the tea-bell rang. Just as we were getting through, Mrs. Loring looked out and said:

"Why the sun is shining: we shall have a rainbow soon."

My eye caught Katie's, and I saw by the luster there that the same thought had flashed through our minds at the same time. We rose, and went together to the little "green room," and stood before the window looking at the west. The sun was beaming forth gloriously, and poured a flood of rich and mellow light over the whole sky, and seemed to gild the underside of the dark clouds around those which were still dropping the rain-drops. Everything was bathed in the golden shower of light, and as I passed my arm round Katie's little waist, I said:

"The darkness is turned to light! I have learned a lesson, and will no longer dread the coming of the storm; let us go and look at the rainbow, darling."

So we did go; and we looked at a splendid, double rainbow, for a good while, that arched the whole heavens. While I gazed, a feeling of peace and trust came over me, and I pressed her dear little hand.

"I wish you could tell me what you love me for," said I, looking up into her face.

"Why, I have told you I don't know, I can't help it," she replied, with a smile and a kiss.

"Will you let me try and tell you then?"

"Yes, indeed you can."

"I'll try. I love you because I see in you those qualities and traits which characterize the true woman, that is, my ideal of a true woman; I mean gentleness, purity, and a strong unwavering deep affection that is always the same, that forgives and forgets the faults of the beloved object, and increasingly points upward. You love me because you think you see the ideal strength of mind and of will, the energetic, masterful power to accomplish, which marks a well-developed man. You want something to cling to, to look up to—" (she turned her head, and looked at me with a meaning[ful] smile) "for protection, I mean, you darling. You know we must both look up, each to different qualities. Reverence is a necessary element of true love, and you revere me because I am the stronger, I revere you because you are the better."

"No, no," she said, putting her hands before my mouth, "you mustn't say better."

"Yes, darling," I said, gently taking her hand down, "it is so, whatever you say. The very knowledge of evil contaminates, and a man is fortunate if he passes through the scenes of life with only knowing evil. This is the office of woman—to guide us, and purify our motives, and impel us to greater goodness by showing us its exceeding loveliness; while man's office is to do the work of life, to accomplish something worthy of life, to accomplish something worthy to be accomplished. We ought not to say that either office is the higher, because they are equally necessary; to use a very homely illustration, if I bring the meat and you bring the potatoes, we can make a very good dinner together; but neither would dine so well on meat alone."

"I have found my hopes of happiness with you . . ."

———

83

"I think that you are right," said she, laughing, "although there is not much poetry in your illustration."

"Never mind the poetry of it, so long as it is true. Now to do my work, I want a very different kind of wife from what most men want. The majority of men need only to be loved, to be encouraged to act their several parts; but not so with me. My work will be intellectual work, and that too, of a kind that requires sympathy; I have therefore sought an intellectual companion as well as one who can love me, and I believe I have found one at last. So you will cultivate your mind as much as you can, I hope; for you must share my pursuits, or I shall not be perfectly happy."

"I hope you are not mistaken in your choice," she said, softly.

"Do not fear," I answered, kissing her, "I have no mistrust.

"When I first knew you, I saw you were wholly different from the rest of them, and I saw also that they did not know it. Now let me guess at something of your past life, of which I know nothing; for you have let me do all the talking. When you were a little girl, a very little girl, you had an indefinable longing which you did not understand, but which made you unhappy. You went with other children, but you felt they were not like you at all, although doubtless you loved many of them. As you grew older, you used to go alone into the fields and woods, and stay out there for a long time; when you were with Nature, you forgot this unspoken and almost blind feeling of loneliness. You used to watch the sunsets, and gaze into the river, and pore over the flowers, and find a sweet solace in their companionship; at those times you felt very happy. Also, whenever any one spoke a word, even in jest; that had the slightest harshness, so slight perhaps that nobody else would have noticed it at all, you would go off by yourself and cry, and feel troubled and wretched a whole day at a time; while a casual kind word would make you proportionately as happy. As you grew still older, you began to understand this hidden craving of your nature, and you longed, oh so earnestly! to find some one who could understand and share these secret emotions. You were not always sad by any means, you often were unaffectedly gay and merry; but sometimes you seemed to be so to others when you were not. At last you saw me; you loved me very soon, not because you thought me handsome, or good, or rich, or wise, but because you felt at once that here was somebody that could read your character alright, and love it, and cherish it, and with whom you could commune of those thoughts and feelings which were a closed book to those around you. Have I guessed truly my darling?"

"Oh Frank! How could you guess so well?"

"Because I read it in those dear eyes and because I knew right well in my own experience that which I read there. We have both that same exquisite sensitiveness to slight impressions, and that is the reason it took us so short a time to love. We at once understood each other's characters, and did not have to reason them out as most people must."

But I cannot recall much of what we said; this conversation was one of the most interesting ones I ever had, because we seemed to be more and more near to each other in those things which will cause our union to be cemented together by ties that cannot be broken. I never loved so warmly and truly as then, and I feel a daily increasing confidence that we are indeed meant to be the companions of each other for time and for eternity.

Cambridge, June 5, 1857

Dear Mother,

You don't know how glad I am that you love Katie. I thought you could not help it, but I feel a great deal better to know it. You say rightly that she understands me; I knew almost as soon as I saw her that she could, and it was because I trusted my instinct that I was so sudden in my action. I saw by your looks that you feel anxious about her health, and I assure you I am not more blind than you; but never speak to me of this—it is enough to let you know that my eyes are open. Whatever may happen, I tell you I shall always thank God for having known and loved Katie—but I won't write so, I dare not.

Frank

"I have found my hopes of happiness with you . . ."

June 14, 1857

Katie spent the May recess with me at Beverly, and the five days seemed to be only five minutes. I went to meet her at Porter's on Wednesday, but did not see her till we got to Boston. Her head ached quite badly, and she felt tired. When we got home, Mother and Emmie greeted her so warmly that she felt little of that restraint that I feared she might feel at going for the first time into my home. I was very much pleased when [my younger brother] Willie began to love Katie at once; he clambered up onto her lap, and caressed her as tenderly as possible. I cannot recall the particulars of these two or three days in their order, for I left this journal behind by accident, and have only just got it again, but as I think of them, I will set them down.

While I was at Beverly, I placed on Katie's forefinger, as a token of our engagement, a slender gold ring which was my grandmother's betrothal ring. It was doubly sacred for me; for I was named for her, and believe her to have been a truly good woman. May we be as happy together as she and grandfather were.

June 21, 1857

I went to Concord last Tuesday evening, and came back last night (Saturday). Katie and I were alone a good deal. Thursday evening the other girls went off to bed quite early, and left Katie with me on the sofa. She seemed rather more silent than usual, and for a long time neither of us spoke. At length she raised her head from my shoulder, where it had rested, and gazed intently on the forefinger upon which I had placed that ring I mentioned before. With her other hand she was slowly, very slowly moving the ring towards the joint, when I instinctively put it back, and exclaimed,

"Don't move it over the joint, Katie!"

As I looked in her face, I saw it was perfectly white.

"Frank, take off the ring, and keep it till I ask for it!"

The words seemed meaningless to me; I could not stir, but it seemed for a moment as if I should stifle. She saw it, and hastily throwing her arms round my neck kissed me passionately, and said,

"Not that I do not love you, Frank, for I do with my whole heart; but I wish you to take it off."

I said nothing for some time; a hundred thoughts passed through my head at once, and I was confused with the strange conflict of my feelings. I could conceive of no possible reason for such a step on her part, and I feared some terrible evil threatened us. For a short time I suffered exquisitely; suddenly the idea flashed across me that, as she was unwell at the time, she feared her health should incapacitate her from maternity. I could not express my apprehension though it made my heart sink within me; but pressing the ring back on her finger, I cried.

"I understand you, perhaps; keep it on. Whatever affliction God may bring upon us, my fate is, and shall be, the same as yours."

Her hand lay passive in my own; and she looked steadily in my eyes without speaking. But I could not endure the uncertainty long; my brain was brimming with bitter fears, and laying my head on her shoulder I said—

"Is it because you fear that when we are married, we shall be alone together?"

I do not know whether she understood me or not; she answered me in the negative.

"For God's sake, tell me what it is, Katie; you must not leave me in suspense. It is my right to know."

She hesitated, and then said,

"Just before I left Crawfordsville, the very night before I came away, I heard a voice tell me "not to love you so much." I don't know whether it was a dream or not, but I heard it very distinctly. I told Mother, but she laughed at me; yet I could not forget it. I have meant to tell you ever since I got back, but have not had the courage to. When you took me home, I knew you were going to give me this ring; but I could not refuse it when you put it on my finger. Now, Frank," said she, looking at me with all her soul in her eyes, "God meant that I should love him first, and you next, but I find I am loving you first."

"But will you love me less if you make me take the ring off your finger?"

She shook her head.

"Then why do it?"

She made no answer; but before I knew it, she had drawn the ring from her hand, and placed it in mine. I started as I saw it, and the poor little thing, trembling all over, in tears threw her arms round my neck. I passionately kissed away the bright drops, and clasped her to my heart as if I should never see her again. Then I took out carefully the little lock of her hair which I have worn next to my heart ever since it was given to me, and laid the ring in it as it lay curled in my hand, then replaced the paper where it was before. She cried again as she saw me do it, but I wiped her cheeks again and kissed them.

"I have found my hopes of happiness with you . . ."

———

"My own dearest girl, I am not going to let this trouble me, for I believe it springs from ill health. When Mr. Frost [her minister] returns, see him and ask him about it. But although you are wholly free from your promise to me, I shall not consider myself free from mine to you; on the contrary, I now renew it. I will love you always as her who, I believe, has been given to me by God, and I will never marry any other woman while I live."

"Oh, Frank! I will never marry anybody else if I do not marry you!"

"I do not want that promise, darling; if you ever love another more than you love me, I pray God he will give me strength to resign you unselfishly. If I know myself, I value your happiness above my own." Dear, dear Katie!

July 4, 1857

This morning I finished my Institute Poem, which contains about 400 lines. It is a very crude, disjointed, and rudely-expressed thing, and does not by any means do me justice, except at the close, which is as good as I can write at present. I have purposely left it ill-conceived and ill-expressed, although it is rather hard to read a poem which I know is not so good as I can write. I feel sure that now I have succeeded in writing it in so ordinary a manner that I need not fear an election as Class Poet. I hope sincerely that my selfishness and vanity will not make me accept that office, in case it should be in my power to do so. Oh God, help me to act generously by my true-hearted, generous friends.

Cambridge, September 3, 1857

My dearest Katie,

The clock just struck nine (our hour, you know) and the great round moon is peeping into my window, although somewhat shamed by one candle, and somewhat obscured by the leaves of the dear old elms in the yard. You cannot guess how it thrilled me to see the old familiar faces again, and "clap palms" with my true old friends. Absence brings its own reward, my darling, in the delight of reunion; as we know, don't we? So we go on alternating from pain to pleasure. I sometimes think life is like the sea in more than one respect, and especially in this, which I never saw commented on: the waves are continually rising and falling, and yet, no matter how high they tower, they always sink into a gulf proportionately deep. So our sufferings are almost always compensated by joys as great and the reverse . . . Write soon to your loving,

Frank

Framingham, October 5, 1857

Dear Frank,

. . . Only a fortnight more and I shall see you! It does not seem as if I was almost eighteen years old. A good many people have asked me if it did not make me feel old to be engaged. I am sure I never felt so young in all my life, as I have for seven or eight months. I wonder when I shall begin to feel old.

Your own, Katie

Cambridge, October 6, 1857

Dear Katie,

Your letter, which I got this morning, was very welcome; although a little tardy. I have been thinking of you all day and wishing I could have a kiss or two. It is an age since I have seen you and the two weeks still to come before I am at home again, seem another age. If you only lived within three or four miles of Harvard, I should consider myself a little better off than if I should find a bag of money.

. . . It seems as if the crush of this world were coming upon me too soon; I cannot help feeling that it is hard to give up on my time for reading and private study, and slave for dollars and cents when I should really be acquiring useful knowledge and cultivating my intellect. Besides, though I cannot really doubt that I have more poetical ability than most young men in college, the dark hours will come sometimes. Then I feel as if I were a fool to incur such a debt and undergo so much anxiety of mind, just to become a rhymester and second-rate poet. I get disheartened, and feel tempted to give up the scheme of education; to enter some active business, and throw all my literary tastes to the dogs. There is nobody on earth whose sympathy extends to such troubles as these, unless you can give me encouragement; and somehow I feel as if you were too young to understand such things. Yet if I could see you often, you could cheer me with a greater power to soothe these fancies than anybody else, if you tried. I know you love me dearly; but you talk so little when I am with you that I cannot tell whether you take much interest in my poetical success or not. To me, it is all in all; I don't wish to be rich, nor powerful; I leave such gewgaws to those who

"I have found my hopes of happiness with you . . ."

———

89

covet them. I propose a higher, nobler destiny to myself; yet so weak and incompetent do I feel at times, that I am sorely tempted to give up in despair. Katie, dearest, can you give me counsel and encouragement? You have the power to nerve me to endure anything, if you do but know it; and I come to you for your comfort, because, if you have none for me, I know not where to look for it.

I am afraid I am selfish to write so to you. Yet it is a relief to unburden my heart to you, and will you not forgive me? I cannot confide such things to any of my friends, lest I seem self-conceited and arrogant, in claiming the sacred gift of poesy . . .

It is almost midnight; my chum is quietly asleep by my side, and I am alone. I hardly know why, but my heart is sick within me; everything seems black. I doubt if I can get money enough to carry me through the year either by begging, borrowing, or better still, by earning. Pupils are scarce, and I have little tact in getting them . . . I am afraid I have made you unhappy by unmanly repinings. Don't be troubled—it is one of my depression fits, which I can't control. Before you write again, I shall be more cheerful.

Your loving, Frank

October 8, 1857

Dear Frank,

Why should you be sorry that you have told me your troubles and you ask me tell you mine, and why should you not tell me of yours! I do not wonder that you think I do not understand what you say or that I care little above your poetical success. I know it must seem unkind in me not to say anything after you have been telling me of your hopes and fears, but if you could only see into my heart you would see that I do understand and sympathize with you. If I take an interest in what those around me wish to accomplish, do you not suppose I should take a greater interest in what you, who are dearer to me than all else, desire most of all. I wish for your sake I could talk more. I do not know why it is that I can not, but I can never say what I wish to. Have patience with me dear Frank, and for your sake I will overcome this fault . . .

I know you will succeed in the work you have undertaken if you only persevere, if my love will help you and you know that you have that, without my letting you know that. I love you better than my life . . .

God bless you, Katie

This is one of my attempts to tell you what I feel, and I have failed as usual . . .

Cambridge, October 9, 1857

My dearest Katie,

If you only knew, or could know, how much help and delight and comfort your letter gave me you would not call it a "failure." If that is what you call failing, I hope you will always fail. Oh my dear, dear, dear, Katie! It is not often that my eyes are wet with tears but they would come while I read your words of love and sympathy; but they were tears of affection, darling. As I said then over and over I could not tell whether my heart more filled with inexpressible yearning to clasp you to my heart or self-reproach for having seemed to complain and not appreciate your tenderness, or whirling tempest of love that stirred me almost beyond self-control. I burn to see you, to pour out this pent-up flood of passionate love. You are my better angel, darling; and nothing in heaven or earth will ever step between our mated souls. Do not think I said anything in my last letter in the spirit of complaint; while you love me, I shall think myself more blest than I ever dared dream of before I knew you. I was only depressed by a constitutional tendency to occasional melancholy, increased by my present anxiety about money matters. But your tender words came to me breathing nothing but unselfish devotions and pure, gentle, maidenly sympathy; and they have touched me more than any words ever touched me before.

Darling, I would pour out my whole soul and lavish all its treasures on you, but I might as well try to describe the sun to a blind man, as attempt to give expression to the up-welling springs of affection in my heart. Let the unwritten love atone for the wretched written words. I can only invoke all Heaven's best blessings on your dear head. You have strengthened me and cherished me; and I hope you will never again think you cannot write to me out of your loving heart. You need not suppose that, because you do not write me studied and elegant letters, you cannot reach my heart; on the contrary, your simple and earnest words have ten times more power to touch and console than the most elaborate expressions could have. It is not words and phrases that I wish for; I can find those in the dictionary. What I do wish and what you have given me, is simply the thoughts and feelings of your dear self.

Your own true, Frank

"I have found my hopes of happiness with you . . ."

Framingham, October 22, 1857

Dear Frank,

. . . You were right in saying I did well in asking you for that ring. I have felt happier since you gave it me, than I have done for a long while before. I see now how

very wrong and foolish it was ever to give it back to you. I thought I was doing right.
I wanted to get rid of the thoughts that troubled me and I thought I could do it by
giving you back the ring. I am afraid I was consulting my own happiness more than
yours then . . . Katie

[This is taken from a manuscript book of poems written by Frank for Katie
on her eighteenth birthday, October 18, 1857.]

To Katie

All can weak speech love's fount unseal
    And bid its stream beholden roll;
All can the trembling pen reveal
    The secret motions of the soul,
The gushing tenderness which finds
    No outlet, save in eager eyes
That gaze and gaze till gazing blinds,
    And tearful mists unbidden rise.
And yet, O best beloved, the day
    That gave thy gentle form to light
Shall forgotten glide away,
    Nor lack my tributary mite
A slight memorial of esteem
    I bring from poverty's small store;
Dear girl, this simple offering deem
    A token of my love, no more . . .
Heaven grant it mine to be thy guide,
    And life's rough path for thee to smooth,
To love thee more than all beside,
    Thy grief to soothe.
Like children walking hand in hand,
    May we the vale of years descend,
And gain at last that heavenly land,
    Where soul for aye with soul shall blend.

October 25, 1857

I have written but very little this term in my journal, I have been so busy. Last Sunday was Katie's birthday, which I spent at Framingham with her. Just before I left Cambridge, Henry called on me, having just returned with Susie from Washington. In the surprise and pleasure from seeing him, I forgot to take my poems with me to Framingham, to my infinite chagrin. However I promised to send them by post soon.

Cambridge, October 30, 1857

My dearest Katie,

In less than a week, I shall be "twenty-one," the former fairyland of imagination, but now only a cold grey milestone in the journey of life. Heigho! I hope I shall not overlook the flowers at my feet while pressing towards the blue mountains in the distance. Yet they are not so very blue after all; at any rate, many a deep ravine and many a sandy desert lie betwixt me and them. I trust you and I will trudge along bravely some day, side by side; you shall pull my nose when I go crooked, and I will carry you over the bogs and rivers.

At last I am going to send my book. It contains all the pieces I thought would interest you, and perhaps a good many more. They are arranged mostly in chronological order, with a good many exceptions; and from time to time I will copy off whatever I may write that suits your fancy, in the same book . . . a few of them possess a slight poetical value; others are valuable to me as indicative of stages of feeling and thought; and, altogether, this may serve to give you a deeper insight into my aspirations and my past experience . . .

Frank

Framingham, November 4, 1857

Dear Frank, I shall love you just as well after next Friday as I do now, unless you think that because you are a man you are too old to play with me, and I don't believe you will be too old for that for a long while . . .

Katie

"*I have found my hopes of happiness with you . . .*"

———

93

November 5, 1857

It is the last day of my boyhood—in a quarter of an hour I shall be a man, at least in the eye of the law. Only think how the period of boyhood has been wasted! Happy and thoughtless once, then stubborn and willful, at last reckless and indolent! Comparing the accounts of my last two birthdays, I cannot but be struck with the decrease in pure aspiration. I wish I were a good man, a true Christian; but even while I record the wish, my heart is cold as an icicle; and I feel as far (if not more far) from God as before.

How swiftly the moments fly! Only five minutes more! As the bell strikes, I will read a verse or two from the Bible mother gave me; may the Commencement of my manhood be prophetic of its close. Hark—no not yet—a minute more—there—no, no—gone!

Cambridge, December 2, 1857

My dear Katie,

Do you think I have forgotten you altogether, because I have not yet written you my promised letter? . . . I reached the classic shades of Harvard in perfect safety, and am now fairly once more in the routine of college duties. It always takes a day or two to recover from the enervating effects of vacation; one feels so dismally homesick when one first comes into the college room after an absence of even a few days! Nobody had got back when I arrived, and I wandered over the buildings like a discontented ghost. One by one they came back, and soon a blazing fire was roaring up our long chimneys from every room. But I had to wait more than a day before I recovered from the effects of the good lazy time I had at Beverly.

Jim [Fay] says he can't let me send off this letter without mentioning him; so I will mention him as having just daubed my face and my hand with ink, out of pure malice and spite. We have got to write a theme tonight, and he is cudgeling his brains for ideas, and sighing most piteously because they won't come. Poor fellow! I should pity him if he had not inked me . . . he says he has left off smoking and swearing, and hasn't been drunk since last Monday, when he tried to drive his horse into the church at Newton, and was put in the watch-house for it. Too bad, wasn't it? But I must stop, and write my theme . . .

Write immediately to your immaculate Francis

Cambridge, December 8, 1857

My dear Katie,

I got your letter yesterday morning; and many thanks for it. You need not fear you will ever lose the "little place in my heart" which you now hold. Perhaps, if you could look into my heart, you might not call it a "little" place.

I never before felt it a hard task to write to you, darling; but now it is, and a very hard task, too. You will not wonder why, when you have read my letter through.

Last night there was a meeting of our Society, which, I believe, includes the whole class, at least, the majority. After the exercises were through, and before the motion to adjourn was made, I got up and spoke these words, as nearly as I can recollect them:

"Gentlemen, I wish to ask your attention for a few moments to a communication of a wholly private nature. I wish to make the statement of facts which must produce a change in your opinion of me, and that for the worse.

Nearly five years ago I foolishly began to wear eye-glasses without being near-sighted. From that time to this I have been acting a continual falsehood, because I had not the moral courage to throw off the cheat. I have tried to find some way of easing my conscience and sparing my pride at the same time; such as feigning a gradual recovery, or taking some other contemptible half-way course. But it was of no use. The only manly course left me was open confession. Accordingly I here publically declare myself to have been for nearly five years a systematic deceiver.

One word in regard to the motives which have prompted this statement. I have made it because, whatever I may have done, I do, in my inmost heart, hate and detest a lie; and because I was appalled at the thought of having to keep up this falsehood through my whole life. It has been a millstone about my neck, and I have at last thrown it off because I would not endure it any longer. This is but the first step in a long series of humiliations; until tonight I never breathed a syllable of the matter to anyone; but it seemed to me just that this first step should be as public as the fault which rendered it necessary.

I have many friends among you whose goodwill I value highly. There are two or three whose friendships I consider my greatest gain in coming to college. But I am well aware that Love and Respect must go hand in hand and I am also aware that I no longer have any title to your respect. I am content it should be so. I came here tonight prepared to meet contempt and ridicule, and I can bear it. But any pity would

"I have found my hopes of happiness with you . . ."

95

be displaced. I gain my own respect at the same time that I forego yours and this exchange is for the better. That is all I have to say."

These are nearly the exact words I used, I need not now speak of the hard battle I have had to fight with my own pride before I could bring myself to publicly degrade myself in the eyes of all my friends; nor of the imploring prayers to God that alone secured me the victory; nor of the mental agony which that victory cost me. It is all over now, that is, the commencing step is over. I have something else to speak of to you now.

I know very well that there can be no true affection where there is not the highest respect. I know that truthfulness is the very basis of all manly and womanly character; and I know also that I have grievously failed of being truthful. So far I have lost the respect of all who before reposed confidence in my honor and integrity. By my open avowal of my fault I have regained a partial claim to their esteem; yet it is only partial. Nobody can ever regard me, an honest and sincere young man. Now for the friendship this diminished esteem will suffice; that is to say, my friends, some of them at least, declare they can love me as well as before. But the case is different in love. My fair name is now sullied with the deepest stain that can be cast upon the character of a gentleman, viz; vanity, moral cowardice, and falsehood. I have no right to expect that the promise you made to one whom you believed truthful and honorable, should be binding upon you after discovering that one to be just the reverse of what you believed. On the contrary, I have no wish that you should do yourself so great an injustice as to unite your fate with a man unworthy of you. I feel that, at the present at least, I am not worthy of you; and I wish to wait till I can assure myself, and you, too, that I may eventually better deserve your love. I therefore release you from your engagement, until you can find your confidence in my honor and integrity restored by a long course of upright and sincere conduct. It shall rest wholly with you whether I may correspond with you and visit you in the interim; I shall acquiesce in your decision, whatever it may be. But your family may be unwilling that you should be connected with me, having such a despicable blot on my character; and before you decide to pity me—no, not pity—but forgive me for the past. Please God, I will try to live a true life hereafter.

I do not mean that you should publicly break off our engagement unless you wish to break it off permanently, but that it should be understood between us two. The world has no business to interfere betwixt us now. May God bless you, and guide you right, dearest.

Most truly your loving, Frank
P.S. Before you decide (for I wish you to take time), will you write encouraging words to me? I think I need some encouragement a good deal now; things look pretty dark.

Beverly, December 12, 1857

Dear Frank,

What can I say to you? I cannot believe that what you have told me is true. It is so different from anything I ever thought of you. I thought you hated everything that had the least semblance to an untruth and you have been acting one for five years. I did not think you perfect, but I little thought that want of truthfulness was one of your faults. Why did you not tell me of this before? Why— But you ask me for comfort and encouragement and I only give you reproaches, forgive me dear, dear Frank. Strange, is it not that while my heart is filled with prayers and good wishes that you may have strength to bear this heavy punishment for your fault; and while it seems as if I never loved you half so well as I do now, that I cannot tell you one word of what I feel? I thank God that He has at last given you strength to confess your faults, and I pray to Him to keep you from again wandering from the path of rectitude you are now stirring to regain. I feel sure that when this is past you will be a better and truer man. Be sure that I shall never love you less than I have done, and although at present I cannot respect you as I could wish, I know that you will prove yourself more worthy of it than you have ever yet been.

I expect to go home next Saturday, can you meet me at the depot if I do? I want to see you before I say anything to mother or father about it. Your own loving, Katie

Cambridge, December 20, 1857

My dear Katie,

I put off writing to you partly because I expected to meet you in Boston, and partly because I felt heartsick and disinclined to write—I wish I could see you . . . You say you "thought I had hated anything that had the least semblance of an untruth." So I did, and so I do. I hate falsehood more than any other vice. What, in heaven's name, but the love of truth could urge me to a public confession from which my whole nature revolted? What else could break my stubborn pride, which was never broken before? What else could nerve me to bear this daily and hourly mortification, which cuts me more keenly than steel knives could do? If you knew my haughty and willful spirit as well as I know it myself, you would know that it would have been easier to face death than the fiery ordeal I had to pass through. I began to wear eye-glasses when I was a mere boy, induced by a boyish vanity. I had no idea of what I was entailing on myself. It was wrong, but owing more to a

"I have found my hopes of happiness with you . . ."

97

thoughtless vanity than any desire to deceive, but having once begun, I dared not un-say it all. Besides, I did injure my sight, and now I am somewhat nearsighted, more so at some times than others. I have the power of making one eye much so at will; and these facts helped to keep my silence.

Fools complain—men endure . . . I would rather have my heart plucked out from my living body. That is why I proposed to suspend our engagement for a time to learn more of your own mind. I know in your trusting little heart my image is not really dimmed; it may show a scar, but it is a scar from an honorable wound. I never before felt what a glorious thing it is to command one's own respect. I can afford to disregard all else. I wish you could be with me; you would calm my stormy moods, Little Mignonetta. I love you very dearly. God bless you, for your love to me; it shall not be a pearl cast before swine.

Goodnight darling, Frank

December 22, 1857

Dear Katie,

I have just been out star-gazing with [William] Everett, the son of the illustrious Edward [Everett]. Pretty good fun, but the wind was cold. We settled the positions of several famous stars and constellations which I have been desirous of knowing for a long time. If you go home before I write to you again, I think there is no need to say anything about this matter of mine at present. I am more and more in doubt whether it was a wise thing to make a public avowal or not. On more sober thoughts, it seems to be a rather ostentatious, and unnecessarily public manner of getting rid of my trouble. I am inclined to think the most judicious way would have been to simply leave off wearing glasses, and when any body asked me the reason, then to state it. There was no need to draw so much attention to the fact . . .

Ever yours, Frank

Oh, Katie! . . . Will my sin ever leave me alone? Just now a classmate asked me if I had a pair of spectacles . . .

Beverly, December 30, 1857

Dear Frank,

I feel low-spirited tonight, and so must need to tell you of it. I am not very well, and that, added to the weather, although I never knew the weather to affect me before, makes me feel so. I am hot and feverish, and I want to feel your hand on my cheek and brow. I suppose any other hand is as cool and soft, but none ever feels so to me, and none ever sends such a thrill of pleasure through me.

They say that a woman's love is calm and quiet. Mine certainly is not. It is like a river, always deep and strong, but sometimes rolling over stones and rocks and sometimes gliding quietly along through pleasant fields and old woods. Tonight it is tumbling over the rocks, and tomorrow it will be flowing quietly through the fields. I have such a longing to see you and feel you and hear you say "my own darling," that it makes me almost unhappy. Am I very silly to feel so? No, I know you will not think so, for it is my love for you that makes me feel as I do. Goodbye, dear, dear, dear Frank.

Katie

1858

Cambridge, January 1, 1858

My own darling Katie,

Your note that I got in my trunk was a beautiful New Year's gift, and I thank you for it very much. No letter that you ever wrote gave such a great pleasure as this, I think, it was so tender and loving, and so beautiful in itself. The words were just the right ones; and the meaning I cannot criticize, for somehow my eyes grew dim, and I almost involuntarily prayed that I might never cause your trusting little heart one single unnecessary pain. You touched the chord of my nature. You say your love is like a river that is tumbling over the rocks. I think you are right in using such a simile, even of a woman's love, which is, at least, less passionate and impetuous than a man's. So is my love like a turbulent river; sometimes calm, it is true, but commonly rushing with no gentle current. Yet by and by, when these two restless streams, shall join in one, (as I hope they will, with God's favor) they will form a deep and broad flood, too tranquil to be disturbed. May we glide smoothly down its surface, and never part till we reach the great sea beyond, still clinging to each other as when we commenced our voyage. I send heaps of love. Heaven be with you, darling.

Frank

"I have found my hopes of happiness with you . . ."

———

99

Beverly, January 6, 1858

Dear Frank,

. . . *Do you know that it is just a year since you were introduced to me? I worried myself a good deal that night as to what you would think of me. It does not seem as if it was a year since that little party and yet it seems as if I had known you a great while longer than a year.*

I can hardly believe that you care about my letters. I know that you do, but I do not know why you should. I generally fill them with commonplace remarks about things in general. I have never given you but one or two glimpses of my "inner life." I do not know how I got into the habit of writing so to you. To others it is very natural for me to write in this manner for I have always cared very little for my thoughts and feelings. I know that it is different with you, and I will begin the New Year with the resolution that I will try and overcome this dislike which I have to writing from my "inner life," for I would like to have you know what that life is, and you can surely never find out if I cannot tell you. Good night and may God bless you my own dear Frank.

Katie

Cambridge, January 7, 1858

Dear Katie,

. . . *I thought Mrs. Dana had her "soiree" on the seventh of January, not the 6th; at least I so wrote in my journal. Nevertheless, it is very likely I was mistaken. But how come you recollect the date so distinctly? I thought my first appearance was not very successful. I have often tried to find out what you thought of me in the early part of our acquaintance, but always received very unsatisfactory answers. If you wish to write to me more out of your heart, (as I most sincerely desire you would do), this is a grand chance to begin. I liked your last letter, so much because it was evidently a faithful transcript of your feelings when you wrote it.*

Since you cannot go to school, I would take pains with my letters. It is a great charm in anybody, especially in a lady, to write a lively, pleasant letter; and it is a charm only to be acquired by practice. The most elegant style is that which gives the least evidence of study; it is by no means necessary to shun commonplace remarks, but there is a great art in saying ordinary things in a piquant, agreeable manner. Anything that plainly comes from the heart, and is simply and naturally expressed, gives a vast deal more pleasure than a studied composition . . .

So it is just a year since we were first acquainted. How well I recollect those pleasant days, darling! Your "sophomore" is half through his junior year, and soon will be fighting in the world, while you patiently await the result of the battle . . .

Good night, my darling, from Frank

Beverly, January 11, 1858

Dear Frank,

You were right about the night at Mrs. Dana's little party, it was the seventh and not the sixth. When I wrote I was thinking more about the time you would get my letter than about the time I was writing it. So you would like to know what I thought about you when I first knew you? I think you would be surprised if you knew what I thought when I was first introduced. Henry Dalton came up and asked me if I would be introduced to you. I said no at first, but afterwards, I said yes: and at the same time determined to make you pay more attention to me than you did to anyone else, merely because I liked to secure attention but I had not talked to you ten minutes before I forgot all about that, and really wanted you to like me.

After you began to come down every night I used to watch for your coming very eagerly. I had to sit upstairs all the morning because I could not walk, and after dinner I went into Mrs. Dana's room, and stayed there the rest of the day. I used to think over what you had said and wonder what you would have to tell me when you came again. Perhaps I should not have learned to love you so soon as I did if I had been able to go about instead of sitting still. I did not see any one but you, and I thought you liked me. I was afraid that you sometimes thought me rather bold, particularly the night when I gave you that piece of chip but I could not help say what I did. What have you done with that piece of chip, I know you kept it for some time?

Do you remember that night when I came in from tea and found you sitting before the stove with your face hidden in your hands? I put my hand on your shoulder and you looked up as if you were frightened, but when you saw who it was, you smiled and I knew from that smile the air-castle you had been building. I had disturbed you, but you told me you would "willingly have your castles so destroyed."

Another time I came in and saw you just rising from your knees, when I asked you what you were doing you said, "I am trying to make my dreams real." I am afraid you think because I never say anything about such things that I had forgotten all about them. I very seldom forget anything you say to me and I believe I remember everything you said to me during the eighteen days you knew me before you told me you loved me . . .

Good bye from your own, Katie

"I have found my hopes of happiness with you . . ."

———

Cambridge, January 12, 1858

Dear Katie,

    . . . You say you feared I should think you bold when you gave me that little slip of wood. If I had loved you less, I should have thought you so. But I read your heart well enough to know that you would not show your feelings until they were very strong. You were too honest to do such a thing for effect, and I was too deeply earnest to win your love to pout at my own success. You have that little worthless bit of pine to thank, that I did not keep silence, when to have kept silence might have changed the destiny of both of us. And do you imagine I could lose it? Do you pretend to wonder if I have it still? You know as well as I do that it is cherished among a few tokens of my real life, of no value in themselves, but speaking whole volumes to me, whenever I look at them.

    Only think, Mignonetta, one year has gone already! How quick in passing will the rest seem, when they are once passed! Today a mere boy and girl, tomorrow a husband and a wife, then two graves lying side by side, I trust. Oh darling, my own darling, may that dark curtain of death, which must sooner or later fall on us both, when it rises, open to us the view of some happy realm where grief and fear are strangers, and where truth and love dwell together forever. One of us must in all human probability go first to that unknown land; but if we act toward each other as lovingly and faithfully as we now both mean to do, that dreadful separation shall be robbed of its bitterest sting. Hope shall spring from the ashes of earthly happiness, and cheer the lonely heart of the one still destined to toil and suffer below . . . Now write me a long affectionate letter, won't you?

Love, Frank

January 13, 1858

    Dear Frank,—Did I ever tell you what "mignonetta" meant? I don't mean the translation of it, but the meaning it has in Floral Language. It is—"your qualities surpass your charms." I hope that it is true; for, if it is not, I cannot hope to keep your love long . . .

Katie

Cambridge, January 16, 1858

Dear Katie,

I did not know the meaning of "mignonetta" in the Floral Language, but I shan't give my name for you on any such account. I think it is appropriate, however. I should never be very deeply in love with a young lady whose "qualities" were not superior to her "charms," even if she were lovely as Venus herself. I think your "qualities" are superior to your "charms," and therefore I love you. I am not to be smitten with a merely pretty face. You are pretty enough for me, and I don't wish you to be prettier than that . . .

Frank

Concord, February 8, 1858

Dear Frank,

I am going to sit for my portrait! Isn't it perfectly ridiculous? Mr. Austin, the gentleman I told you was trying to paint Sue's, was in here yesterday, and he pounced upon me in such a manner I had to say I would sit for mine. I went today for the first time. I rather like it. Besides, I feel rather curious to know what sort of thing he will make of me. I had a compliment from Mr. Sanborn the other day. He said I have a 'very beautiful profile'!!! What do you think of that? I suppose I ought to feel very much delighted at it, but it does not please me half as much as when you tell me I am "not very pretty, but pretty enough for you."

Your own Katie

Concord, February 15, 1858

Dear Frank,

Mr. Sanborn was perfectly delighted to see me back in school this morning. Someone told me the other day that, if I grew strong and healthy (as one of my friends was wishing I would), I should be so handsome that all the young men would break their hearts for me! Don't you begin to feel jealous? Don't you think I am a little goosey to tell you all the silly speeches people make to me? I don't care one fig for them; for I don't believe they mean anything by them, and, besides, I know they are not true . . .

Your own Katie.

"I have found my hopes of happiness with you . . ."

———

103

Cambridge, April 21, 1858

My dearest Katie,

Of course I met no very wonderful adventures on my journey back to the antique halls of Harvard. That diary of yours pleased me very much. The motion of fastening flowers in the margins is a very tasteful one, and I hope you will continue the practice. What numberless little fancies of that sort ladies have! It is very pleasant for us stupid hobgoblins of men to see the dainty devices invented by you airy sprites, you lightsome fairies, you sylph-like essences of grace and beauty!

I wish I could take an unmixed satisfaction in your project for next winter. How I shall miss my little Katie! It is a long way to Texas—oh dear! It is a long time, six months—oh dearer! It is hateful to think of you so far off, oh dearest! Even though I see you occasionally now, it is some consolation to reflect that an hour's ride at anytime will bring us together again. But to be a thousand or two miles away,—that is not good to think of. However, it will be an excellent thing for you, and you need not fear I shall grumble much . . .

Your own, Frank

Concord, April 29, 1858

Dear Frank,

. . . Father is going to sell his house in Framingham, and go West to live. It is useless trying to stay this way any longer . . . Father would have gone earlier if it had not been for us girls. I know he feels worse about taking me than any of the others, he knows I have more to make me wish to stay here . . . I shall probably stay here until Lydia goes to Texas, and go with her then next year go to mother and father . . . Good night and pleasant dreams of your own, Katie

Cambridge, July 1, 1858

My dear Katie,

. . . When I see you, I have a great many things to say. It is time to think of life in earnest, not any longer mere children. I want to see you become a woman in the highest sense of the word, just as I wish to become a man. We must both of us make a plan of living; by which I do not mean to settle before hand every individual action, but to determine what shall be our motives and highest aims. It is not well to *work in an aimless manner, living from day to day and from year to year just as cir-cumstances may direct. We must rule circumstances, not let them rule us. This world is not the end of things, neither are we to consider ourselves as the center of the world. Unless we make usefulness our chief object, the threescore years and ten will bear little fruit. I want you to think of these matters, and make up your own mind according to the light given in the Bible. If you really wish to be my wife, you must give up the idea of ever being rich. I will never make wealth even so much as a sec-ondary object; I will devote myself heart and soul to my Master's service, and leave all else to him . . .*

Good night, darling, love me always, and strive to fit yourself for the highest kind of love, as I will likewise strive—then our reunion shall be real and lasting . . . God bless you, ever your own, Frank

Concord, July 8, 1858

Dear Frank,

. . . I could not help thinking today how short a time it would be before my con-nection with Concord would be almost entirely broken up. After this year I shall have very little to do with it . . . Sad thoughts always make me feel that I am no longer a child; and the thought that I must soon leave my old home is very sad. I do not al-ways feel that as if I was beginning to be woman instead of a child. My play time has seemed so very short that I can hardly believe it has been as long as most girls. Yet I would not give the pleasure of being a woman for the sake of a few more years of girlhood . . .

May God bless you and keep you Frank, Katie

August 6, 1858

FRAMINGHAM

I do not expect to either go to Dunbarton or Wilton this summer. I haven't money enough, and Katie wants me all the while she can, for her father will certainly go West in the fall. At any rate, he is going to sell the house next month and Katie will go to Texas with her sister. She would rather go to school another year, but she does not think her father can send her.

Cambridge, December 3, 1858

My dear little Katie,

Are you wondering why I do not write? I am pestered with work, the Hasty Pudding meets before long, and I seize Time by the forelock to send you a line, just to let you know I am alive. It seems an age since I kissed your dear little face in the entry, Monday morning. I fancied I saw a tear in your eye—was it my egotism?

Good night and God bless you . . .
Your Frank

Framingham, December 29, 1858

Dear Frank,

. . . When you asked me Saturday night, why I sighed, I did not tell you simply because I did not know myself. As I sat by your side in the twilight and darkness gathered round us, a gloom seemed to settle down on my heart, I sighed to relieve myself of it. Then came the thought that has sometimes troubled me: "What if Frank should grow tired of me? Perhaps now he wishes he had never asked me to be his wife." Do you think I doubt your love because I think such things? You are mistaken if you do. It is because I know I am not what you wish or need for a wife, and I am afraid you will some time find it out, too. God help me if ever you do! You need a wife who will open her mind and heart for you to see and read all that is in it, and for whom you can do the same, feeling that she can understand and appreciate all your desires and aspirations. It is my nature and habit to keep my thoughts and feelings to myself, and there must be a great change before it can be otherwise. God grant it may not be long before it does take place! You cannot know how deeply I felt those words of yours, "Katie never tells me anything," because you have not known the struggle between nature and inclination, and had nature conquer, and then felt that you had caused pain, when you would have given anything if you could only have told what was in your mind. Many a time, when I have been sitting in your lap and you have asked me what I was thinking about, I have tried to tell you and failed, and then your arm would loosen its hold round my waist. I knew it was wholly involuntary on your part, but it showed that you felt hurt that I did not answer you, and I have prayed so earnestly that it might not always be so. Sometimes I feel as if it would not last, but I cannot tell. At least I shall try to fill my mind with all pure and lovely things, that

you may have something worth looking at, if I am ever permitted to show it to you. It is almost one o'clock. Goodnight.

Your loving Katie

1 8 5 9

Cambridge, January 16, 1859

My own darling Katie,

I am so sorry you were disappointed in your letter Saturday night! My vacation begins Wednesday, and [it] is provoking to lose you just at its commencement. But I wouldn't keep you back for anything.

A poor half-witted beggar is sleeping on my couch at my left hand, while I am writing to you, "Jimmie Candyman." The poor fellow was burned out a week or so ago, and literally has no where to lay his head; so I offered him the use of my room tonight. Tomorrow I shall try to hunt him up a room. It is a pity he is not a little less odorous; but I should be a poor disciple of my Master if I let my charity be stifled by a little Irish fragrance.

This afternoon I took leave of my little Sunday school class. Dear little things, I hated to leave them, even for six weeks; I love them much. I had made a kind of farewell address of the highest description—told that I hope they had gained as I had by our meetings, that they had won greatly upon my heart, that I often prayed for them, and trusted we should at some time all meet in a holier and happier home above. I shook hands with them and kissed them all round; and they seemed to love me, which cheered my heart . . .

Oh how I wish I could at once begin my life as Christ's anointed servant. I would so love my work, so earnestly devote myself to His service, that I know He would bless my efforts. And I can work now; I hope I do work now. Good night, my dear little wife-to-be, and blessings fall upon you like a shower of flowers this night.

Your own, Frank

"I have found my hopes of happiness with you . . ."

———

Framingham, January 18, 1859

Dear Frank,

I miss you so much, after your visits, that it sometimes seems as if it would be better not to see you at all than to see you for so short a time. The evening after you left me, when I knelt to say my prayers I wanted to feel your arm round me and hear your voice . . . I wish the time were come when we kneel together every night. Patience, patience, patience . . . I meant to write a longer letter but the clock just struck twelve and my eyes have been crying out ever since I began to write. Goodnight, may God bless you my own darling,

Katie

Philadelphia, January 27, 1859

Darling Happy,

I thought you would like a letter before I got to Texas and this is my only chance for writing for some days . . . Oh Happy, I felt so homesick and heart-sick when you left me in the cars. I wished you had not come to the depot. I hate to say good-bye in such a place . . .

Your loving Katie

Beverly, February 20, 1859

My dear Katie,

It was three weeks last Friday since you started for Texas, and three from Wednesday since I last saw you in the cars. Yet it appears as many months since you and I read Schiller together by your parlor stove. How long these real months will seem, and into how many years they will metamorphose themselves, I hardly dare to think.

My time passed so quietly here that it hardly leaves room for my egotism to display itself in writing much about myself. Father is just now giving me a lecture on health in general and my cough in particular, which the poor gentleman believes will speedily terminate in consumption. Don't be alarmed though, there is no ground for apprehension, it is not half so bad as twenty coughs I have had in my college course, and can't hold a candle to the one I had in Concord when I first had the pleasure of dancing with you. Do you recollect that? I shall never forget it, nor the strange events and experiences of which it was precursor and partial author. The whole year looks to me like a dream, an extract from some unpublished romance, a motley compound of glimpses into fairy-land and hand-to-hand encounters with some bitter realities. Of what varied scenes is the most tranquil life in outward semblance, really composed? A stranger who should learn the outer history of my brief existence, rehearsed by some observer not behind the curtain, would think there was nothing worth reflection in it. But I might tell him what would most certainly change his opinion. And so it is, I suppose with the meanest of mankind. What a lesson of charity we ought to learn from this thought! I have no patience with the idle gossips and harsh judgments which fly around me like snow-storms. What impertinence to tell me that Mrs. Brown or Mrs. Smith hasn't paid for her last pink bonnet, that Mrs. Jones does certainly spend a great deal of money in perfumes and kid gloves. Well, I must stop my tirade, and send an assortment of kisses, prime quality, to my dear little kitten out West.

Frank

Beverly, February 27, 1859

My darling girl,

I have really become anxious lest your journey made you sick, when I got your letter from New Orleans, which, I assure you, was most welcome. To hear you talk of violets and bananas seems rather paradoxical to one who has more to do with snow-balls and icicles . . . I feel rather sad about entering upon my last term of college life; I would not clip Time's wings if I could. Still as one chapter of my life is closed and finished, so full of meaningful events, so rich and hallowed and cherished recollections, a dimness will gather in my eyes in spite of myself; and Hope seems less bright than her sister Memory. So much I have suffered, so much enjoyed, in these four years, that I doubt if my life after can match them. Well, when the sun has set on Class Day, I trust I can say then as now—"God's will be done."

Goodnight, dear Katie, your own, Frank

Galveston, Texas, March 2, 1859

Dear Frank,

. . . I went out to the cottage not long ago, and got a great many roses and other garden flowers; but I found some houstonias that pleased me more than all the rest. To be sure, the others laughed at me for hunting such flowers, when there were plenty of others much handsomer; but those were more homelike. Beside, I love wild-flowers

"I have found my hopes of happiness with you . . ."

better than those which are cultivated in gardens. They have always been my friends. Many times when I felt lonely or sad, I have gone into the fields or woods and talked with them, and they have always comforted me. To the wild-flowers I owe my belief in God's love for me. Do you wonder why they are dear to me? I always feel as if they were something more than flowers, and never liked to gather any that I should throw away, or pull to pieces thoughtlessly.

Your own Katie

March 8, 1859

My darling Katie,

What has become of you? I have not heard from you for nearly two weeks, and I must say such rare communication is not very pleasant. However, when there are thousands of miles between us, we must not expect they will establish a special mail for our own accommodation. Please don't forget that every letter of yours is worth its weight in gold . . .

Frank

Cambridge, March 31, 1859

My dear Katie,

I have just received a pleasant letter from you—I wish I could take my little pet in my arms and kiss her till my lips ached! Your description of your Texan home is delightful; your figs and pomegranates, oranges and mocking birds, honeysuckles and horned frogs bring up a gorgeous picture before my imagination, perhaps brighter than the original. I am filled with a yearning for beautiful things, flowers, birds, sunsets, spring glories of air and earth and sea; and if we could only roam together in such loveliness and beauty it seems I might learn the hidden secret of the word contentment. Write me full descriptions of all you see to love and admire in your little "paradise" of a cottage; and believe that though I am thousands of miles away, my heart is enjoying it all with you . . .

Frank

Galveston, March 31, 1859

Dear Frank,

I have been running all over town this morning getting "fixin's" for a great party tonight. I wish I could stay at home but it would not do to refuse my first invitation.

I know you wish to have me go into company as much as possible. In revenge, however, I shall do my best to make an impression on the first rich, handsome young Texan I see—you are so far off you can't prevent it. If you could look into my chamber just now you would be quite disgusted with the appearance of it I am sure. Gloves, slippers, ribbons, dresses, etc., etc. are strewn indiscriminately over chair and bed. Just think what you will have to endure when you get married! Perhaps you will have been out all day and come home tired and on entering the room won't be able to sit down. I think I hear you scolding at it now.

Will you be satisfied if I tell you that I have missed you a thousand times more then I ever thought I should! I have sometimes lain awake thinking of you so long that after I have fallen asleep I would dream you were with me to hear you talking with me.

Goodbye from your loving, Katie

Cambridge, April 14, 1859

My dear Katie,

Your letter of March 31 reached me yesterday, and was like it predecessors, very welcome. I trust the grand ball to which you were expecting to go proved a pleasant one, although, after expressing the hope of meeting a rich young Texan for the purpose of falling in love with him, you hardly deserved to have a very extraordinary time.

I am gradually getting towards the end of my college career, and begin already to hear the roar of the great world beyond. Before long I shall turn a sudden corner, and then the vast sea of life will burst upon my sight. I half tremble at the thought of launching my little skiff upon untried waters, and yet feel the secret stirring within which always prompts a young man to try his future where so many have gone to the bottom before him.

Oh dear! If I had not debt to pay, and no other charges upon my conscience, three years hence would see me preaching God's word will all the power there is in me; but the duty that is nearest is the one whose voice I must hearken to. I do feel compunction at the thought that you are waiting for me, and that while I cannot offer you a home, you must wait. I sometimes question the honorableness of my course in having asked you to marry one whose prospect of maintaining a wife is so far distant; but I was a mere boy, and you not much more worldly-wise. I have often told you that I consider you perfectly free, while I am not; that is, not free to be dishonorable to myself, and unfaithful. As your heart is, so it shall be, be sure and consult your heart. God bless you darling.

Ever yours, Frank

"I have found my hopes of happiness with you . . ."

———

III

Galveston, April 14, 1859

Dear Frank,

I am homesick and heart-sick, the weather is cold and strong and that makes me feel worse I suppose. I have just heard that Father and Mother are going off to Winona, Minnesota. I feel as if I had no home . . . I want you here to pet and comfort me. I wonder if it was ever intended that you and I should live quietly together—it scarcely seems as if it was, at any rate we have not been much together so far. At first I must go off to Indiana, then here, and lastly to Minnesota. But I ought not complain; everything is in God's hands and he will do all for the best . . . The rain falls patter, patter on the roof and windows. At any other time it would seem so pleasant and soothing, but tonight it makes me feel sad and gloomy.

The flowers I have pressed are hardly worth sending. I cannot press them well here; for some reason I cannot understand, they will not retain their shape and color. However, I send an orange blossom and a cherokee rosebud—I wish you could have seen them fresh.

Katie

April 26, 1859

My own little darling way off in Texas,

This morning I found two letters from you awaiting me at the Office, and you may judge the eagerness with which I went back to my room to read them. The news you told me made my heart sink at first, but now I have firm faith that all will go well. Under God, I am resolved in some way or other to prevent your living out West. I will tell you the plan I have hastily formed, and which, under some modified shape or other, I am determined to put in execution, unless God plainly shows me it is my duty to abandon it.

In a few months Stanley will probably go out West to join his uncle John. The family will then be reduced to Mother, Emmie, Willie; for Father lives in Boston mainly. Henry and Edwin have supported them entirely since I entered college. Now I am at the point of graduation, and shall be able then to do something practical by the fruit of my labor.

I claim the right, then, of anticipating our marriage a few years more or less, and asking you to share this home which I am to help support. Here in the North and in my house, you will have more opportunities of reading, studying, and becoming acquainted with my immediate family and friends. I shall be away mostly, it is true, but as often as I can, I shall be at home. Besides, it will relieve your father of as least some care, although of course that care would not seem a burden.

I will go and see Jennie next Saturday, and if I find your father is really going to live in Minnesota, I shall see Emmie and Mother, find out their feelings (which I know will be with me) and then it will be no slight difficulty and opposition that shall turn me from my purpose.

I cannot and will not make up my mind to let you go off in the unlooked for manner. No, Kitty, you must come back, or something will happen. Our love must not end so.

Your own, Frank

Galveston, May 7, 1859

Frank darling,

You may feel sure that I shall not go off to Minnesota till after I have seen you. If it rested with me alone to say whether I would go at all, I should certainly say "no." But Father and Mother have something to say about it. As yet, I feel that my duty to them is greater than to you; and whatever they think best, that I will do.

You ask me to share the home which you are to help support. But you are not able yet to support a wife, too, and I feel as if I could not become part of your family in any other way. That seems and really is selfish, but it is no foolish fancy that makes me say it, and I hope this same selfishness may spare us both a great deal of pain. However, it will be time enough to decide what to do when I see you. I shall at least spend the summer in Massachusetts. Good night, darling.

Your loving, Katie

May 16, 1859

Dear Frank,

You need not fear that I shall go to Winona without first going North. I could not make up my mind to go without seeing you. Father has gone there to live. I think it is the very best thing he could do, but it is certainly anything but agreeable to me. I want to be in some place where I can see you . . .

Katie

"I have found my hopes of happiness with you . . ."

———

113

May 20, 1859

My dear Kitten,

Your news that you expect to come North in about a month was most welcome; I long to hold you in my arms once more, and feel how long a kiss tastes again. Besides, that will bring you here before Class Day, and that will be pleasant. I want you to be here . . . I got a letter from your sister Susie the other day, and she asks me for a daguerreotype of my ornamental self! Perhaps you will not be jealous if you grant her request, by which, of course, I am greatly flattered. Please state any objections you may happen to entertain, and I shall listen with the most consummate request. I am going to keep quite a number of my class photographs, which I fancy to be very successful, and if you wish, I will reserve you one. It may be, however, that possessing the original may render the counterfeit unnecessary. I do not doubt my homely face is stamped indelibly on your loving little heart.

I have been writing my Class Ode this morning. It is disagreeable to have the job to do, for I did not want it at all. It was pure good nature and desire to avoid giving trouble to my classmates who made me accept it . . . they wanted me to accept it, after I had declined standing for poet. I have written two stanzas which I think are better than the average of college productions in this line.

Your own, Frank E. Abbot

Galveston, May 21, 1859

Dear Frank,

I hope to go up to the country before I go home but I am not sure whether I shall or not. Now is the pleasantest time to go, the prairies are covered with flowers and the magnolias are in blossom. I want very much to see a grove of magnolias. A lady sent me one of the blossoms a few days ago. I tried to draw it but I did not succeed.

God bless you, darling! Katie

May 29, 1859

Dear Frank,

I haven't any objection to your giving Susie your daguerreotype. I shan't be very jealous of her. You must reserve two of your photographs for me. I want one and Jennie wants the other. You ought to feel greatly flattered to think that your likenesses are in such demand at present. I send the thousand kisses I wish I could deliver in person.

Katie

June 3, 1859

My dear Katie,

I have not written for two or three days after your letter, and I think you will find my reason to be good. Day before yesterday, about eight o'clock P.M., all the class except nine individuals entered four omnibuses behind Holworthy Hall, and after a ride of three hours or more which nearly broke all our necks, owing to the darkness and bad roads, arrived at Point Shirley House to enjoy our Class Supper. Here we spent the night, having a jovial time, eating, drinking, singing, and laughing, until half past four o'clock in the morning. Didn't we feel sleepy that day! At Professor Lovering's lecture, twenty-seven were sound asleep, and I keep nodding all the time, sleeping five and ten minutes at a time, then waking up to catch indistinctly a word or two about "terrestrial magnetism" and to see the old Negro Clary grinning like mad, behind the worthy Professor, and then falling into another daze of equal length. After dinner, I lay down, and took a regular nap. I drank but a little, but there were many intoxicated. I long to see you darling, and have one more kiss.

Ever yours, Frank

June 16, 1859

My darling Katie,

Are you sufficiently magnanimous and forgiving to pardon my not writing . . . I have been waiting to get information in regard to Commencement, that I might save you some unnecessary delay. I wish you and Lydia would come down to the colleges, on Wednesday morning; I will meet you at the station. Oh Katie, I want to see you and to have you to myself for at least a little while; I will, at Wilton; where we will go for a "few weeks of happiness" you spoke of. If I can only make you really happy, I shall thank God from my very heart. Dear little Katie, your lot has not been an easy one; I hope I may lighten its cares, and sorrows at least a little.

Kisses, kisses, kisses from Frank

"I have found my hopes of happiness with you . . ."

115

[On June 24, 1859, Frank Abbot and fellow members of the Harvard Class of 1859, observed by their families, celebrated their Class Day. The "programme" of the festivities indicates that the ceremonies began with a prayer by Harvard president James Walker, followed by an oration by

James Balch, a poem by William Reed Huntington, and the class then sang Frank's Class Ode.]

Once again has the earth lightly whirled round the sun
    In the jubilant dance of the spheres;
Ever youthful, another bright gem she has won,
    To flash in her circlet of years.
But our spring-tide is ebbing, our morning is o'er;
    The moment of parting draws nigh,
And our Mother—God bless her!—stands here at the door
    To throw us a kiss and good-bye.

Like the arches and spires that with marble of frost
    The Winter-elf builds on the pane,
Hope's castles may melt and in tear-drops be lost,
    Ere our sun its proud zenith shall gain.
But friendship has rung a sweet chime from her bells,
    Whose echoes, when youth shall decay
Like the music that lurks in the sighing sea-shells,
    Will haunt us and cheer us for aye.

As the rain-drops that wed on the river's gray breast
    Are divorced in the broad heaving main,
From the north and the south and the east and the west
    We have met but to scatter again
The noble old elm waits our time-honored song,
    Let us join "hand to hand, heart to heart";
We have laughed and been merry full long,
    But the summons is come, and we must part.

Yet the friendships of youth, like the Pleiads that weave
    Their soft meshes of splendor on high,
O'er our paths a bright glory of starlight will leave,
    And smile all the gloom from our sky;
Oh cleave to the love that has hallowed the past,—
    It shall hallow the future's long years!
For today, ere life blows her stern clarion blast,
    We baptize it immortal with tears.

HARVARD COLLEGE.

ORDER OF EXERCISES

FOR

CLASS DAY,

Friday, June 24th, 1859.

[While a light rain fell on the freshly shorn grass of Harvard Yard, Frank and friends George Chaney, Samuel Haven Hilliard, and Ellis Loring Motte held a "spread" in their rooms in Hollis Hall. Later, members of the Class of '59 gathered at an old elm in Harvard Yard, known as the "Rebellion Tree," sang "Auld Lang Syne," and performed the traditional "running" around the tree (when the seniors, with hands joined, encircled the tree and ran around it in one direction, while underclassmen, also holding hands, circled them in successive circles to run in opposite directions—until they collided). The chaos was followed by a lunge for garlands that decorated the trunk of the old elm. At five thirty, the students moved through the yard and cheered the college buildings and faculty. That evening there was a "Levee" that was "terribly jammed" and featured "the fastest waltzing this side of Paris." From ten to eleven P.M., the Glee Club sang in the Yard.*

Class Day was followed by Commencement Day on July 20, 1859. At the close of the exercises, President Walker conferred degrees on Frank and the eighty-nine other members of his class. In his journal Frank's description of July 20, 1859, was uncharacteristically brief: "Commencement Day—and the death of my college life."

During a holiday in New Hampshire, Frank and Katie's patience to postpone their wedding evaporated. On August 3, 1859, Frank and Katie left Wilton and went eighteen miles east to Nashua, New Hampshire, where they were secretly married by Reverend Austin Richards of the Olive Street Congregational Church. Their arrival at the Church was preceded by the following note.]

Reverend Sir: For two years and a half I have been engaged to be married; but as I have not yet acquired my profession, am unable to support a family, and shall be unable to for at least four or five years. The lady's parents have recently removed to a western State, and she expects shortly to rejoin them. It is the wish of both of us to be privately married before she leaves this part of the country; and to ensure secrecy, we have preferred to request a stranger to perform the ceremony. Will you render us this kind office? You need feel no scruples of conscience at this request; no unworthy motives prompt the step, which is taken in an humble and God-fearing spirit, and not without His blessing first invoked.

*Accounts of Class Day and Commencement based on news clippings from the anonymous diary of a member of the Harvard Class of 1859 (reprinted in the *Records of the Class of 1859* in 1896) and the *Daily Advertiser* and the *Courier*, June/July, 1859.

The only person beside yourself to be present, are the bearer, a classmate and tried friend of mine, and some lady of your own family. Will you give us two certificates of marriage, signed by yourself and the two witnesses, in case you are willing to perform the ceremony and preserve our secret inviolable? When we arrive at your house, or at the church, as we should prefer to be equally convenient, I will furnish you with the names. With great respect I remain,

Yours truly _____

[The ceremony was performed by Reverend Richards and witnessed by Frank's Harvard classmate Albert Stickney. Frank and Katie's wedding certificate read "This certifies that Mr. Francis Ellingwood Abbot of Boston and Miss Katharine Fearing Loring of Concord, Mass., were by me duly joined in marriage this 3rd day of August 1859.

Austin Richards, Nashua, August 3, 1859"

We know little of Frank and Katie's newlywed life in August and September 1859, because, on January 7, 1897, the fortieth anniversary of their meeting, Frank cut the ten pages from his college journal that recorded that period.

Throughout the autumn of 1859, as Frank commenced his studies at Harvard Divinity School, Frank and Katie continued to exchange letters. A particular message from Katie delivered some life-changing news.]

Framingham, October 5, 1859

My own Frank,

I know I am very naughty to write you by lamp-light but I felt as if I must send you a letter by the morning mail. I meant to write this afternoon but was out riding two or three hours and felt too tired when I came in. I reached Boston safely after you left me on Monday . . . I spent the afternoon there . . . and went up to Concord at night. Lydia [her sister] was very glad to see me, we sat and talked some time but I did not tell her anything that night, and as I had a severe headache I went to bed soon after tea. With my headache, a feather bed, wishing I could see you and thinking what Lydia would say. I managed to pass a most miserable night and got up in the morning feeling half-sick. However, after breakfast I felt better and I told her about it. Of course she was very much surprised and wanted to know why we got married in such a way. I told her our reasons and she did not appear to think it was wrong . . . She was very kind indeed and offered to do all she could for me,

"I have found my hopes of happiness with you . . ."

————

besides which she took the trouble to go up to her brother-in-laws to find some little baby things for me, thereby saving me a good deal of work and some eight or ten dollars . . . I am very well except that I feel very hungry all the time and the mention or sight of anything to eat makes me feel sick and towards evening I begin to feel restless and uncomfortable . . .

Your loving wife, Katie

Cambridge, October 7, 1859

My dear little wife—

I would have written before, if I had had the time; indeed, I meant that a letter from me should welcome you. The day after you left Beverly, I told Emmie and Mother of our marriage. I will not conceal from you that they were both much distressed by the information. But the next morning, Wednesday, Mother went up to Boston, with my full consent, of course, and told Father and the two oldest boys. That afternoon, I received a letter from Lydia, urging an immediate and public avowal of the marriage. I postponed answering it until yesterday (Thursday) afternoon, that I might show it to Mother, and learn the result of the interview with Father and Henry and Edwin. She returned in the noon train; and after consulting with her, I wrote to Lydia that Mother would meet her Monday morning—and would go to Concord to see her.

Thursday night Father had a talk with me; neither he nor Mother are angry with us, but think that we have probably drawn much sorrow on ourselves and friends. He said that he himself, Mother, Henry, and Edwin all joined in thinking the marriage should be kept secret, if possible. It will, I fear, injure my prospects very greatly in Cambridge, to have it known there; and our interests now are one and indivisible. There is one reason why it will be bad for you to publish it now . . . I wish to God I could bear all the sorrow alone; it cuts me to the heart to reflect that I have brought misery upon you, when I had no aim but to make you happier. I did not see the true character of my plan till now; before God can declare I was completely self-deceived. All the blame should fall on me alone, for it was wholly my doing. But you must not think our case desperate. You must go West as intended.; I shall stay here and work as hard as I can. Then, whether divulged or not, our marriage will seem what it is, merely a piece of ill-judged sentiment. Let us hope firmly with a living faith in our Heavenly Father, that He will save us from suffering worse things than our folly really deserves. I only love you more deeply, little darling, because I fear I have unwittingly injured you. Let us bear this chastening with a meek and submissive heart, we yet bless this very trial as the source of great good. Dear, dear little wife, say with me, Oh God, thy will be done.

Ever your loving husband, Frank

October 9, 1859

Dear Frank,

I wrote to Mother this afternoon telling her that it would be impossible for me to stay this way and also the reasons which rendered it impossible. I heartily wish I had told her everything when I first found I could not conceal our marriage but I hated to do so then and have delayed doing it until today . . . Do not let Lydia persuade you to disclose our secret. It is better for us that our trials come upon us while we are young than when we are old, and if we cannot thank God for them let us at least try to bear them cheerfully.

Ever your loving wife, Katie

October 10, 1859

My dearest Katie,

I got your letter this morn, and it gave me pleasure, great pleasure that you will look to God for help in all of your upcoming trials. Surely His hand is strong enough to deliver us out of all our troubles; blessed be his name forever. Let us bend our whole strength to seek Him, and submit ourselves to His christening with meekness and loving trust. All this is the result of my own unwise act, and my wrong concealment of it from my parents . . . no sin lies at your door, my dear darling little wife. Dear little heart, I know you forgive me utterly for all I have done that may cause you suffering; and, please God, I will try to make you happy the rest of my life as well as I can. I thought this marriage would make you happier; my conscience is at peace there. Little wife: take good care of your health, and look up, up. My love remains with you.

Ever your own Husband

"I have found my hopes of happiness with you . . ."

October 20, 1859

My own darling wife,

Would you like to have a letter from your husband? You must keep up a good heart, you know, and trust in God; and we shall be so happy by and by, when we *get nicely established in a little home of our own, shouldn't we darling? Mean-while we both have duties to fulfill, you of womanhood, and I of manhood. You must wait patiently without repining, doing your part as the faithful daughter and sister, and by and by as mother; and I must work bravely without disheartenment, looking to God and not to man, striving to earn money, first for my creditors and next for my wife.*

I will copy my poems you asked for as soon as I have a chance; I wish I could give you a better gift. Only think, no birthday present at all from your own husband! But by and by he will give her his whole life to comfort and help her, to make up for his past folly; and will she live cheerfully in the hope of that, and all the while keep loving her own loving husband?

Goodbye—God bless you ever—Frank

Concord, October 21, 1859

Frank, my own dear Frank,

I have just received a letter from Mother in answer to the one I wrote her in-forming her of our marriage. She is not, nor is Father displeased at our marriage but they are [disappointed] at our keeping it a secret and she says it must be made known immediately; if not publicly, that is, by having it put in the papers, at least among friends. I am very sorry that it must be so.

Dear Frank I have so wished to see you this week, and now worse than ever. God help us to do our duty. Have you found anything to do yet? I hope your Father was able to get you the work that he had tried to obtain. By the way, what did Mr. [Ralph Waldo] Emerson want of you that he should write to you? Do you wonder how I know anything about it? Ellen came to me for your address to-day, and said her father wanted to write to you. Am I very inquisitive? If I am you must answer my question.

Good night darling, your loving wife, Katie

October 25, 1859

Dear Katie,

. . . I got your letter yesterday morning, and went with it directly to Beverly. In the afternoon, I returned with Emmie to Boston . . . Of course, the question as to concealing our marriage is at an end; the question now is, how best to divulge it. My own opinion, and that of all my family, is that it would be perfect madness to put it

in the papers. That would excite notice among perfect strangers; they would ask, "Why publish a marriage nearly three months after the date? There is nothing wrong about it?" A false impression, therefore, might easily get abroad, which no subsequent efforts could correct. If it is told among friends, and allowed to spread naturally, the account our friends would give would be the one which others would receive.

So much for the manner of making it known. As to the time, it ought not to be mentioned till you go West. If it is revealed before people will ask, "Why was it concealed so long?" The only answer would be, "Because the friends of the parties were ignorant of it all this time." But if it is divulged after your departure, the answer would be "The friends of the parties thought it best to wait till Kate went out to her parents." This course is best in itself, for now, while you are here, people might naturally suppose we meant to live together at once, and this would make the matter a hundredfold worse.

The sooner you start, therefore, the better it will be. If it is divulged now, I cannot wisely see you again; if not, I can see you if you come to Boston, otherwise I shall be unable to, for I cannot now leave Cambridge. I have entered the Divinity School, having first informed President Walker, Doctor Francis, and Doctor Noyes of my marriage; they all declared no impediment to taking this step, and that, too, knowing that my parents were not aware of the fact till subsequently. It must be acknowledged that we were married without the knowledge of our friends.

Your query as to Mr. Emerson is not answerable by me; he has not yet written to me. I am curious to know what he may have to communicate.

Frank

Cambridge, November 16, 1859

My own darling,

How long it seems since I held your hand in the cars, and after the last kiss caught in the last glimpse of you as you bowed your dear head to me from the window, while the cars rolled you away out of my sight! How much has passed in these few weeks! I am fairly established now in the School, and begin to get accustomed by degrees to the strangeness of my present living in my dear old haunts. But I am ten years older, at least; are you still the little girl I knew and loved? Were we not both children, ignorant of the world and living in dream-land? We will yet prove that the love of husband and wife is deeper and truer than that of maiden and lover. Do not now tell me, please, that you are less happy than you would have been; when you feel so, think of these words—I shall love you tenfold more than I could have done

"I have found my hopes of happiness with you . . ."

123

before. You must not think that I shall love you less because we have made each other suffer innocently; until now, I have not been so firm in the faith that our love will grow and ripen and bear blessed fruit . . .

Frank

Cambridge, December 19, 1859

Dear Katie,

    I am sorry you have a cold; do not forget that caution is doubly a duty now, for my sake and that of the little child—our love yet to be. I wish that I might be with you; but I can serve you better by diligence than by wishes at present . . . Frank

PART III

"Ethel's diary is unwritten . . ."

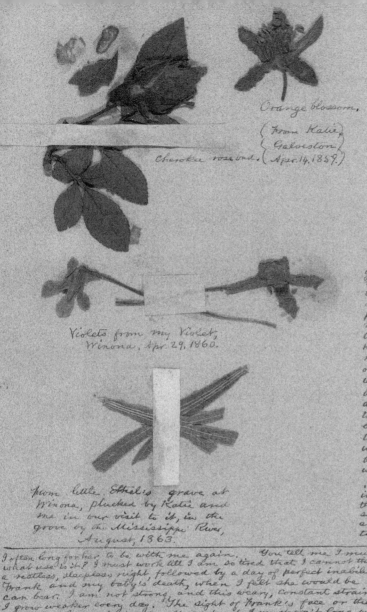

Orange blossom.

(From Katie
Galveston
Apr. 14, 1859.)

Cherokee rosebud.

From Katie, Winona, Apr. 3, 18

Violets from my Violet,
Winona, Apr. 29, 1860.

From little Ethel's grave at
Winona, plucked by Katie and
me in our visit to it, in the
grove by the Mississippi River,
August, 1863.

Galveston, March 2,

... I went out to the cottage not long ag
got a great many roses and other garden fl
but I found some houstonias that pleased
than all the rest. To be sure, the others lau
me for hunting for such flowers, when there
plenty of others much handsomer; but those
more homelike. Besides, I love wild flowers
than those which are cultivated in garden
have always been my friends. Many times,
have felt lonely and sad, I have gone into
or woods and talked with them, and they
ways comforted me. To the wild-flowers I o
belief in God's love for me. Do you wonde
are dear to me? I always feel as if they
thing more than flowers, and never take
or any that I should throw away or pull
thoughtlessly... I got some orange buds t
when I was out walking. I couldn't reac
blossoms, but I have the promise of some,
will send them to you... Your own Katie
... The flowers I have pressed are hardly wort
ing; I cannot press them well here, for some o
that I cannot understand. They will not retai
shape or color. However, I send an orange bl
and a Cherokee rosebud. I wish you could
them fresh... Goodby, darling. Katie. (Copied Ma
Galveston, April 14, 1859.

I often long for her to be with me again. You tell me I must take care of myself, and I try to do so, bu
what use is it? I must work till I am so tired that I cannot think of anything save bodily weariness, or el
a restless, sleepless night, followed by a day of perfect inability for any regular work. The separation f
Frank and my baby's death, when I felt she would be such a comfort to me, is almost more th
can bear. I am not strong, and this weary, constant strain upon my heart is wearing my very life a
I grow weaker every day. The sight of Frank's face or the touch of his hand would do me more go
anything I can do for myself, and yet I must wait long, weary months for that. I know God does
ingly afflict us," and I try to be patient under this trial, knowing that it is his will, and that it is no
without some good purpose; but it is hard to bear, and I cannot always say, "Thy will, not mine," be
I cannot tell Frank of this, for it would do me little good and only make his trouble harder to bear
know that the thought of my suffering is more painful to him than anything else, and his burden
enough without my adding needlessly to it. I only hope that with cooler weather will come renewed
and strength. I did not mean to fill my sheet with complainings when I began, but I cannot sp
these things to any one else. Mother is not well, and the least excitement makes her sick, so I d
go to her; the girls sympathize with me, and do all they can for me, but they do not, cannot un
my sorrow. I wish I might see you for a little while now; I should feel so much better, if I could
instead of writing. Well, patience, patience — the time will come when I can look back on all
row and suffering, and read plainly the lesson God would teach. Till then, may He give me stre
bear whatever He may send. Lovingly, Katie.

Cambridge, Sept. 16, 1860.

My dear little wife, ... As soon as I heard of our little Ethel's death, I was greatly distressed about
knew your nature too well not to understand the inevitable results of such an overwhelming sorrow. U
come to you, I foresaw that you would suffer from your accumulated griefs so much as to injure
health; and this fear was confirmed by a letter of yours to Mother which I almost insisted upon
against her will. Fortunately, George Chaney, who has told schemes of bringing us together which I
told you of on account of their impracticability, heard of a vacancy as teacher in the Meadville High
in the Seminary a week worth at least $1400 per annum. I applied for this situation seve

1 8 6 0

Cambridge, January 3, 1860

Dearest wife,

Merry Christmas, Happy New Year, all other kind and loving wishes! Last night I went to Mrs. Vaughn's, who had a little charade party, and most successful it was. One of the charades was "The Game of Life," representing two men playing chess, one of the players being the devil. Behind his opponent stood the angel of protection, looking sadly at the board. The position of the chess-men showed that the game was nearly over; and the anxious look of the man, contrasted with the exulting leer of his antagonist, indicated that the evil one was gaining. The angel was my sister Emmie; she was enveloped in a white haze of muslin, floating indefinitely on every side, with a head-dress of the same, showing only her face, and the long dark hair that streamed down beside it. She looked beautiful; very beautiful; the tableau will dwell in my memory. If she should ever leave us before her time, I shall dream of her standing behind me in this game of life, watching and yearning over me, in very truth my guardian angel.

Dear little wife, you too must be my guardian angel, here in this world. You must go before me, leading the way; if you grow in grace and spiritual beauty, do not fear I shall be backward in following your guidance. We must each lead the other, by *different means; you by a womanly gentleness and purity and love, I by a calm wisdom and manly strength.*

Frank

Winona, January 4, 1860

Dear Frank,

. . . No one here knows the circumstances of our marriage and of course I have nothing to trouble me save the knowledge of the suffering I have caused. Would to God dear Frank I had never married you! I am even tempted to say that sometimes would that I had never seen you! If I sinned and caused pain to those dear to me it was ignorantly not willfully, I would have died rather than made you suffer knowingly for a moment. Oh Frank! I sometimes hope that the child may not live to see the light of this world! I know it is wicked . . . my heart is full and I have written as the thoughts came uppermost.

Katie

Cambridge, January 10, 1860

Darling wife,

For anything you did or said last summer; for as truly as I love you, I believe you guileless and self-sacrificing and loving to the utmost I can desire. And do not say you wish you had not married me, or even seen me; least of all, that you wish our little child may never see the light. Such things make me shudder, for I know how bitterly you must suffer before you could utter them. I would not have things other than they are, for our Father is turning the sorrow into a blessing which will bind us closer to Him and to each other.

Dearest, I wish I could press you to my heart and kiss away your tears and chat nonsense until the smiles should come back again . . . only think, what a little treasure you will have to remember your husband by, when the little one lies in your bosom and smiles sweetly at its mother's face. My dear child do not think of the bitterness [of] our lot, for how much more of a joy than of sorrow is mingled in the cup!

Cheer up, and take heart, poor fluttering little bird; by and by you shall nestle again by my side in peace and tender love. Now goodnight, and our dear, dear Father bless and keep you always. My last thought as I fall asleep shall be of the little wife I wish to see.

Frank

January 27, 1860

Dear Happy,

Did you remember last Tuesday night that just three years ago you and I sat together in Mrs. Dana's room and by the firelight you told of your love and asked me to be your wife? I thought of it a long time and of all that has passed since then . . . how long we then thought we should have to wait before we were married and now I have been your wife nearly six months, does it seem so long as that? Shall I be any dearer to you by and by when the little child comes? I cannot help feeling that you will be nearer to me then . . .

Katie

February 4, 1860

Dear Katie,

. . . To answer a few of your interrogatories (which you seldom condescend to do to my own, Mrs. Abbot!). I did remember, that the 25th of January was the anniversary of the first kiss I ever received from your lips. (How many have I had since, I wonder?). Yes, darling, I was thinking of you then, and wishing I could fold you in my arms again. That was a happy week, the first week of our engagement. I do not doubt that many a happy week is still in store for us. And now for six months you have been my wedded wife, and before long will be the mother of my child. What a world of solemn thought is hidden in those words!

"Shall I be dearer by and by, when the little child comes?" Let your own heart answer your own question. When the helpless little infant lies upon your bosom, drawing its nourishment from its heaven-appointed fountain, and when you gaze on the tiny hands stretched out to its young mother, I know well that your soul will gush forth to cling to him with whom the priceless treasure would never have been yours. I am sure that you only asked the question for the pleasure of seeing me write once more, how dearly and tenderly I cherish my little wife who waits for me in the far West.

Frank

"Ethel's diary is unwritten . . ."

Winona, March 4, 1860

Dear Frank,

The nearer the time approaches for the birth of the babe the more I feel how little fitted I am to have the care of such a treasure. God help me to be a true mother to *it, in every sense of the word! How I wish you would be with me to help and teach me and how I will long to see the little one in her father's arms.*

The ice in the river is beginning to break, and it makes ugly work with the mails, so I have had reason to know . . .

Ever your own loving wife, Katie

Cambridge, March 5, 1860

My darling little wife,

You can guess, I suppose, from your own feelings, how I long to be with you now when you so greatly need a husband's tender and loving care. You must often feel this want of the affectionate soothing and sympathy that no one else can give you so well, and I wish sincerely I could give it to you; but all I can do is to thank you, and love you, and pray for you. I want you to write me of your present condition frankly and freely and particularly; you must know how anxiously I desire to hear all that concerns your health at present. Between husband and wife there should be no false delicacy. I shall be greatly pleased if you will tell me fully and minutely about your symptoms, feelings, desires, thoughts, and bodily ailments.

Nothing you can write will interest me so much as the little items about yourself; and especially such information as concerns the dear little child of our love. I know that in pregnancy [a] wife needs the tenderest and gentlest and most soothing care; and I know that her husband ought then to be with her. But through my own want of wisdom I am unable to watch over you during that trying period of your life.

I am glad, very glad, you still want any of my poetry, which you shall have more of before long. But just now I am very busy, and cannot stop to copy any for you. Goodbye, little darling, and God bless you and keep you with his love.

Your own loving husband, Frank

Cambridge, March 12, 1860

My own darling,

. . . I shall want to hold the little one in my arms, you may be sure, darling. What a beautiful gift to bring your husband by and by! It must remind you always of me, and kindle a stronger love in your bosom for its father, as you will be doubly dear to me because of being the mother of my child. How I shall want to see its tiny little face, and how I shall wonder if it will resemble you. We will try to fit ourselves for being the

parents of a new human soul by making ourselves more obedient and loving children of our heavenly Father . . . Goodbye, dear Katie; be very prudent about your health . . .

Your own husband, Frank

Winona, Minnesota, April 3, 1860

Frank darling,

It is so very warm today that I should be glad to put on a summer dress. I took a short walk this morning for flowers, with which the prairie is covered. I will send you one as promised. They grow in clusters close to the ground and look much like the crocus . . .

Katie

From Katie, Winona, Apr. 3, 1860.

Winona, April 13, 1860

Dear Frank,

Only think how your wife has been honored: she has shaken hands with Tamaha, the grand sachem of the Sioux Indians. Last Thursday, Mother, Jennie, Sue, and I were sitting sewing in the parlor when the doors opened and in walked three Indians. Tamaha came first and shook hands with all and then they sat down. I think I never saw a more disgusting looking person than he was. He is over one hundred years old, one-eyed, having lost the other in the revolutionary war, and so dirty! Jennie and I, however, quite lost our hearts to one of the others—he was so neat and handsome. They are fond of little white squaws so don't be astonished if I run away with him some day. They came for bread and butter!

Katie

Cambridge, April 21, 1860

My dear little wife,

 Last night I dreamed of you. I stood beside you while the little child came into existence, and he put his little arms around my neck (for it was a little boy.) And I thought you suffered but little pain, darling; but as I turned towards you, I awoke. And so I went out, thinking of my wife and little son. May that last part of my dream, at least, prove prophetic! I have at last got a professorship, although a temporary one. Professor Sophocles has just gone to Europe, and I occupy his room, and have charge of his entry till he returns . . . I do not value the appointment much except as a stepping-stone; for it will not give me more than $30.00, I suppose when the time comes that you cannot write yourself, cannot you get your sisters to send me news of you at least as twice a week? I shall be so anxious and sad if I have to wait in suspense, while my dearest wife is sick . . . Oh how I long for a loving kiss and embrace from my little Katie, to cheer me up. Write me tender words of love, darling, for I need them much . . .

Ever lovingly, Frank

Cambridge, April, 28, 1860

My dear little Mrs. Abbot,

 What unparallel distinction, to shake hands with an Indian sachem! I wonder Tamaha did not Tomahawk you, since you say that he is fond of white squaws, and I suppose his fondness would be apt to assume a scalping guise.

 I go to the gymnasium every day, and I exercise an hour or two. I found I was running down from hard work, and so made up my mind as a matter of duty to take vigorous exercise in order to recuperate. But I did hate at first to sacrifice my little leisure to legs and arms; although now I begin to take an interest in the physical again, as I find my old skill and strength returning. When I see you next, you will probably find me a mass of knotted muscles. Nothing will stand against my gigantic power.

 Now I hope, dear Katie, you will be very careful of yourself, and not fatigue or expose yourself in the least degree . . . God help you, my darling, and be very gentle with you. When the little cheek is laid for the first time against yours, think that your husband's blessing and love are with you then.

Ever lovingly your husband, Frank

Winona, April 29, 1860

Dear Frank,

. . . I wish you might be with me when the little child is born. Your baby and my baby, thank God for it!

Katie

Cambridge, May 5, 1860

My darling wife,

Many, many thanks for the little violets you picked and sent to me, and more still for the loving words which accompanied them. As I read them, my soul grew so restless that I was unable to sit longer in my room poring over my books; and the evening bell that was inviting weary hearts to prayer drew my steps to the little vestry of the Baptist Church. It made little difference to me that they held dogmas I could not write in my creed; they were sincere and met for real worship and living devotion, and through the uncouth phrases a something stole to my heart and soothed the wild tumult there.

This morning my aged grandmother died at Wilton, New Hampshire. Do you recollect, on the morning of our wedding day, how she blessed us both as we took leave of her? And in three or four weeks, my little Katie will hold a child of mine in her arms, and the tiny lips will press the bosom I have kissed so often! Oh my darling, I yearn to be with you, and help and strengthen you now when you need me most.

Ever your own husband, Frank

Winona, Minnesota, May 14, 1860

Dear Frank,

Katie has asked me to write to you, and I assume that you know I am very happy to be the first to congratulate you upon being a father, and of such a nice baby-girl, as we have all been rejoicing over this morning . . .

Katie was sick about four hours, and the Doctor was quite anxious about *her . . . At present she is asleep for almost the first time since the baby was born, which I forgot to say was half-past one this morning, and now it is almost noon.*

We have just weighed the baby, and she weighs six pounds and a quarter, not as much by two pounds as we thought she did. Enclosed you will find a very small lock of hair, that I have cut from the young lady's head . . . My head is so confused from excitement, and from want of sleep that I cannot write anymore at present . . .

Your affectionate sister, Sarah Loring

Winona, May 16, 1860

Dear Frank,

I felt as if I must send you a few words to let you know how nicely I am getting along . . . Baby is on the bed with me asleep—I wish you could see her. I have not had one good look at her yet myself. I only have her to nurse and that is not often, but when I feel her little lips and cheek pressing against my bosom I thank God with my whole heart for the treasure he had given me. And oh! I love its father infinitely more than before! God bless you and keep you papa! A name for the baby please.

Katie

Cambridge, May 20, 1860

My darling wife,

How glad I was to hear of your safety you may perhaps guess by imagining your own feelings if I had to pass through a dangerous operation at the Hospital. Thanks to our Heavenly Father's ceaseless love, my wife and little daughter are both safe at last. And now my Katie is a mother, and has a sweet little comforter to console her in long separation from her husband. Blessed gift of God! How I almost envy you its sole possession. Let its silence speak eloquently of your own Frank's love, and cheer you in your hours of sadness . . .

Be prudent and hopeful and of good courage, and by and by we shall rejoice together over the dear little one. The little lock of hair sent to me I shall put in a locket, and wear on my chain; so I shall ever bear with dear tokens of my wife and child. What a pleasure it will be to take care of the little darling baby! I shall be fancying you all the time, with your tiny burden in your arms, playing with it, dressing it, kissing it, and telling it stories of papa.

By and by, when you are well and strong will you have a daguerreotype of yourself taken, holding little Miss New-come in your arms, and send it to me?

My darling, how I wish I could sit by your bedside and stroke your forehead, and hold your hand in mine, and be your loving, clumsy, good-for-nothing nurse. Kiss Dot for me, and tell her to be a good girl, and not trouble mamma . . . Ever your own, Frank

Cambridge, May 25, 1860

My dearest wife,

You and your little one have filled my thoughts ever since I heard of its birth, and I keep trying to picture to myself how it would seem to my little Katie with a child of mine lying in her bosom. Only to think of our having a daughter, darling!

Sometimes I draw my hand over my forehead, as if it were all a dream, and it was time to awake; but no, there is no delusion about it, and I am really a father. And you are a mother, the mother of my child, my little daughter. How I long to take the tiny burden in my arms, and gaze into its eyes to discover a miniature Katie is lurking there. What a wonderful thing is the birth of a human soul!

Your loving husband, Happy

Winona, May 27, 1860

Dear Frank,

. . . I am much better than you think me. I have sat up almost every day for the last week and went downstairs. I have not suffered much since the night the baby was born, but I have very little strength, just enough to walk a few steps without help. Shall I do as the Doctor says? He tells me I must "live high and drink hard," and would have no objections to my getting "gloriously tight" every day. Unfortunately, I can not get anything to get "tight" on, so they make a perfect beer jug of me instead . . . Baby is getting along nicely and is as good as a little kitten . . . I wish I could see Father with her. He thinks there never was so pretty or good a baby in the world. The first thing in the morning and the last thing at night is to come and kiss the baby . . . By the way, did you know your daughter rejoices in the name of "Topsy Chloe Dorothy Ann"? It is Father's selection . . . love and kisses to papa.

Goodbye darling, your loving wife, Katie

"Ethel's
diary is
unwritten . . ."

———

Cambridge, June 14, 1860

My dear Mignon,

. . . You must do all the Doctor says, and not hesitate even to get "gloriously tight," if that is the prescription. But you must not attempt to do too much . . . If I were with you, you should ride round in my stalwart arms, which are growing sinewy and stout under their gymnasium regimen, although they were not puny before. How I should like to feel your arms round my neck, and your cheek on my shoulder, as I carried you softly upstairs or round the house!

Yesterday I was looking at your photograph which Jennie gave me in Concord, and I longed to kiss you and pet you, and hear you talk of our little darling. I protest against "Topsy Chloe Dorothy Ann" being the appellative of the young princess; if you cannot wait till I am satisfied with a permanent name, choose some pretty little name as a pro tempore substitute, such as Dot, Puss, or the like. But I suppose I shall grumble in vain, so I must hurry up the real article. None of the names I have thought of please me nearly so much as Ethel, and if you like it, and my friends here do not seriously object, I doubt I can suit myself better . . .

You have not yet given me a description of Baby. My dear Mrs. Abbot, do you not know that your views of the little dame's appearance are highly important to papa? Has she blue eyes, or grey, or green, or brown, or pink, or purple, or yellow, or white, or orange, or scarlet? I have been asked, and felt quite ashamed not to know. Now I want a very minute description of her charms, feature by feature; and as soon as you are able to do it with perfect safety, dress yourself and her in your prettiest robes, and be daguerreotyped for my benefit. I shall want a new picture every three or four months, so that I may keep the run of her growth. Besides, I want to see how my own darling looks with our child in her arms.

Your affectionate husband, Frank

Cambridge, June 16, 1860

My own darling,

. . . Since you like the name Ethel, and since Mother likes it too, I should like that to be her name. It is better for a girl not to have a middle name, I hold, so we will not trouble our heads to hunt up one. Ethel Abbot—let that be the child's name . . . I am very glad that you are better yourself; do not relax in your caution at all . . . How I should love to come in unexpectedly, and see your face light up, and have you run to my arms, and throw your arms round my neck, and look up in my face as you did the day after our wedding . . . your eyes seemed to say—"Take me to your heart, dear Happy, I am all yours, forever! Your will shall be my will, your praise my happiness, your blame my sorrow, your love my deepest joy!"

Ever lovingly, your own, Happy

Winona, June 18, 1860

Dear Frank,

For fear you may have occasion to be ashamed again at not knowing the color of your daughter's eyes, I will immediately give you a description of her personal charms. The head comes first, that is shaped like her papa's and is covered with real golden hair full an inch long. I shall make it curl one of these days when I feel able, now I am too tired by the time she is washed and dressed to trouble myself about it. Forehead, like papa's. Doctor says she will do her own thinking by and by. Eyes, dark blue at present, don't know what they will be. I think they are inclined to turn grey . . . Sometimes she has her father's deep earnest in them. There? You needn't laugh and say it's my fancy and that babies don't have any expression . . . Nose, straight and well formed, none of the turned-up pug noses such as most babies have. Mouth, just the prettiest, rosiest little mouth you ever saw. Everyone speaks of baby's mouth, so whenever you look in the glass you can admire your own mouth, for the little one's is shaped like yours.

Altogether, Miss Abbot is a very pretty lady without being at all baby-pretty. Do you know what that means? When a baby is fair, clean, and fat without being really pretty it is called baby-pretty. Now, our baby has none of those charms, except being clean, she is thin and looks old enough in the face for a baby six months old instead of one month old . . . I wish you could see her now as she lies sleeping on a chair by my side.

Dear Happy, I would like so much to have you here to pet and carry me wherever I wanted to go. I do long sometimes to lay my head on your shoulder and feel you stroke my hair and cheek and hear you call me darling. You will have to wait a good while for a picture of Dot and me, for it is a long walk to town . . .

Your own loving wife, Katie

"Ethel's
diary is
unwritten . . ."

Cambridge, June 24, 1860

My darling,

My heart has been full of you today; full of longings to fold you to my breast and feel your heart throb against it. I want to look into your eyes, and see the strong *love, deep, unspeakable, which I know is burning within, shine out and warm me with its heaven-kindled light. I am restless and pained by my solitude now; my whole soul yearns for my young bride, yearns for the closest communion of spirit with spirit and body and body, yearns to pour forth the intense love which is too powerful for my own peace, yearns to draw her whole being and absorb it into my own. Oh my darling little wife, you have grown dearer to me since the currents of our being mingled together and became merged into a third, a new life. The mystery of parentage, of birth, broods over me in the solitude of thought; and I boldly strive to pierce the unfathomable with vague and hardy guesses, while yet I almost shudder at my own temerity.*

Have we, under God, created an immortal soul out of the substance of our own immortality, as we have created a mortal body out of our mortal flesh and blood? So the little one really is life of our life, spirit of our spirit, the eternal blending of your secret nature with my secret nature consummated in silence and mystery within the hidden chambers of your womb? If so, what revelations of our own innermost essence shall we behold in the developments of the child's character? Perhaps, dear wife of my bosom, in the unrolling of that scroll we shall read the soul of another as our words have always failed to image them forth.

But perhaps, after all, our human bodies have been only the framers of the caskets. Then what an awful responsibility rests upon us, to guard the precious charge from stain and spot and blemish, and return the gem of God back to its Creator unsullied.

You must not buy a cradle for Dot; for before a great while, in a month or two, you will probably be honored with the arrival of a most magnificent one, sent by the "Class of '59" to the first baby of one of its members. This has been the custom of late years, and the cradle is a costly and handsome one . . . Miss Ethel will be a highly distinguished baby, and the westerners can see how we Harvard boys do things for one another. I must stop now . . .

Your own, Happy

Winona, July 14, 1860

My own darling Happy,

I went to town yesterday with Dot to have her daguerreotype taken. I could not have hers and mine taken together, and I almost despaired of getting even hers. Miss Ethel is never very still when she is awake and it seemed as if she is never so restless as when she was sitting up for her picture—hands and feet were in constant motion and her head was first one side and then the other. However, I got a much better likeness that I expected, though I am afraid you will not have much idea how your baby looks from the daguerreotype. The darkest one looks like her, only not half as pretty . . . the other one is not so good . . . When the baby is old enough to sit still and look at anything I will have a better likeness for you but she is too little now.

At present she only cries when she is hungry or has the stomach ache but I have to consult the comfort of all in the house. Father thinks there is no need of a child's crying and loses all patience if he hears one for any length of time, and here when the baby cries she can be heard all over the house. Mother [thinks] Ethel is the best baby. She is pretty too, but even I am unwilling to confess that I have seen prettier babies—I wish you could see her!

Your own loving, Katie

Winona, July 22, 1860

Dear Frank,

I have had a new experience this week; that of nursing a dying child! If simply doing what was in my power to ease the last moments can be called nursing. I happened to go to one of our neighbors and she said her little grandchild had been taken sick the day before and she did not think it would live through the day. I went in to see it but I could do nothing then, so after telling the baby's mother to send for us if she needed help. Later, I went home I went back alone and found the baby lying perfectly rigid in the mother's arms, who was sobbing as if her heart would break and saying she could not part with her babe! I cannot help but get anxious for our little one sometimes; for it seems as if a child is sick here, it is sure to die. Within the last week three babies have died; two older and one just a fortnight younger that Ethel. But she is in God's keeping and he will do what is best.

I wish you could see the little one. She grows so fast and begins to take a good deal of notice of things. Last night I dressed her in a flannel night dress high in the neck and with long sleeves. I never saw her look so cunning as she did in that with her little hands coming out of the great loose sleeves! This morning she saw her own hand for the first time . . . The other day she made the discovery of your photograph, which hangs in my chamber, and stared at it a long while. I wish you could spare a fortnight this summer, that would give you a week with me. It is growing dark and I must get Midget's supper ready . . .

Good night . . . much love, Katie

"Ethel's diary is unwritten . . ."

139

Cambridge, July 27, 1860

Dear Katie,

    Your last letter gave me a fright, beginning, as it did, with saying that you had been nursing a "dying child." My heart stopped beating for several seconds. Of course, reading a few lines further dispelled the sudden fear.

    I have never seen my little one, and I can hardly say I love it, for love requires sight to convenience with; yet there is a deep emptiness in my heart which my child only could fill, and a restless longing that sometimes stings my peace. Perhaps the best way I could express that what I mean is to say that I feel robbed of the opportunity to love. Every little baby I see makes me ache for my own, and I yearn to fondle her and press her to my heart. Your lot is easier that mine, darling, in some respect, though I doubt not you have your own peculiar cross to bear. How I wish I could see Ethel in her little flannel night-dress, and see her dear young mother's pride in her pet! Oh that I may humbly learn what my Father is trying to teach me by all this soul weariness! Kiss Ethel for Papa; and fold her close to your breast and think it is your own Happy.

Love, Frank

Winona, July 30, 1860

My darling,

    Pray God for strength to bear the great sorrow that has fallen upon you. Our little one is no more—she died this morning about six o'clock. Weep, Frank, weep! Shed for me the tears I cannot shed for myself! Oh, may you not know the agony of tearless grief! It seems sad news to send you, yet had you been here you would have rejoiced as I did when she drew her last breath. Poor little thing, she suffered dreadfully.

    She was taken sick Monday and was a little sicker the next day. Wednesday and Thursday she was better and Friday morning seemed perfectly well; towards afternoon she grew sick again and I sent for the Doctor. He said she had the cholera infantum. Jennie and I were up with her all night. I could only wait on her, I could not hold her for the little thing knew me and wanted to nurse when I took her in my arms. I did not dare to let her for fear she would eat too much. Saturday morning she was worse—I scarcely thought she would live through the day. The Doctor came and gave her some medication to keep her quiet—it was all that could be done for her. Towards night he came again but could do nothing more.

Saturday night I went into Mrs. Sewton's to get a little rest. I could not have it at home for the baby's groans could be heard all over the house, and they promised to call me if she grew worse. About half past eleven o'clock, Mrs. Tucker (one of our neighbors) came for me thinking the babe could not live till I got home. From that time till this morning we thought every breath might be her last, and yet the little child lingered in terrible agony till it seemed that she never would die. I never prayed for anything more earnestly than that she might die. The Doctor said she was unconscious of her sufferings but it seemed to me it could not be so for if she was moved at all or even had her little parched lips wet with cold water it would throw her into a spasm. Mrs. Beasley sat for eighteen long hours with the babe in her lap without moving once for fear of disturbing the little one. Thank God for our kind neighbors. I do not know what we should have done without them for all at home were sick. The last two hours of the babe's life were very quiet. We have at least one treasure in heaven now, darling. I shall miss her and I feel very lonely—but I would not have it otherwise. I cannot mourn for her; for she is happier where she is than she could ever be with me.

I am thankful you were not here to witness her sufferings. My poor Frank how I wish I could be with you to comfort you in this trial.

Ethel's diary is unwritten, but there are few things in her short life that I cannot remember. God's will be done . . .

Katie

Cambridge, August 3, 1860

My noble, darling wife—

What shall I say to you, what prayer shall I send up for you to our Father's throne to still the agony of your little heart? My poor, poor little wife! Oh how my soul is rent with fear and anguish for you, poor childless mother! May God be near you, and fill you with all soothing peace and trust!

The little angel at our Father's bosom will watch our faltering steps, will draw down blessings unnumbered on our stricken heads, and heaven will be closer now that earth has lost its charm. I must kneel beside you in prayer to God, feeling that He who has sent me such an angel by my side will keep the lost angel safe until our coming.

One year ago, my darling, one year ago today, you gave me your heart and hand and soul. And thus has our Father seen fit that I should celebrate the day of anniversary. Your husband's heart is sick for you, not for himself.

Love your own Frank

"Ethel's
diary is
unwritten . . ."

Ethel Abbot, 1860.

To Ethel in Heaven

Sleep like the wind-nipped bud, my daughter, sleep!
Untimely dropping from the parent stem;
Sleep in God's boundless love, like some fair gem
Sunk in the bosom of the azure deep.
Thine are the joys of God,—'tis owns to weep;
Ah! Thy young mother's warm impassioned tears
Will gush unceasing through the desolate years,
While o'er life's dial plate the shadows creep.
Yet art unsunned by the Heaven's sweet beams of love,
Nor faithless in our Father's care, we dwell;
Through misty tears the bow shines bright above,
And grief still sighs—"He doeth all things well."
Take, oh my God! Our offering of cost,
And in thine own dear home, give back the
Loved and lost!

Winona, August 19, 1860

My darling Happy,

. . . For the last few days I have felt very lonely and missed my baby more than ever. My heart cries out for you in my loneliness, and I cannot be content; sep-

arated from my husband, my babe taken from me, I am tempted to say that the burden is almost more than I can bear. And yet, if my burden is so heavy with dear ones around me to make it lighter for me, what must yours be who have to bear it alone, with no one to help or comfort you! For myself I could bear it, if only I could feel that you were free from sorrow and trouble. Dear, dear Frank, I do so long to be with you once more! You tell me to pray for strength, and I do, but I cannot always still the rebellious thoughts and feelings that will rise. I dream of you often, darling, and seem to feel you with me; but when I stretch out my hand for you, I wake, and find that it is only a dream. May it prove a reality before long! Good night, my darling; may God bless you and keep you forever, it is the prayer of your own wife,

Katie

Winona, August 19, 1860

Dear Mamma [Frank's mother],

 I have not had the heart to write to any one for the last few weeks, else your letter should not have been so long unanswered. It is so lonely and sad without my baby that I scarcely feel like doing anything. I cannot get used to working without interruption; even now, when I am busy, I often stop to listen for the baby's waking. I know God took her in love and kindness, and feel glad she is spared all the pain and suffering that would have fallen to her lot, had she lived; but for all that I long for her to be with me again. You tell me I must take care of myself, and I try to do so, but what use is it? I must work till I am so tired that I cannot think of anything save bodily weariness, or else comes a restless, sleepless night, followed by a day of perfect inability for any regular work. The separation from Frank and my baby's death, when I felt she would be such a comfort to me, is almost more than I can bear. I am not strong, and this weary, constant strain upon my heart is wearing my very life away. I grow weaker every day. The sight of Frank's face or the touch of his hand would do me more good than anything I can do for myself; and yet I must wait long, weary months for that. Know that the thought of my suffering is more painful to him than anything else, and his burden is heavy enough without my adding needlessly to it. I only hope that with cooler weather will come renewed health and strength. I did not mean to fill my sheet with complainings when I began, but I cannot speak of these things to any one else.

Lovingly, Katie

"Ethel's diary is unwritten . . ."

———

143

No. 37 Divinity Hall, Harvard University. On the 30th of July, my little Ethel died of cholera infantum, and I did not hear of her sickness till I heard of her death. I had just returned from Cohasset, where I had been spending a week with Frank Balch and Nellie Noyes. Friday, the day I came back, was a beautiful one, and in the morning we all sailed down to see Minot's-ledge Lighthouse, which was on the point of completion. It was the anniversary of my wedding day, August 3, and my thoughts, although sad, were yet peaceful; I loved to think of the day when I should take my little daughter in my arms, and feel her soft cheek against mine, and hear her call me "papa."

On my return, I found Katie's letter awaiting me, telling me of her agonized death. The shock was sudden and terrible, but I felt it more through her mother's bleeding heart than through my own. I suffered much that night.

About the middle of August, Professor Sophocles came home, and I moved down here. I was proctor during his absence in Europe. This week I heard from Sarah Loring that Katie's health is suffering from her secret grief, and that they all think that she should come East to be with me. I am greatly distressed about her. I knew, as soon as I heard of Ethel's death, that such would be the result of it, and at once racked my brain to find some contrivance for giving her a home. I could think of none, except to apply for a school in Meadville, Pennsylvania which would enable me to support my wife, pay off my debt, and study my profession at the same time. This afternoon I shall probably hear. I have been longing for the place more than words can express; I have not prayed for it, however, as an unquestionable good, for God only can see whether it is really best for me to get it. God, who hast shown me my duty, make that duty possible, even if I must give up my dearest plans, abandon thy ministry, and do daily toil as a drudge in some office.

Cambridge, September 16, 1860

My dear little wife,

. . . As I soon as I heard of little Ethel's death, I was greatly distressed about you. I knew your nature too well not to understand the inevitable results of such an overwhelming sorrow. Unable to come to you, I foresaw that you would suffer from your accumulated griefs so much as to injure your health; and this fear was confirmed by a letter of yours to Mother which I almost insisted on seeing against her will. Fortunately, George Chaney, who has tried schemes of bringing us together which I never told you of on account of their impracticability, heard of a vacancy in Meadville High School [Female Seminary, Meadville, Pennsylvania], a place worth at least $1400 per [year]. I applied for this situation several weeks ago, have not yet learned the result of my application . . . I tremble to excite delusive hopes, but Mother thought I had better inform you of this, that you might have something to oc-cupy your thoughts. Goodbye, darling.

Your loving, Frank

Cambridge, September 19, 1860

Dear Katie,

Joy, joy, little wife! Come to my heart, and find your home there now! We will never more part, please God, until the last parting on earth shall come. I have got that place! Fall down on your knees, and thank God with your whole soul that He has showed us such boundless kindness! By the 19th of October I shall probably be in Meadville myself, and shall at once make arrangements for your reception. It may be that as I soon as I get there, I shall want you to come; so immediately on reception of this, write me and send me word whether you have money to come as far as Meadville with, which probably is not the case. If you have to come alone; I shall pay to go for you; but I want Sallie to come with you and be my assistant teacher. I will promise $300 and board now, and very likely may be able to increase it.

I am impatient to clasp you in my arms, and call you my little wife once more. Bring me a blade of grass from Ethel's grave, darling; I hope to pray there sometime.

Your loving, Frank

*"Ethel's
diary is
unwritten . . ."*

———

145

Winona, October 7, 1860

Dear Frank,

 Now that I know that I can go to you it seems as if I could hardly wait till I can get to you . . . It is hard to leave Father and Mother and not know when I shall see them again. And dear Baby, I used to think so often of the home we should have together and our little one with us—I went to visit her grave today for the last time before leaving here . . .

      Good bye my darling until I see you . . . your own, Katie

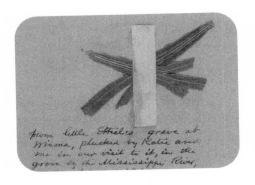

from little Ethel's grave at
Winona, plucked by Katie and
me on our visit to it, in the
grove by the Mississippi River,

PART IV

"Glimpses of Katie"

July 1, 1883. — This leaf is from the wreath of leaves laid on the coffin of my grandfather Sarcom, and preserved by Mother under glass, in a black walnut frame. At the funeral of my dear Mother, June 2 1883, by request of Eunice and Edwin, I carried this wreath to the cemetery at Beverly where we laid the precious dust, and placed it on her casket just before it was lowered into the grave; but previously I had taken this leaf, and Willie another, as last memorial. For over twenty-one years Mother cherished fondly this memorial of her father; I lay it reverently here as a memorial of her.

"Gather up the fragments, that nothing be lost."
*"Why did I ever write of anything but her? If we could only foresee! She was the
air I breathed, the sunshine I lived by—I wrote of almost everything but thee!"*

[In 1902 Frank copied out references to Katie from his letters to his mother
to form a journal he entitled "Glimpses of Katie." These entries, with salu-
tations of "Dear Mother," 1860–1877, follow.]

September 30, 1860

MEADVILLE, PENNSYLVANIA

Dear Mother,

*Here I am at last, safely lodged in the hospitable mansion of Mrs. Shippen till
I can feather a snug little nest for Katie. She will probably get here in eight or ten
days, by which time I shall have two or three rooms ready to receive her. There is a
considerable amount of furniture in the house already which belongs to the establish-
ment. The house is a very nice one, airy, roomy, and sunny, and is probably a better
inn than I shall come across again in the journey of my life. Sarah is coming on
with Katie, which will save me considerable in traveling expenses myself. My school
will open October 5.*

October 13, 1860

Dear Mother,

Monday, I opened my school as I expected to do, and had just a dozen scholars to start with . . . All the week I was expecting Katie, and Sarah after Tuesday. They arrived Thursday, having come on in two nights and two days from Winona, 800 miles. That night when I had met the stage downtown at the Barton House, and saw my two proteges snugly packed in it, I jumped in too, and we drove to the house. They were so tired that I recommended instant retirement, and while they were getting ready for their repose, I fumbled around the cupboards, found some preserved peaches and bread, and I smuggled coffee, toast, and cakes up to them, and they regaled themselves.

Next morning, they were introduced, and have been most hospitably treated ever since. Katie is well, but very delicate, and lacks strength; she only weighs 89 pounds! However, she looks better than I anticipated. She wears half-mourning, and, although she is very happy in the prospect of her new home, I feel rather than see that she misses the baby and is almost constantly thinking of her.

1 8 6 1

January 5, 1861

Dear Mother,

I have nothing new to tell; the stream of life with me now forbids hardly a pebble to ripple over. Not without care, not without the inalienable heritage of human nature, anxiety; yet peaceful, with no noise or din or discordant voices. A little family altar sanctifies each day, and strengthens us for the daily duties; a common trust in God binds us all closely together. How near we all seem, when humbly confessing our sins together at our common Father's knee! What a different home shall we have had, if we had not such a daily tryst! By and by, in that painless world, we will all meet thus at last, with no vacant place in our little circle.

January 20, 1861

Dear Mother,

Katie is well, and has gained in health immensely since she came here. I cannot but think of the little one that would have been such a sunbeam in our simple home. But she may now be reading her father's heart better than he can read it himself. I shall see her at last.

April 14, 1861

Dear Mother,

I was thinking the other day how little I wrote you about Katie, and wondered if you supposed I kept silence designedly or from any indifference. I only wish you could see what a model little wife she is, how she makes it her first object to please her good-for-nothing husband; and how skillfully she steers our little flat boat round all the snags of housekeeping. She has a quiet way of her own, I find, of stealing people's hearts here, and she never was half so pretty or vivacious as she is now. One young man called her, I was told, "a perfect angel," another said she was "perfectly charming."

So you must reckon me as having got just the disposition and character in my wife best adapted to the wants and crookednesses of my own. Her happiness is my love, and I should be a lump of granite to withstand her little winning ways and contrivance to secure my smile.

April 23, 1861

Dear Mother,

The war news absorbs all thoughts, and especially this evening, when we have just heard that Washington is surrounded by enemies and on the point of capture. We cannot tell whether this rumor is true or false, but it fills me with anxiety for Henry and Susie. Do you know anything of their movements? Is Susie still in Washington? Do just send me a line to tell of their safety. God rules as in the calm—may He give us strength to do our duty.

May 12, 1861

Dear Mother,

Katie is as well as ever, and looks much better than she used to. This week I have a vacation in my school, as my third term ended last Friday. I am glad it comes now, for Tuesday is Ethel's birthday, and we would like to spend that in quiet together . . .

October 21, 1861

I have been teaching here for a little (a few days) less than a year. During the year I was bitterly pressed in money matters, and we remained here all summer. I found my school work very hard, but my conscience tells me I have been faithful; I gave up everything to it. My little wife is grown very dear to me this year, and my home is peaceful and happy; I turn away my eyes from the past as far as possible, and fix them on the present duty and future hope. In February Katie expects to be again confined. So another year has slipped away, and the end is nearer.

1 8 6 2

[On February 3, 1862, Katie gave birth to a boy, Everett.]

February 9, 1862

Dear Mother,

Katie is again recovering from her temporary difficulty and is no longer at all feverish. But I am scarcely allowed to see her, and so Emmie will write you the news in regard to her much better than I can. The baby is a funny little thing and is growing pretty already. Everybody seems anxious to have Katie get well soon. You may imagine the relief I feel in having safely passed such a crisis. I could not see my little

*wife enter into the Valley of the Shadow of Death, and issue from its awful mystery
in safety, without a mountain weight of suspense being lifted from my soul . . . I rejoice most of all that the aching void of the young mother's heart is to be filled with a
new delight, and that her life may flow in the beautiful channel of maternal love.
But the thought of the fresh responsibility laid upon me is almost awful in it sublim-
ity—what am I that I should shape the destiny of a young immortal? Give me a
mother's prayers in this great work—prayers for a wise and understanding heart.*

February 15, 1862

After Everett's birth at Meadville, Katie's mother died at Winona on February 6. But Katie was so sick that her life was in the greatest danger, and
her physician said that the news would kill her then. With great difficulty
she was kept in ignorance of it, for she knew her mother was in feeble
health, and made inquiries very hard to parry. It was in this agony of suspense and fear that I wrote these verses. When, after seven or eight weeks,
she was permitted to come down stairs, and it became impossible any
longer to hide her loss from her, I sat down alone with her in our little parlor, took her tenderly in my lap and arms, and gave her the poor lines, purposely vague, to break her as gradually as possible to the bitter tale I had to
tell. She read them, burst into tears, threw her arms about my neck, and
hid her face on my shoulder in a storm of sobs. She had divined it all. I
did not let her go till the first paroxysm of grief was over, and she had
sobbed herself to stillness on my loving and ailing heart: "Must I, dear
gazer, speed the dart / I shut the sunlight from thy brow / With darkening
veil of grief, whilst thou /Art still the sunlight of my heart? . . ."

1863

January 25, 1863

MEADVILLE

Dear Mother,

    *We have been having a wearisome and anxious time with little Everett. He has
been quite sick, and I do not feel out of the woods yet. This evening I had to walk*

with him a long time and soothe him to sleep. But I think he has got over the worst of it. Doctor Cotton said that there is an influenza quite prevalent in the neighborhood just now. Poor Katie's rest is very much broken nights, and she feels tired out.

May 10, 1863

Dear Mother,

As to what is to follow my graduation I know nothing. I think I shall have to see Katie safely in Winona, for I dare not let her travel alone with Everett; but how long I shall stay in the West will depend entirely on how much I wanted to preach.

June 20, 1863

Dear Mother,

My Ordination [as a Unitarian minister] takes place on August 31, and I hope you will stay up country [Wilton, New Hampshire] until you have fully picked up health and vigor. I got through preaching on Sunday tolerably well, but missed the inspiration of your presence and sympathy.

July 6, 1863

Dear Mother,

You told me Katie was going to write to us as soon as she got to Winona, and I will not dwell long on what happened up to our parting. It will suffice to say we got nicely through our packing Monday, and made our parting calls that evening; which were very pleasant to me and gave me some sunny recollections to carry off as mementos of my first home. After waiting a few hours, we started for Cleveland and got there about five o'clock. Katie seemed quite tired, but bore the fatigue very well. The baby was as good as a kitten, and set very contentedly in my lap, sleeping part of the time. The heat was oppressive, and indeed continued so throughout our whole journey. About nine o'clock we started in the night boat to cross Lake Erie. It was beautiful moonlight at first, but, as I sat in the bow of the boat enjoying the cool breeze, a *thunder shower came up and drove me into our hot stateroom, where we passed a somewhat unrefreshing night.*

We reached Detroit next, Wednesday, and got on board the Michigan Central cars en route for Chicago. Everett was quite fretful part of the time. When we reached Chicago, we crossed the city to the Galena and Chicago Union Railway, at last I got some berths in a sleeping car on the night train from Chicago: a double one for Katie and Everett, and a single one above for myself.

Next morning we awoke about six, and had time to dress and wash comfortably. Only one other family were there in our part of the car, and they were very respectable people. I put Katie, on arriving at Dunleith, on the Mississippi River, opposite Dubuque in Iowa, on board the up-river boat [to visit her father in Winona, Minnesota, until Frank could set up their new home in Detroit], had just time to make the necessary arrangements for her, and then, without time for breakfast, or even to buy another return ticket, jumped on the train again for Chicago.

July 12, 1863, Winona, Minnesota

Dear Happy,

. . . I suppose you are very busy and I ought to be satisfied with one letter a week, but somehow it seems a long time to wait before hearing from Happy. I have heard his voice, and seen his face, and, what is more, felt his love every day for three years, and I miss them sadly now that I am away from them. I cannot be long away from you now, darling . . . I cannot tell you how much love I send . . . but you may be sure it is all my heart can hold.

Your own wife, Katie

[On July 8, 1863, Frank's brother, Stanley, was killed at the Battle of Gettysburg.]

Detroit, Michigan, July 20, 1863

My darling Katie,

More than ever I have longed for your society and love the last three days; for I have been under a cloud of sorrow, and the darkness makes me long for your unfailing affection. My young brother Stanley is dead, and he has fought his last fight for the cause he loved so dearly. As I wrote you, he was wounded at the Battle of Gettysburg, being shot in the right breast; and the surgeon told him the wound was not mortal. But the shot had passed through his lungs, and the wound bled internally; and about noon, on July 8, his breath grew shorter and shorter, and our anxiety for him is over; he is "safe" now. Edwin did not reach the Hospital until he had been dead two days; they had laid him under the grass on the hillside, beneath the trees, and on the bank of the little brook, the only peaceful spot in the midst of infinite turmoil and confusion. In the distance Edwin heard the thunder of cannon, softened into the indistinct roar of battle afar off. Stanley did not suffer much pain, and was very happy at the thought of dying for his country. The body is probably now at home, and I suppose the funeral has been performed.

The letters telling me of all this reached me Friday afternoon. The first shock was stunning, for I had given up all fear of his wound's being fatal. I could scarcely read, so fast did my tears flow. The agony of loss was bitter; but not a thought of complaint, not a murmur, passed through my mind. Although alone, I was not lonely; for in every deep sorrow I find myself in the presence of God, and his love never deserts me. I am cheerful now, though the tears will come sometimes. My worst pain comes from the thought of Mother and Emmie, to whom I have written. Could you not write to Mother, and tell how you loved Stanley, and what goodness you saw in him when you and he were together? It would comfort her, I think.

Early Saturday morning, I was called on by a Captain Barse to perform funeral services for his son the next day. He was a corporal in the 5th Michigan Calvary, had been wounded at Gettysburg on the same day with Stanley, and, like him, had died in the Hospital before his friends could reach him. I found on inquiry that he had been a most excellent young fellow, and during his short life of only 18 years had been everywhere faithful and true to his duty. I felt nearly overwhelmed at the thought of performing the last rites, as it seemed to me for my own brother; there was something so solemn in such a summons at such a time. But God gave me strength; and I went up stairs and wrote a short funeral sermon.

Next day . . . I went at 3 o'clock to the church, where the funeral was to be held. It was crowded, many strangers being present. I felt miserably weak at the thought of trying to console other hearts when my own was so bleeding; but in God's strength I found support. I took as a kind of text, "The Lord loveth a cheerful giver," showed how cheerful a giver of Life and all dear to him the young soldier had been, said the call to give now came to us, and there briefly mentioned the loss I had sustained, saying that I did not stand there to utter words of exhortation, but spoke as one weighed down by a common sorrow. I spoke right out my own soul, and I know I touched the souls of those who listened; there were many wet eyes, and I could not perfectly command my own voice. It was a new and solemn experience . . . I want to get back to Boston more than ever . . . Frank

Winona, July 22, 1863

My darling one,

I have only a few minutes to spare but I feel as if I must send you a little note. I received a letter from Emmie this morning telling me of Stanley's death. My heart aches for you all and for myself. I loved him as if he had been my own brother. I wish I might be with you now. I know I could not do much to comfort you but all sorrows and trials seem lighter to me when I have you with me and so I think I might help you now.

Dear Stanley, all his sorrows and trials are over! He died, nobly doing his duty and that at least makes it less hard to bear. I wish that we could have seen him once more even though it were in death. Your poor mother, I know how her heart must yearn after him with all a mother's love, but she will bear it nobly, for she is a true woman—God help and comfort you, my own husband.

I received a letter from Lydia this morning in which she says she shall not be able to have me stay with her this winter. If it were possible she would be glad to have me, but that she does not see how it can be arranged. I shall not fret, for I know some place will open to take us in, and you must not be anxious either.

Sometimes I almost fancy that I am not pregnant. I do not think I have grown any larger than I was when I left Meadville, and I have not as yet felt any motion in the child, for which it is time. I do not dare to build any hopes upon such slight foundations, still I cannot help feeling a little doubtful at times as to the fact of my pregnancy, but time only can show whether my suspicions are correct. Love and kisses from, Your little wife

Frank Abbot with son Everett, circa 1863.

[On December 13, 1863, in Beverly, Massachusetts, Katie gave birth to a son, Edward Stanley Abbot.]

1 8 6 4

[In August 1864 the Abbots returned to New England, as Frank was appointed as minister of the First Unitarian Society of Dover, New Hampshire.]

1 8 6 5

March 3, 1865

Dear Mother,

We are all pretty well now, though Katie has had a week or two of sickness [the mumps]. Stanley is learning some very cunning ways, and is the most winsome little creature I ever saw. I do not think it partiality that makes me say so, for I never thought Evie was a particularly attractive baby—he has become interesting in proportion to the development of intelligence and never had those graceful ways that Stanley shows. I often wish you could see this or that little cooing exclamation. I know he will soon entrench himself in "Mamoo's" heart, if he once gets near her.

1 8 6 6

April 27, 1866

Dear Mother,

I would have answered your letter immediately, if Katie had not been threatened with a miscarriage the very next day, I believe. Thus far we have staved off everything serious, but Doctor Horsch say she is not yet out of the woods. As she is at the end of the sixth month, a miscarriage might cause a dangerous hemorrhage, and I still feel quite anxious about her; but, so she can get along so well hitherto, I have very strong hope that we can avoid a catastrophe.

[On April 29, 1866, Katie gave birth to a unnamed premature girl, who died a day later.]

April 30, 1866

Dear Mother,

Last Friday, I wrote to you that Katie was threatened with a miscarriage. Saturday she seemed very bright, and with Doctor Horsch's permission she sat up for about an hour in my study. That evening and night she was very well. Katie had pains that kept increasing. I went out and bought two quarts of ether, in case she should need it. In the afternoon, at five minutes before four, Katie gave birth to a little girl, alive, and it is still living now at half past ten, though it cannot live long. Katie had a very easy time and is doing well in all respects. I feel so grateful for Katie's safety that I can hardly realize my own disappointment in losing the little daughter I have so longed for since Ethel's death. I have nothing but thanks for the great mercy God has shown us, and shall forget as far as possible the empty place in my heart.

1867

April 9, 1867

Dear Mother,

This morning, at twenty-two minutes past twelve, A.M., Katie gave birth to a little dark-haired girl. I was out during the evening at my German class, and on coming home about nine found that Katie was expecting to be sick at once. Doctor Horsch came with me about half-past ten, and a little past midnight all was safely over. Katie took ether, just enough to help, not to hinder, and Doctor Horsch seems converted to the policy of using it, at least in some cases. Katie seems to be doing very nicely—is asleep now, or would send love, which I do in her name. The child is fat and strong, with an abundance of dark curly hair. We are so blessed that my heart is

"Glimpses of Katie"

———

159

only full of the deepest gratitude. The little boys, of course, are full of interest in the new advent. Stanley asked, when I told him that God had sent him a little baby sister, if "God has come, too?"

"No," said Evie, "God is everywhere." Please inform Willie that little Miss New-comer is patriotic, as she chose to be born on the anniversary of Lee's surrender.

August 14, 1867

Dear Mother,

I have not written to you before, since leaving you at Beverly, partly because I have been too busy and tired to write, but mainly because I wished to spare you the anxiety you would have felt under the circumstances. Now that all is over, I write to say that I found little baby sick on my return, and that yesterday afternoon we laid her away in the ground. She was taken Friday of Commencement week with a kind of dysentery, just after Jennie had come up to see Katie on a visit. I found her a little better on my arrival, but she soon grew worse again.

Tuesday morning, about quarter past twelve (just the time she was born) she must have died; for Katie awoke just after and found her dead. At the last she suffered little, and passed away in utter quietness. Katie and I at once washed and dressed our little one, and laid the coin-weights on her dear blue eyes. We telegraphed at once for George Chaney at Hampton, who came just in season for the funeral at six o'clock, P.M. We could not keep her longer. I wish you could have been here, but it was impossible. It was the most simple and touching of services, and will remain beautiful beyond description in our memories. So we have no little daughter on earth now, mother, but three little daughters waiting for us in heaven. I do not think our tears have been any impeachment of the boundless Love on high.

August 1867

> *Little Gertrude*
> From her brow, so pale and smooth,
> Brush the silken hair . . .
> Lay each dear, thin, tiny hand
> Gently by her side;

None will ever their aid demand,
    While the seasons glide.
Little hands have nought to do,
Little feet are idle, too;
All their baby task is through, . . .
Lay her in the cradle-bed
    That no rocking needs;
Pure and white, the blossoms spread,
    As her beauty pleads.
O Thou Shadow of the pall!
Shall the Gardener of All
Into nothingness let fall
    Even the least of seeds?

[After the death of Gertrude, Katie convalesced with family and friends in Massachusetts.]

October 4, 1867

JAMAICA PLAIN, MASSACHUSETTS

Dear Happy,—Will it make Saturday night any pleasanter to get a letter from me? I must tell you how I long to see you. I wish I could go home this very day. I want to sit in your lap and feel your arm round me and to be kissed and petted and made a baby of. I know, if it were Saturday night, you would be too busy to do it; but then I could sit close beside you now and then, and I could have a good night kiss when I went to bed. Now I don't have any. I should be so glad to see you when you come down—you know how glad . . . Katie

November 4, 1867

BEVERLY

My own precious darling Happy, I was so disappointed at not getting a letter from you tonight! I was feeling terribly homesick and Happy-sick, and, when Mary came home without a letter for me, I felt like crying . . . I wish I could go home to-morrow. It would be so much nicer than anything else: why won't you send for me? Can't you say you are tired of being without me, and I must come home? Oh,

Happy! I should be so glad to get back to the old nest again! I want everything that belongs to home, and most of all I want you! I want you now, this very minute. It seems as if I could not wait! Frank darling, mayn't I come home? I am so homesick. It's too bad. I meant your birthday letter should be a nice bright one, and I have written a dismal one so far. But I can't help it; I feel just so.

Love and kisses from your own, Katie

Dover, N.H., November 6, 1867

My own little wife,

 I have just got out of the Office [a letter] from a dear little wanderer for whom my heart hungers and thirsts daily . . . that made me cry like a baby for me, a bearded man on his thirty-first birthday! If you cannot answer the question, I shall not. And you are "home-sick and Happy-sick"! And you ask, "Mayn't I come home?" Do you ask me? Is it I that can answer your pleading call? If the answer could come from me, how long would it be before you would nestle close to my heart? Do you think I sent you off to please myself? No, poor little beating heart, you must ask that dumb Power that molds our lives not at all after the pattern of our wild wishes. I am helpless as a bird in the fowler's hand. See! I sent you off because I thought your health might gain by a change of scene after our great sorrow of the summer,—and also because I could not afford to keep you when friends were eager to have you visit them. You know that I have had to borrow $115 already to eke out the necessities of the hour, and must save this out of this quarter's expenses or else go deeper inside the slough of debt. And Katie, when your husband must choose between dishonor on the one hand, and on the other the bitter pain of separation, of anxiety for absent dear ones, of loneliness that no words can measure,—you know he cannot hesitate. Be sure of this, my darling—that I hold happiness, love, life itself, cheap as dirt in comparison with integrity. During all these dreary weeks, I have resolutely repressed all complaints or lamentations in writing to you, wishing not to make your absence any harder to bear.

 I ask you, as the dear wife of my bosom, to put forth the strength of character I know is in you, and rise so far above adverse circumstances as cheerfully to accept the inevitable.

 You know how dearly I love you. Let me feel that you are willing to do what I am doing—live apart from most precious love for honor's sake.

Most loving and tenderly yours, Frank

Beverly, November 7, 1867

Dear Frank,

If I had dreamed of all the pain my letter caused, you should never have seen it. I cannot bear to think that I have made your burden heavier, even for a moment.

Lovingly, Katie

1 8 6 8

August 2, 1868

STOWE, MASSACHUSETTS

My dear little wife,

Tomorrow is the ninth anniversary of our wedding-day, and I wish I might spend it with you. But I can only think of you with love, and must make that do. Kiss the dear little boys for me, and thank the mysterious Power that determines human destinies, that our union has been blessed with so much happiness. With all the shadows that have darkened our path, I know that we both are grateful for the inward light of love which has edged the clouds with gold. Fidelity to each other and to the high principles of life has proved the wisdom of what the world judged superlatively unwise. Not for worldly favor nor all the gains of cheap ambitions, would I relinquish the faithful, tender, unselfish love you have made me so happy with. May you receive what you have given!

Frank

1 8 6 9

"Glimpses of Katie"

163

[In June 1869 Frank accepted a position as minister of the Unitarian Society of Toledo, Ohio. As Frank set up their household, Katie and the boys lived in Winona, Minnesota, with Katie's father.]

Winona, August 2, 1869

Dear Frank,

Last night I dreamed that you had come to see me. I thought it was very early in the morning. We were still in bed, Evie and Stanley on either side of me, and you came in from the boat. You kissed both the boys, and leaned over to kiss me. I had just put my arms round your neck to draw you down close to me, when I woke and found it was only a dream. I wished it might come true.

It is ten years ago tomorrow since you and I took that journey from Wilton to Nashua—ten years that we have been one; and, if the body has been separated, I do not think the heart ever has. We have seen trials and sorrow in all these years, but they have only drawn us closer together, and we love each other far more now than we did on that bright August morning ten years ago. They have been happy years, in spite of all the trouble and anxiety; for we found our happiness in each other, not in things outside of us. If we did a foolish, unwise thing in getting married as we did, surely the All-loving Father has overruled it for good.

Dear Frank, whatever there was in me that was true and good and womanly has been broadened and deepened by my intercourse with you. I know that I am a truer woman for all these years of my married life, and from the bottom of my

Frank Abbot with sons Everett and Stanley, circa 1870.

heart I thank you. If I have been to you all that you have been to me, I am satis-
fied . . . Katie

[Frank and Katie remained in Toledo, Ohio, throughout 1870–1871, where Frank was editor of the *Index*—a publication that promoted "Free Religion." In the spring of 1871 Frank sent Charles Darwin copies of the magazine and expressed support of Darwin's views on the theory of evolution. In response, Darwin wrote: "what you tell me about the interest felt in America on my own and allied views impresses and highly gratifies me."]*

1872

May 20, 1872

TOLEDO, OHIO

Dear Mother,

Katie is nearing the time of her confinement, but is better than she ever was at such a time, I think. She sends you her love—and she does love you. The two girls [her sisters] (Jennie and Susie) are with her, and everything is ready; and the little boys are well, too. So you need have no anxiety about any of us. Before long I hope to send you good news.

June 14, 1872

TOLEDO, OHIO

Dear Mother,

I must not let your birthday go by without telling you of the birthday in our Ohio home. Yesterday Katie was delivered of a fine healthy girl-baby, which we have not yet weighed, but which the nurse thinks weighs over eleven pounds. She is a fat little thing, and seems very thriving. Katie had a labor of about three hours, taking ether freely, and she is doing very well. The baby was born ten minutes before seven. We both hoped the day would be June 14, and I cannot quite be reconciled that it was not.

"Glimpses of Katie"

165

*Abbot papers, Harvard University Archives.

June 30, 1872

TOLEDO, OHIO

Dear Mother,

Katie is getting well, I hope, although her strength is returning but slowly. The dear little baby is thriving and gaining daily. She is going to be a "good baby," eats well, sleeps well, and cries but little. Katie nurses her, and will do so as long as she can. We have named her already, and the name is Fanny Larcom. This was my earnest wish, and Katie cheerfully consented.

[A note from Katie to Frank's mother.]

Toledo, August 5, 1872

Dear Mamma,

While I am waiting for baby to wake and be washed and dressed, I will try to scratch a little note to you. We are getting along very nicely, baby and I. She grows fat and strong on my milk and I do not find that I am the worse for nursing her, in spite of what Doctor Torrey said. I did not think when I began to nurse her that we should either of us be as well as we are, but I dreaded the bottle for her, and determined to get through the hot month well. I wish you could see her—she is so sweet and cunning, we all make fools of ourselves over her . . . and I am afraid that she will be completely spoiled before long.

I think I never took such real comfort in any of my babies as I do with this one and yet I am constantly haunted by the fear that she will leave us as the others have . . .

Katie

IF EVER
TWO WERE
ONE

———

166

September 24, 1872

TOLEDO, OHIO

Dear Mother,

Katie and the boys are very well. Dear little Fanny, your baby, is also well now, though she had a sick turn a week or two ago that filled us with alarm. It proved to be only a severe cold, and not that terrible trouble that deprived us of little Gertrude, and Ethel, too . . .

December 2, 1872

Dear Mother,

Your letter fills me with grief. I can scarcely bear to wait while my dear Father is in such a state . . . I will try to be prepared to leave on short notice, but I trust there will be no need . . . My father's life has been so pure and upright that the natural vigor of his constitution cannot be broken yet . . . It is surely something to be grateful for, if we are spared the sight of seeing pain added to weakness . . . Katie is well and so are the boys, excepting colds. Darling Fanny is very well indeed, as sweet a baby as the fondest soul could wish. I wish you could see her. She could nestle herself in your heart, I know.—

[Frank's father, Joseph Hale Abbot, died on April 7, 1873. At the end of 1873, the Abbots relocated to Cambridge, Massachusetts.]

[In March 1874 Frank sent Charles Darwin a copy of his essay entitled "Darwin's Theory of Conscience." In response, Darwin wrote to Frank: "you have put with remarkable clearness and correctness my views on the moral sense; and you must allow me to say that your eulogy on what I have tried to do in science is the most magnificent one passed on me, and I heartily wish that I deserved the half of what you say."*

On August 12, 1874, Katie gave birth to a daughter, Margaret. Two months later, Margaret died. Frank's diary is silent during the months preceding her death. Around 1902, Frank transcribed his mother's diary en-

"Glimpses of Katie"

167

---

*Abbot papers, Harvard University Archives.

tries into the diary entitled "Glimpses of Katie." Those entries for October and November 1874 follow.]

October 12, 1874

Day very bright and beautiful. I went over to Frank's as soon as possible after breakfast. I found the dear little Margaret fearfully changed indeed, when I saw her awake in my arms. Katie had written to her sister Jennie, but, as she could not come today, I put by my own plans and stayed all day to help as I might be able. Lydia and Lucy came from Concord. The dear baby got no rest all day. Doctor Wesselhoeft told me it had "no chance whatever of life, but it might linger some time."

October 15, 1874

Baby had a better night, but poor Jennie is so ill with nervous headache that I begged her to return to bed, and I would help Katie through the day. I returned to Berkeley Street, changed my dress, returned, held the baby, and darned stockings for the children all day. I can never forget the appealing look of this dear baby's eyes—it appears to me now.

October 18, 1874

We came to Frank's. Baby is fearfully wasted—how long, O Lord, how long? The beautiful little appealing eyes grow more touching in their expression, as the little frail body wastes away.

November 1, 1874

A clear, bright, cold morning, but no snow. I dressed myself after breakfast for church, and went over to inquire for little Margaret. Poor Katie is attempting to change its dress, and I certainly never conceived such utter emaciation. When the task is performed and the little sufferer composed on the pillow in Katie's lap, I could only stand to look at her as a new type of Madonna, where the most perfect type of motherhood was expressed as I never before saw it—the perfect patience of love.

[Margaret Abbot died on November 3, 1874.]

1875

CAMBRIDGE

Dear Mother,

 Last Thursday, Katie went to the post-office mail-box near the Arsenal, and took Fanny with her to give her a little airing; but the walking was very slippery and the little thing could not keep her footing on the ice at all. So Katie had to bend down and lift her along, getting very tired before she got home. In the evening she went to Cambridgeport to meet me at Mrs. Joshua Kendall's at tea, as Miss Maria Mitchell, the astronomer and professor at Vassar College and a sister of Mrs. Kendall, wanted very much to meet me, having failed to do so last year. I wish now that she had failed this year; for Katie, who took the Main Street car at the Square, had to walk Inman Street through Cambridge Street, and so got tired anew.

 On coming home in the evening, she was obliged to stand up in the horse-car, which was very much crowded, and got an internal strain, a displacement of the uterus, in consequence. Next day she felt poorly, but did not let me know how much, thinking it was only fatigue; but the day after, finding she was not well, I insisted on her having the doctor. Now she is laid up for three or four weeks in bed, at the least. I have had to get a nurse, at ten dollars a week, and so I seem to be plunged into another expensive period. Dear me, every radical ought to be made an old bachelor by law, as incompetent to support a family! My life has been one long, persistent battle thus far, with patches of peace at intervals; and here I am thirty-eight with only a debt of hundreds of dollars to show as the savings of fifteen hard, toilsome years.

                     Frank

1 8 7 6

[On October 20, 1876, Katie gave birth to a stillborn girl.]

November 22, 1876

Dear Mother,

First of all, I must tell you about Katie. When the birth of her babe came on October 20, Doctor Sewall feared a terrible inflammatory fever, as I afterwards learned, on account of her carrying the dead child two weeks, and then giving birth to it three weeks before the time. But she escaped all fever wonderfully, and has had no back set at all. She has not yet sat up, however, except to be propped up in bed for a few minutes. The doctor intends to keep her in bed until the ulceration which (she thinks) dates from childhood, and has been the cause of her feeble health all these years, has passed away; and everything looks very favorable now. Probably she will have to stay in bed a week or two longer, perhaps more than that. But the prospect of her getting up "a well woman" at last is enough to keep me patient. Katie herself is very cheerful and comfortable, though she feels the tediousness of her long confinement severely. Her strength is, of course, reduced for the time being, but I cannot help thinking that this long rest will be excellent for her over-tasked nervous system in the end. I try to be as cheerful as I can over the heavy expenses of doctors, nurses, apothecaries, etc., and have contrived to keep out of debt . . .

So much for sickness and pecuniary circumstances. Over against these is my profound home happiness. Never did a man have a better or dearer wife, or better or dearer children. No jarring or heart-burning at home, thank God!

PART V

"You have been just the best wife that ever was . . ."

"You ask me when I first suspected that I loved you. I will tell you when I first kn—
at I loved you. Do you remember the night we sat by the stove, playing with th
ips, and I gave you one and told you that, when I found the ebony, I wou
e it to you? I knew then that I loved you as I could never love another, a
knew, too, that you would think me that piece of ebony. God grant that
ay prove true ebony! Perhaps you think it strange that, knowing what I d
should have told you so. But I could not help it — something seemed to so
me, 'tell him so', and I could not resist it."

(See p. 132.)   [Copied Jan. 25, 1894.]

(See p. 132.)

(Extract from her letter at Beverly, Jan. 11, 1858.)

" I was afraid that you sometimes thought me rather bold, particularly that night when
we you that piece of chip, but I could not help saying what I did. What have you done with
at piece of chip? I know you kept it for some time."   [Copied Feb. 8, 1894.]

(Extract from my letter at Cambridge, Jan. 12, 1858.)

" You say you feared I should think you bold, when you gave me that little slip of wood. If I had loved you less,
ould have thought you so. But I had read your heart well enough to know that you would not show your feelings
y were very strong. If you had been a coquette, you would never have done it; if I had been flirting with you, I sh
it have been pleased with it. You were too honest to do such a thing for effect; and I was too deeply earnest to
ur love to point at my own success. It certainly was a strange thing; but, as Kingsley says in ' Two Years A
is the strange things that keep the world alive? At first I was too diffident to believe you meant all you d
lean; but, after I got home, I saw you could mean nothing else. You have that little bit of worthless pine to this
at I did not keep silence when to have kept silence might have changed the destiny of both of us. An
n imagine I could lose it? Do you pretend to wonder if I have it still? You know as well as I do that it
rerished among a few tokens of my real life, of no value in themselves, but speaking whole volumes to me, whereve
ok at them. Only think, Mignonette, one year has gone already! How quick in passing will the rest seem, when they ar
assed! Today a mere boy and girl, tomorrow a husband and wife, then two graves, lying side by side, I trust. Oh d
y own, own darling, may that dark curtain of death, which must sooner or later fall on us both, when it rises, open
a view of some happy realm where grief and fear are strangers, and where truth and love shall dwell together forever!
us must in all human probability go first to that unknown land; but if we act towards each other as lovingly and f
ly as we now both mean to do, that dreadful separation shall be robbed of its bitterest sting. Hope shall string f
shies of earthly happiness, and cheer
lonely heart of the one still
stined to toil and suffer below.
earest, let us never have to
proach ourselves with harsh
ords towards one another, for
ey bring untold suffering
it is the speaker and the
roken to." [Copied March
      2, 1894.]

The first letter from my darling,
written as she was starting for Crawfordsville, Indiana, Feb. 2, 1857, and
handed to me by Jennie Loring on
the same day.

Dear Frank, please direct your letters to the care of
Jacob Kim. The reason why I sent you off so
early was because I did not want you to see Mrs. Dixon
again. I could not forget what she said to you.
                                                            Kate

Dear Frank, you must be satisfied with this without
a letter this time. I hope it will say to you as much
as any of my letters have, and tell you how much I love
you. Your own Katie.   (Received Mar. 17, 1857.)

1 8 7 7

January 1, 1877

Before I go to my office (I cannot take a holiday this New Year), I am determined to tell the story of our Christmas, or I fear it will never be done. Doctor Sewall consented to Katie's coming down on Christmas day to dinner; so the boys and I devised a little bit of a celebration in honor of dear Mamma's appearance after a nine or ten weeks imprisonment upstairs. I proposed a Coronation! So, after grave deliberations and plannings, we settled upon a programme. I bought a young fir-balsam tree for fifty cents, and we decorated the parlor, study, and dining-room. With some Bristol-board and gilt paper, we made a splendid crown, all pure gold inside and outside, with a red band and a red star on the front—a marvelous piece of magnificence. Everything was arranged elaborately beforehand, with great whisperings and fun of all sorts.

About noon, I went upstairs, and told Katie it was getting towards turkey-time, and said she was to appear with her pretty brown hair floating down her back! This was to lay a becoming foundation for the Crown, which would be sadly interfered with by that big bun on the back of her head; but the quick-witted little matron sniffed mystery in the air, of course! So I carefully helped her downstairs, as she would walk herself, and ushered her into the study, where an easy-chair, with a scarlet table-cloth spread over it, had to do duty as a throne. The conspirators were all in the dining room, having been previously drilled to their parts. So I left Katie alone, wondering what was up in the study, and organized a stately procession in the dining-room. I led the way, with a wooden sword (an old Roman gladius whittled out by myself in the far-off boyhood) stuck under my blue dressing-gown cord, and a round mahogany ruler, tipped at each end with a pink tape knot, for a baton. Evie and Stannie came next, bearing between them the sofa cushion with the crimson damask cover (a relic of the great curtain behind my old Dover pulpit), and the Crown resting on the cushion. I approached near the throne, halted the procession (I forgot to say that Fanny and Addie, the servant girl, brought up the rear), and, with a profound obeisance, addressed the enthroned lady somewhat as follows—I will not swear to every word, as the oration was extemporized,—while Evie and Stannie, kneeling side by side, held the Crown before her in readiness for me to take, when wanted:—

"Most august and gracious Sovereign! Your dutiful and loving subjects, over whom you have ruled these many years with a gentle sway which they have acknowledged in their hearts with a delight and grateful obedience, desire to signalize your resumption of authority by a formal testimony of their loyalty, placing upon your brow the visible symbol of your unquestioned rule. Hitherto you have been directed the destinies of this vast empire with the aid of external marks of the royalty we all so gladly recognize; but, in their profound joy over your partial restoration to health, your subjects would fain celebrate this auspicious occasion by a Coronation ceremony whose solemnity and magnificence shall set the seal of legality to your de jure queenship and thus impress foreign nations with new respect for your reign. Now, therefore, I in virtue of my high-office as the Ace of Spades, do hereby lift this golden symbol of sovereignty, place it upon your royal head, and solemnly proclaim you, in the presence of these assembled thousands, the rightful and lawful Queen of Hearts! And I command all principalities, kingdoms, and powers to pay you the honor due to your exalted position."

With this, I crowned the laughing Queen, and motioned the procession to retire. Presently, little Fanny re-appeared, bearing the silver cake-basket full of peanuts, and holding it out the Queen, said with her exquisitely sweet voice and bewitching childish manner:—

> "Please take these peanuts, for we've got no tarts,
> And give me one, most gracious Queen of Hearts!"

Stannie next marched in, bearing me a salver (an old tin pot cover concealed with a red napkin!), a new Russia leather pocket-book, containing a checkup for One Million Dollars made payable to the Queen of Hearts by the King of Diamonds, and kneeled and said:—

> "My royal lord, the King of Diamonds, bends
> Low at thy feet, and here his tribute sends."

Next Evie appeared, bearing in the same way a new jasper-ware butter-dish, and said, kneeling:—

> "The King of Clubs with many a loyal wish,
> His tribute adds, although 'tis but-a-dish."

Then Evie and Stannie (who officiated, I forgot to say, as the Jacks of Diamonds and Clubs) went out, returned with a bright, handsome, silver-plated and gold-lined spoon-holder, which I bought with Mother's five dollars and a trifle of my own, and presented it, kneeling and saying in unison:—

> "Our mistress, Grandmamma the Good,
> Has sent us two gossoons
> To give the Queen a hearty kiss,
> And say, she'll hold your spoons!"

"You have been just the best wife that ever was . . ."

175

With some indignant expostulations to the bronzed plaster-casts on top of my book-cases for disturbing the ceremonies by indecorously making a great noise in the galleries,—telling Shakespeare to stop playing with the little Milton boy, and Bonaparte to take off his cocked hat or I'd knock his head off, hat and all, and Apollo Belevedere to stop shooting arrows at the glass window panes, and go up stairs to put his clothes on or I'd tickle his skin with a stick,—I brought the Coronation to a close; and with lots of fun we went out to the turkey.

Katie got very tired, however, and soon after dinner I had to carry her upstairs in my arms. She has not yet been downstairs again, though none the worse for her Christmas venture.

January 25, 1877

The twentieth anniversary of my engagement to Katie. Wrote the dear woman a little note in honor of the day. She had not remembered the date, but was much moved and pleased at my remembering it . . .

My darling wife,

    Twenty years ago this day, in the little town of Concord, I wooed and won the hand of a dear girl who has blessed my life with a love as pure, as tender, as faithful, as a woman gave to a man. It was a Sunday afternoon, you know, and I told you my "dream." I shall never forget your sweet "I hope so!" that told me all; nor, when I exclaimed, "And now that little hand is mine, and the heart, too!" how softly and lovingly you whispered, "Indeed it is, and both hands, and all the heart!" And ever so it has been, my dearest, dearest Katie!

    Twenty long years since that winter's day, that made a summer in my life and soul! And now your husband bears his testimony, in manhood's prime, to the truth, and worth, and blessed wealth of love, of her who then won his boyish heart. The hope has proved a fact, and more precious, even, as a fact than as a hope. I love you, darling, with my whole and undivided soul; I bless you for all you have been and are to me, with a gratitude that fills my eyes with tears. God bless my darling!

April 6, 1877

I am thinking over my future. I shall probably open a "Harvard Training School" on a new plan, desiring ten or twelve pupils at $400 each, to instruct on the private tutor arrangement substantially.

April 9, 1877

Ten years ago this day Gertrude was born, only to die on the 13th of the August, and leave an eternally beautiful baby-memory in her parents' hearts. She lies in the little lot in Beverly Cemetery, with a little white cross at her head and two other little white crosses beside it.

May 27, 1877

This afternoon, I left my usual Sunday labor to go with Katie, Evie, Stannie, and Fanny after wildflowers down by the Water Works. We got many houstonia, violets, and wild geraniums. Katie got excessively tired and a bad headache followed—the poor little woman is very feeble still.

1878

January 1, 1878

After a very busy day in town, William James Potter came out to tea with me by appointment. We chatted after tea in the pleasant flower-adorned study, and about ¼ to 9 he took his leave. As I came back to the study from the door, Katie handed me a letter Potter had secretly left with her on behalf of friends "from Maine to Nebraska," containing a cheque for $885.00! It was a "testimonial" to my character and services!!! Enclosed also was a note from Ralph Waldo Emerson with a cheque for $50 towards the amount.

"You have been just the best wife that ever was . . ."

Potter's letter was very touching. I was quite overwhelmed, and Katie was as silent as a mouse to see what I would do. Well, I endorsed the whole thing to Katie, and shall deposit it tomorrow in the Suffolk Savings Bank. It was a blessed kindness, not to be refused; but I prefer to have it Katie's absolutely. I don't want a penny of it for myself, but it will save me a world of anxiety to have it for my family, in case I am unable to provide for them.

January 10, 1878

I had a great frolic with the children just before tea. Stannie and I made an "elephant" with my old college shawl, and we romped and rolled over the floor together.

February 25, 1878

This afternoon, at 3½ o'clock, Ralph Waldo Emerson lectured at the Old South Church on the "The Fortune of the Republic." It filled me with venerating love to see and hear this simple, grand man, with his spotless character behind him, speak his word of hope and faith, of ceaseless reverence and emphasis of the moral sentiment in man. That is Emerson's great mission—to be a testimony to Mind and Conscience as the supreme fact of Man and Nature. My whole soul says amen. And I love this sublime soul which stands for that.

April 9, 1878

I see in a little trundle bed the sweet, still, tiny form of my dead child. How solemnly beautiful was the face of baby Gertrude, as she rested in the small chamber over the front door at Dover! Today is her birthday, the sweet daughter of our love, the sacred memory of our souls. O God, thou art!

April 24, 1878

After working all day, I took Evie to hear Ralph Waldo Emerson at the Old South Church at 8 P.M., on "The Superlative." I wanted him and Stannie to hear him once, for they may never have another chance. Stannie did not care to go, but Evie did. The lecture was in every way to Emerson's high-water mark; I listened with emotion to this greatest and noblest of America's sons.

June 14, 1878

Today, at 10 A.M., William Cullen Bryant was buried at Roslyn, Long Island, where Mother called upon him so pleasantly a year or two ago. It impresses me deeply to associate his funeral with Mother's birthday. Bryant exerted a vast influence on my boyhood dreams and aims. I wrote him an enthusiastic letter while teaching school at Concord in 1856–57, and he sent me a kind little reply, which I cherish now more than ever.

1 8 7 9

January 25, 1879

Twenty-two years ago this day, I told Katie my love for her and heard her blessed "I hope so!" That was the first kiss of two happy young lovers—what is more sacred? Nothing but the first kiss the mother gives her babe, and the last kiss upon the dying lips. We both remembered our day tenderly.

February 21, 1879

I went to Katie and found her in her blue wrapper, with her hair, smoothly done up and a bright face full of happy love to greet me. She is fairer than ever in my eyes, with her beautiful soul peering forth in every feature. Though in her fortieth year, she is lovely in complexion and expression as she was when she was seventeen; and her dainty, perfectly formed ears are still wonderfully pretty. But it is her eyes that tell the story of as loving, pure, unselfish a life as was ever lived; they mirror her inmost heart. The nearly twenty years of our married life have brought us daily closer together; we love each other for eternity, I hope.

"You have been just the best wife that ever was . . ."

179

April 11, 1879

Katie and I spoke of the summer to come. She said Doctor Zakrzewska advised her last summer to get through the winter as well as she could, and then take a long sea voyage. The idea flashed across my mind that she might go to the Azores, as Mother did in 1865. Katie said it cost Mother $600, and where was that money to come from?

"Why," I said, "you have a cool thousand of your own in the Savings Bank!"

"Oh!" she laughed, "that is a mere form; it was your present."

"No!" I replied rather warmly, "it is yours in good faith—I shall never touch it. That will easily pay all the expense, if I cannot."

Her eyes filled with tears. She did not want to go without me, or leave me at home all summer to work. Katie threw her arms around my neck and kissed me, and her great tender eyes full of love, and pressed my head to her faithful heart. Am I not a millionaire?

April 14, 1879

I am delighted to learn that instead of $600, it will cost less than $200—$100 for tickets and $1 dollar a day for board, with a few extras. The *Veronica* sails from New Bedford early in June—a fine barque better than the steamers that now run to Fayal. Could I contrive to go with Katie? That would be too good.

May 1, 1879

This afternoon I told Evie about my will, and said I might not be able to leave the written directions about my books and papers, but wanted him to know something of my wishes. I told him I wanted nobody to write my life till he was old enough to do it himself, with the help and counsel of competent advisers—and wanted nobody to do it except a thorough radical. I told him the keys to all my public and private life, with all its struggles, was the desire and resolve to live out the highest moral ideal in logical consistency with all its requirements, even in details seemingly trivial—to square action with thought and apply religion to conduct logically.

June 24, 1879

On board the Barque *Veronica,* of New Bedford, Massachusetts, June 24, 1879. The tug is towing us down the harbor. The day is very warm and clear. Katie is happy and bright, lying in the steamer-chair that kind Cousin Annie bought for her, with a pillow, and her nice new blue blanket all ready if she needs it, and her blue glasses on her nose to keep off the glare from her eyes.

We two are off together alone for the first time; we jokingly call it our wedding journey twenty years belated! Nonquitt Beach, where we spent our summer of 1875 in Rock Cottage, is already passed; the sea is beautifully green all about us, and the summer sky is bright overhead.

June 28, 1879

Here I lie on the poop-deck of the *Veronica*, in Katie's steamer chair, while she lies in the hammock I bought for her at New Bedford the night before we sailed. She protested against my buying it, and vowed she should not want it; but I remembered how much she likes the hammock on our piazza at home, and obstinately purchased it! Now she is very glad indeed to have it. On the whole, she is a very good sailor, and has suffered very little from sea-sickness—far less that any other lady aboard except for Miss Coleman, who is never sick at all. But she does not like the warmth and the moisture of the breeze the last two days; it is not at all bracing, and I begin to fear that she may not get all the benefit from the voyage in the hope of which I undertook it with her. Still it is the mental rest and nervous recuperation which will do her the most good.

As for me, this rest and laziness for three months will make me ten years younger. I delight in the rolling motion of the barque, and have done so every minute since the rolling began, with an almost idolatrous love of the sea . . . there is something of the sea in my very blood, I believe: grandfather's life upon the ocean, perhaps the sea-rovings of far-remoter ancestors, have somehow told on my very constitution, and joy and health come to me like milk from the maternal breast whenever I get out fairly on the waves.

"You have been just the best wife that ever was . . ."

181

June 30, 1879

Katie does not gain at all in this humid and almost sultry air, which seems more like the muggy atmosphere of dog-days than in the invigorating, cool winds we expected. She is listless and tired, does not relish her food or have any appetite, and said just now she wished she were at home. I cannot help feeling the shadow of bitter disappointment standing over me. It has cost me a desperate effort to take this voyage, in the fond hope of seeing her gain strength and spirits and health under its influences; it will be a gall indeed if she returns at last no better than she started. To be sure, the nights in our berth are suffocating and hot . . . but there is nothing to fatigue or excite . . . I yearn inexpressibly to see some return in her rapid improvement for the sacrifices entailed by the voyage, and I cannot contemplate unmoved the prospect of seeing them all go—for nothing. What more can I do; if this costly experiment fails; with worse than exhausted resources and all the sickness of hope deferred? Ah Katie, you little understand what it has cost me to redeem the secret vow of twenty-years ago! Only be well and strong again yourself, and all will indeed be well!

July 1, 1879

The nights are surpassingly lovely on deck . . . last night I sat by myself a long time in the Captain's yawl, which is suspended from the davits and makes a nice retreat, dreaming and musing for an hour or two without interruption, and wandering in fancy far away from the ship and its little company. The mystery of Nature, the inscrutable and tantalizing secrets she buries in her own breast, yet infuses into ours in the form of vague questionings, the divine glory and poetry of the universe, all these things live in the soul of the man as they did in that of the boy!

July 3, 1879

Day before yesterday, Captain Hathaway told me after dinner that he had something to show me. Presently, he brought up on deck a very handsome, ivory-handled, nickel-plated pistol, inscribed: "Henry C. Hathaway. City Marshal of New Bedford."

This, he said, was given to him by a member of the Colt family, of revolver fame, in acknowledgement of his service in arresting and returning a boy who had run away to go to sea on a whaler from New Brunswick. Finding it rusty, he went again below, and brought up a bottle of olive oil, and began to clean the pistol. I had in my satchel below the Smith & Wesson seven-shooter, which I had bought in 1875 to practice Katie in shooting at a target. Before leaving Boston, I had brought twelve hundred cartridges to amuse her in the same way at Fayal, in case she needed outdoor amusement. Thinking this a good chance to clean my own pistol (which I had not cleaned in a year), I went below and brought it up. It was loaded; but I carefully turned back the barrel on its hinge, and tried to loosen the chamber containing the cartridges, in order to unload and then clean the pistol all over. It seems that it was rusted, and stuck; and in trying to dislodge the chamber, I must have touched the hammer, which fell and exploded one of the cartridges, before I had withdrawn my hand.

The explosion was a great surprise to me, and at first I thought this surprise was the only cause of the severe nervous shock I received. But almost immediately, I felt a growing pain in my hand, which was blackened with the powder, and began to trickle blood on the deck. I saw that I had shot myself in the forefinger of the left hand, and I saw the protuberance of the ball between the first and second joints of the finger, under the skin, where it had lodged. I could not tell how severe the wound was, but supposed that I had broken the bones of the finger. At the sound of the explosion, the Captain turned to me. The pain had grown excruciating. I said,

"Captain, I have shot myself in the hand," and stood holding it out, while the drops of blood fell pretty thick and fast upon the deck.

"Wait till I can bring up some bandages from the cabin," said he, after hastily wrapping a rag round the finger. My first distinct thought had been a dread that Katie, who was below, would be made dreadfully frightened, and perhaps very disastrously shocked in the nervous system, by the accident; so, while the Captain had gone below, I descended to the cock-pit, behind the poop-deck, and took my seat on the "bits," and tried hard to fight off the growing faintness. But the pain was most intense, and I found I was getting very faint. As the sun shone full upon me, I staggered to the stairway leading up the poop-deck, and began to say something indistinctly to Captain Sylva, when I lost all consciousness. The next thing that I remember is the sensation of being carried in the arms of a man and laid on one of the steamer deck chairs. People were about me, holding hartshorn and bay-rum to my nose, bathing my forehead, etc. Miss Coleman chafed and rubbed the wrist of my right

"You have been just the best wife that ever was . . ."

183

hand, while the Captain was examining the wound of the left. It was pretty hard to get rid of the faintness, though the pain helped to this result as much as the hartshorn held by Mr. Lane. The Captain was pretty white round the lips, I was afterwards told, as he examined the wound; and, he found I could move the joints and judging that the bones were not broken, he said he would bind up the wound, and, as we would be in Fayal in a week, leave to a surgeon there the job of cutting out the ball. I simply said, "Go ahead—do all that is necessary;" for I knew that the ball had got to come out. But he evidently did not want to do the cutting himself, so merely bound up the finger and poured on the bandage some soothing liniment.

As I lay there, Katie came and sat by me, quite collected, to my infinite relief; for she told me that she had not been frightened, had heard the shot, but feared nothing because everything was so still afterwards. When she heard someone say I was hurt, it was so long after the shot that she did not connect it with the injury, and she did not at first imagine it serious; so I found she had not been shocked to a dangerous extent, and was relieved of a great fear on her account. I persuaded her to go below and finish her rest, assuring her that there was [no] reason to be alarmed, and not mentioning that the ball was still in the wound.

Miss Coleman came and insisted on reading aloud to me a story by Henry James, Jr. It was a very great service—far more than she guessed in the kindness of her heart; for the agony was constant. While she was reading, old Mr. Gill passed in front of the chair where I lay, and, interrupting he said he had had experience in this line when commander of a vessel, knew how to extract the ball perfectly well, and would be happy to do me this service if I desired. I thanked him, and I said I would speak to him again about the matter. Miss Coleman then continued and finished the story.

When the tea-bell rang, I got up and went down with the rest—not wishing to be a "baby" or let Katie know how I was suffering. Of course I could not eat very much. After tea, I was sitting by Katie, when Mr. Gill came up on deck. I went and sat by him, and questioned him about his experience in surgery. That the ball must ultimately be cut out, I knew; that inflammation and swelling and increased pain would probably attend the delay, I was confident; that the fear of the impending operation would haunt me, I suspected; and that I should be better able to care of Katie if the wound were well on in getting cured on reaching Fayal—of that I had not a shadow of doubt. So I made up my mind—and it taxed my resolution to the utmost. Mr. Gill cheerfully consented, and was for doing it there; but I said, "Such things should be done away from the women" (who were not far off and could see when we stood).

So I descended to the cockpit, while he went for a lancet, and a bowl of water, and another chair. I am not physically brave; my dread of pain is intense. I had to set my teeth, and go through the operation by sheer will, which fortunately I have also. While I sat by the vessel's railing, with my sleeve stripped up, waiting for Mr. Gill's return, Miss Coleman came up the gangway, and looked surprised. I said, "They are going to cut the ball out."

"Oh," said she, with her beautiful great eyes full of pity, "let me sit by you and hold some hartshorn."

"No," I said, "Mr. Lane is going to do that. But I shall be grateful if you go up on deck and engage Mrs. Abbot's attention until the job is over; for I dread any nervous tension for her in the present state of health."

"I will!" said the noble girl, with emphasis and promptness; and go she did, God bless her.

When Mr. Gill came up, we pulled chairs to the vessel's side. I held out my left hand to him and grasped the railing with my right, and fixed my gaze on the horizon and said, "Now cut." But Mr. Lane came up behind me, and insisted on holding my hand against him, while he put the hartshorn to my nose and rubbed my forehead. I think this prevented my fainting again; but if I had known then what I learned afterwards—that he had almost fainted himself in the afternoon after carrying me in my fainting-fit to the steamer chair—I should have refused to let him stay by me during the operation. He has been a brother to me.

After all was done, Mr. Lane told somebody to go and tell Mrs. Abbot that it was all over, but I said no—she did not know it was going to be done at all, and I had better tell her myself, to prevent all anxiety. So, as soon as my hand was wrapped up, I went up on deck to tell her. As I approached, she sat by the hatchway as cool as a cucumber, and she said she was glad it was over. I looked at Miss Coleman in astonishment.

"You have been just the best wife that ever was . . ."

185

"Oh," she said laughing, "I came right up, and began to talk very earnestly with Mrs. Abbot about the sardines we had for supper, but she knew all about it!"

It seems that the quick-witted little woman had heard Mr. Gill's offer in the afternoon, when I thought she was down below; and after tea, when I spoke to him and we went off together, she inferred the whole thing without a word from anybody. So all my precautions to protect her became ridiculous. She is the most imperturbable of womankind. How did she ever get so prostrated nervously, when she never had an equal among women for self-possession?

Captain Hathaway gave me 40 drops of laudanum and no end of brandy for the first night, but I was so feverish, and the wound ached so, that I scarcely closed my eyes. It has continued to pain me much ever since; but now it is just beginning to ease off a little. The kindness and sympathy I have had from the Captain, passengers, and crew have gone straight to my heart.

July 6, 1879

Katie is weak and tired. If she does not pick up on reaching Fayal, my enterprise will prove a costly and most disheartening failure. It will do me little good, if it does not a great deal for her.

July 7, 1879

Before leaving home, the idea struck me to offer myself as a candidate for the degree of Ph.D. at Harvard. It would take two years, I find, and very probably more, as I could only give odds and ends of time to it. To be sure, I am forty-two years old; and some would think it undignified at my age to take such a step. It would help to re-introduce me into the pursuits, the fellowships, and the sympathies which I have had to sacrifice to the duty that seemed laid upon me.

July 10, 1879

At 8 A.M. the yawl carried Misses Coleman and Holt, and Mrs. Bassett and Benton, with Katie, Lane, Rhodes, Mumford, Mr. Perry, and me to

Santa Cruz. We "did" the town. We went to the house of the consul, a Mr. Mackay, where his wife and eight other females of his family received us very kindly. Mrs. Mackay took us to a garden where we saw bananas, oranges, lemons, yams, bamboos, etc. growing. English ivy ran like groundspine over the ground, and we adorned ourselves therewith. We went to the old church and waited for the key till our patience gave way—then we left. I gave a Spanish dollar for three quart bottles of Dublin Stout, and Rhodes did the same. It was fun to march the street with bacchanalian ivy-crowns and a bottle of porter in each hand!

At Fayal

July 12, 1879

By four o'clock the bustle and uproar began. Everybody was talking and sleep became impossible. On reaching the stone pier, we all marched in procession to the Custom-house, where an hour or more was spent on the farce of opening our trunks and valises. Then we went to the Hotel, and got our rooms and some breakfast. The Fayal Hotel is kept by Mr. and Mrs. Edwards. Katie and I occupied No. 18, in the southeast corner; and it was the best room of all in our opinion. It commands an unbroken view of the beautiful harbor, with the Magdalena Rocks and Pico beyond. Here we watched the lofty and lonely summit of Pico, sharp against the sky, when the clouds permitted it to be visible. Now and then at sunset we caught glimpses of ravishing beauty, as the declining sun cast a deep, indescribably rich glow over the whole mountain, rosy and darkly red and warm, which slowly climbed away from the base as the sun sank lower, and finally vanishes from the sharp peak of the cone into the kindred glow of the heavens beyond and above.

In the afternoon, we visited the fine old garden back of the Hotel, where bananas, oranges, figs, lemons, pineapples, sugar canes, and flowers of all kinds flourish. Miss Alice Dabney sent superb baskets of flowers to Katie and Miss Coleman.

At night, Katie and I leaned together on our window-sill, watching the resplendent pageant till the last glow of the sunset had faded into the cold, dark coloring of night.

"You have been just the best wife that ever was . . ."

View of Pico, Fayal, Azores, circa 1879. where Frank and Katie

August 3, 1879

Today is the twentieth anniversary of our marriage. Katie covered me with kisses and smiles this morning. After breakfast, I arranged her pillow and blue blanket in the garden in her steamer chair; and she went out there for the first time for a week. We played cribbage, spite of Sunday! Miss Coleman invited us to go with her party and Miss Mitchel to a country dance at Castello Branco, but Katie did not feel strong enough. While she rested upstairs after dinner, I wrote her a letter in the garden, as a memento. She read it (I was my own postman!), and said, with her eyes full of tears: "You have made my whole life very happy!" And I felt very happy, indeed, such a testimony from one who never prevaricated:

IN THE GARDEN BEHIND THE HOTEL,

HORTA, FAYAL, AZORES ISLANDS

My best beloved!

You have returned to your chamber to rest, after a morning's sojourn among these grand old chestnuts and shady aisles, and I cannot help wishing to give you some lit-

IF EVER
TWO WERE
ONE

———

188

Abbot celebrated their honeymoon "twenty years belated."

tle memento of today—our "Crystal Wedding." I told you I had tried in vain to write you a little poem. It was because I had too much, not too little, to express. The love I bear you is too deeply rooted and too powerful, too much a matter of my very life, to lend itself to poetry on this twentieth anniversary of our marriage. I cannot rhyme about it now; imagination seems a trespasser in the domain of the holiest reality. I must use only the language of soberness and truth, and belittle our sacred love by no simile, or metaphor, or idle fancy.

Twenty years ago, you gave me your whole soul for life. The world thought us very foolish, perhaps; but the world knew nothing of what it so flippantly judged. Today let me say that I never regretted our "foolishness" so little as I do now—never loved you so wholly and unreservedly as after twenty years' experience of your womanly love and faith and truth. From that day to this, you have steadily deepened my reverence for woman by a constant showing forth in my own home of all that entitles woman to the reverence of man.

As a daughter, a sister, a wife, a mother, you have made your dear name a synonym of every virtue that commands my home, and illustrated that unsuperstititous religiousness of spirit which is the supreme beauty of human life. I cannot tell you

"You have been just the best wife that ever was . . ."

189

how dear you are to your husband; I can only say that there is no corner of his heart that is not wholly yours. In joy or in sorrow have we lived together this score of years, growing continually nearer and more near to each other; in our smiles and our tears we have been truly one.

If ever I caused you a moment's pain, I ask your forgiveness now. May I always deserve the dear kisses and smiles of love with which you hallowed this day's dawning light! And may Death only prove to us that love shall be eternal!

Your husband forever, Frank

September 9, 1879

Katie certainly bears the voyage much better than before. The motion of the ship, when pitching before headwinds, troubles her head; but she is not prostrated utterly by it as before. I hope devoutly that the experiment will prove in the end a great success. [Later, Frank added in the margin of his diary: "It proved a partial success only. She was better on the whole after her return; the five weeks in Fayal did her real good, but the two voyages did her only harm. We always thought it would have proved more beneficial, if she had spent the whole summer alone with me at some retired place on the seashore."]

September 12, 1879

Lighted Nantucket Light last night at 10 P.M. and passed it at 1 A.M. Everybody jubilant, in spite of the perfect calm with which the day came in. About 50 miles out from New Bedford. If a breeze starts up, we may easily land this afternoon. If so, I may be able to run up to Wilton and hug my dear babies once more!

December 25, 1879

"Our honeymoon will shine our life-long; its beams will only fade over your grave or mine." *Jane Eyre*, given to me by Katie, "in remembrance of Meadville days."

1 8 8 0

January 10, 1880

Katie went to Concord today, by the forenoon train, so as to rest a little. She will be gone till Monday, January 12.

January 11, 1880

The house is empty enough without Katie. Little Fanny wanted to sleep with Papa, and I was glad to have her; the sweet childish face, softly breathing, seemed to shed a blessing through the room. Dear little Canary, what a treasure you are to Mamma and Papa!

January 12, 1880

I read and explained [William Cullen Bryant's] "Thanatopsis" to the two boys (after Stannie's Latin) and tried to kindle the love of poetry in their young souls. Have I succeeded?

January 28, 1880

If I get 8 seats engaged by October 1, I shall go on to New York alone to open the school, and board cheaply as I can. Katie will keep house here still, with the children, who must go to school themselves. My lease is up August 1, 1881, when Evie will have entered College, I hope; Stanley will have one year longer to study, and I may take him then to my own school, if we all remove to New York. Dismal enough, at best.

"You have been just the best wife that ever was . . ."

February 4, 1880

I tried to get up to Concord on Lydia's invitation to hear Emerson close the Lyceum course tonight.

February 10, 1880

At the very urgent solicitation of Albert Stickney, I took the Fall River boat for New York tonight to consult with him and James Fay as to my school plan. Stickney promises to send his little boy Weston to my school, and Fay wrote me that A. G. Paine, 31 West 50th Street, promised him to send his boy too. If I can get 8 pupils privately pledged, I will advertise at once, and try the experiment.

August 3, 1880

Twenty-one years ago two young souls pledged themselves irrevocably together—and the pledge has been faithfully kept by both. Today, they are knit more firmly than ever. Let the ghosts slumber in their graves: memory is at peace with herself, and all is well. But nothing sacred is forgotten. Take courage, O my soul!

Katie was too tired to make the excursion to Nantasket Beach I had planned in honor of the day; so we quietly stayed at Emmie's—perhaps the wisest thing for both.

August 22, 1880

Wilton, New Hampshire. Katie was tired, and I spent the forenoon alone in Chestnut Glen—now, alas, so defaced by the new Lily Pond road. Here the dreams of my boyhood, solitary and poetic, have hallowed the spot to me; and later memories doubly endear it to me. The maples are still there, and one of the grand old chestnuts also. My poem, "Chestnut Glen," of twenty years ago, still expresses all the loveliness of this fairy glade as it was.

In the P.M., Katie and I sat on the grass under the maples in the orchard, and she read to me.

August 26, 1880

This is the last week of my family life, with the dear home circle all unbroken. I am to be in exile at New York all winter, and can only be a rare visitor at my home. Evie passed his preliminary examinations for Harvard College successfully June last, and will enter next June: so that, if I then remove my family to New York, he will be absent in College here. The shadow of this great separation lies heavy on my heart; what would I not give to remain in Cambridge, as I fondly hoped to do in 1873, till my boys are both through College and the professional schools!

Alas, I must plunge into the maelstrom of the great metropolis now to try my fortune, begin life all over again at 44, and endure anxiety for Katie in her feebleness, left alone to guide and care for our shattered household! This is the reward of a life of labor for truth and higher religion for the world. So be it: I do not complain.

September 2, 1880

I was busy all forenoon in preparing my study for a long absence. Express took my trunk at 2 P.M. to Providence Station.

I took my last meal at 1, with the dear ones I must leave . . . At last, at 3 P.M. the time had come. Katie was upstairs by sick Fanny's bed; she bore up bravely, and did not cry as we gave each other a long embrace, and kissed each other sadly with tears in our eyes. Ah, but she cried, when I was gone, poor thing! It was bitter, bitter.

Evie and Stannie carried my valise, etc. to the corner of Brattle Street. When the horse car was coming, I kissed them, and tried to say goodbye, but my voice failed. We watched each other out of sight . . . O home, home! Shield it, thou Silent Power.

Cambridge, October 17, 1880

My darling Frank,

How shall I thank you for my birthday present! It is the best thing to seeing you to look at it; and you know how I shall prize it. But, oh! I do so long to see you and to put my arms around your neck once more! It is hard only to have a photograph, when I want the original so much! Dear Frank, if I have not said much about needing you, and longing for you, it is not because I have not wanted you, but because it seemed cruel to say one word that could possibly make your share of the burden any harder to bear. Sometimes I have been afraid that I have said so little that you may have thought I did not care about this weary separation. But in my heart I know it is

"You have been just the best wife that ever was . . ."

193

not so. You know me too well to ever think such a thing as that, my darling. What-
ever else happens, our love will last always; that, at least, we can keep, if we lose
everything else. And we will keep it and prize IT above everything else . . .

This afternoon Evie brought me the two bird easels, and told me they were your
present to me. I would kiss you for them, if I could reach you; as it is, I put my kisses
O O O here. They may be little ones on the paper, but they are big ones in my heart.

Katie

October 18, 1880

Dear Frank,

Forty-one today! It is just twenty years ago that you and I began our first house-
keeping in Meadville, on my twenty-first birthday. How long ago it seems. It was our
first home, and it was a happy one, as all our homes have been, in spite of the trou-
bles that came from outside. Thank God! The troubles have always been outside and
not inside, and they always will be, won't they, darling? . . . You do not know how I
enjoy being here with only the children. If only you were here, it would be perfect . . .

Love endless and untiring from your own, Katie

New York, December 12, 1880

My own dear love,

I fear it was a foolish choice for you, when you gave me your innocent girlish
heart, and linked your fate with mine. Truly have I loved you—but I have involved
you in a weary life, a hard life, a sorrowing life, my own! Better for you if I had
never crossed your track, I fear. If that I could make the happy future atone for all
of the past! Yet the future looks darker than the past itself, and all that remains is to
endure. We must make our brief and rare reunions yield all of the happiness that
we can—for in the strength of that meal we must go many days. Good night, my
dear, dear wife.

Yours with love unbounded, Frank

Cambridge, December 13, 1880

My darling,

Do you really think that anything that has come to me since I have been your
wife could make me regret it, or, if I could have foreseen it all, have made me give

you any other answer than I did? No! A thousand times no! I would not change my lot now with any one, no matter how much happier their lives may seem to be. We have each other, and firm faith and true love enough to carry us through harder trials than have yet fallen to us, hard as many of ours have been. I would not have had you do differently, for all the ease or money that might have come to us, and in your inmost soul you know it. Whatever else you may regret, never for one moment regret that you made me your wife! And do not fear to tell me all your loneliness and longings. I know what they must be, and how much you need me . . .

Always with love untold, Your own Katie

1 8 8 1

New York, January 25, 1881

My dear wife,

    Do you remember tonight, I wonder, that this is the twenty-fourth anniversary of our first kiss—given when you first promised to be mine? I shall never forget it, nor cease to bless God for the treasure he gave me then in one little girl's heart. You were nothing more than a little girl then, nor I much more than a boy either; but we knew enough to love and be happy. Well—I think tenderly and reverently of our first love, Katie darling, and I trust that it will live in the soul of each as divine fire forever . . .

Kisses like snowflakes to you, from Frank

Cambridge, May 13, 1881

Dear Frank,

    . . . It is pleasant to have you tell me that you "love me dearly," even if it is an old story. It is fresh every time you say it, though I have known it so many years. My darling, that is the one thing that has kept fresh and strong, and will while life lasts. I am sure of our love for each other! Whatever else fails, we have that left. I wish your vacation might begin now. I long to have you home again.

Ever your Katie

"You have been just the best wife that ever was . . ."

———

195

Cambridge, May 14, 1881

Dear Frank,

It is Ethel's twenty-first birthday. Do you remember it? I need not ask, for I know you do. What a help and comfort she would be, if only we had her now! She has escaped all sickness and trouble, and for her it is doubtless best! . . .

Ever your loving, Katie

Cambridge, May 14, 1881

Katie darling,

Dear little wife, it is just as sweet to me to hear you love me for yourself as it can be to you to hear it from me. All the preciousness of life is centered in our love for each for each other and for our common children—the visible utterance of that love. Frail as is our human lot, there is a divine strength, in the love we bear each other. May it be denied to neither of us for many long years!

How I wish you had our Ethel now to comfort you and care for you now in your feebleness! To think that she would be twenty-one now—how far back that puts our youth! I never could get reconciled to never having seen her. But I remember sacredly how you and I went together to her little grave by the Mississippi River in 1863, and plucked some leaves of grass there. She will never lose her place in our hearts, darling. May she welcome us on the other shore!

Your own loving exile, Frank

June 29, 1881

"Doctor of Philosophy." I attended Commencement exercises at Memorial Hall, or rather Sanders Theatre. I received my degree of Ph.D. and diploma from President Eliot, who smiled cordially as he gave it to me.

September 28, 1881

I returned to my rooms [in New York] and vigorously began packing my three trunks with books, etc. . . .

September 30, 1881

The long nightmare ended . . . I took the 11 A.M. train for Boston, and arrived at home about 7 P.M., not expected so early, but quite as welcome for all that.

December 4, 1881

. . . in the P.M., I had a call from Mr. Lothrop Thorndike and his little boy, Sturgis, whom I am to hear three times a week, an hour each, in Latin, at $5.00 a week.

1 8 8 2

January 31, 1882

Oscar Wilde lectures in Boston tonight at the Music Hall, with a reputation full-blown by Gilbert and Sullivan in "Bunthorne." I desire to hear him, but cannot feel justified in dismissing little Sturgis, whom I must hear recite at 7 P.M.

February 4, 1882

My happiness centers wholly in my family, in the faithful doing of my work as an instructor, and in the consciousness of at least having lived as nobly as hard circumstances permitted.

"You have been just the best wife that ever was . . ."

March 24, 1882

The poet Henry Wadsworth Longfellow died this afternoon. The bells all tolled, and every one is sad, even though he had passed his 75th birthday recently and was full of years as of honors.

Katie has taken a dreadful cold—coughs very badly, and is losing strength to hinder it. This alarms me. I know how serious a thing one of her colds is, and fear its affects. Poor wifie, she cannot escape these constant pull-backs. If she were only well and strong, the heaviest part of my load would be lifted. I am willing to toil till I drop, if I can only see her and the children well cared for.

March 26, 1882

At 4 P.M., I went to Appleton Chapel to attend the memorial service for Longfellow, whose funeral was strictly private today. Professor Everett and Frank Peabody conducted the exercises. Terrible jam, but at least I got a seat.

April 21, 1882

Charles Darwin died yesterday—the greatest scientific man of the century, and the most modest and upright and candid mind of whom its literature can boast. I well remember how his first letter to me in 1871 delighted me and how speedily I learned to love the unrivaled simplicity and purity of his spirit. The letter he wrote to me in 1874, on my lecture entitled "Darwin's Theory of Conscience," ought to be printed, for his character shines in every word. He has wrought a mighty revolution in human thought, and his fame is immortal.

April 28, 1882

Ralph Waldo Emerson died yesterday, at 8:50 P.M. The greatest of all America's writers, noblest and grandest figure in the history of its thought, the "whitest soul of all," as the dying Sumner called him, all the world now honors him whom it once despised. A pang goes through me as I recall his gracious presence and generous friendship. He showed me many an act of kindness, and I sorrow for him. Prophet of the Moral Idea in Nature, he built on the eternal truth, and his house will stand, though the rains descend and the winds blow.

April 30, 1882

I took the 2 P.M. train for Concord to attend Emerson's funeral. The train was crowded, and I had great difficulty getting into the church, where I stood in the aisle in a dense jam. The proceedings were "stale, flat, and unprofitable." Hoar, Furness, Clarke, Brown, Alcott—no one dared to voice the true significance of that great life: the priest-spirit prevailed, and the dead Emerson rebuked it not. Alas!

I went to the grave at Sleepy Hollow, took a sprig from the hemlock boughs that lined it, and retired: I had no heart to see any more desecration of his ashes.

May 13, 1882

Katie and Stanley put down the old Dover green carpet in our chamber, and put up the new cretonne hangings at the window. Our modest home is, after all, a very happy one, so long as I can sustain it. I have real joy in my wife and children.

July 1, 1882

The hurry and bustle of the departure is over, and I sit alone in my deserted home, while the rain patters dully on the roof of my bow-window—now bereft of all the beauty that lately gladdened my eyes. Wife and children are all gone to Nonquitt, and I linger in hopes of work, though little sanguine of it.

I have been sorting and packaging this year's letters. But the chill strikes in—the ghost of dead hopes, of perished possibilities, of unconquerable yearnings, haunt me still—grateful that I need not be ashamed of my past.

July 9, 1882

I wrote all this hot day on my philosophy, pondering and musing on its form. Philosophy and poetry are alike in that they both are little without beauty of form. Every great work of thought must be a work of art: and I aim only for the greatest. The truth I have is deep and new: may it not lose power in my hands.

"You have been just the best wife that ever was . . ."

———

199

July 15, 1882

Nonquitt. I left Susie Loring this morning to shut up the house and took the 11:40 train at Old Colony Station. Nonquitt has not changed so much as I expected since 1875, when we took Rock Cottage for the summer. Our present cottage is that of James Church, the 5th from the extreme Point, in the front line. It is quite a nice one.

July 16, 1882

About 10 A.M. we all went into the water. The boys are strapping youngsters now—quite unlike the little fellows I taught to swim here seven years ago. And Fanny is no longer the wee thing I then held in my arms, afraid of the water. But she still is timid about swimming. Katie is better already from her fortnight here.

July 17, 1882

In evening, I went with Fanny and the boys (Katie was not well today), to the Hotel, to see the charade performance of the "Nonquitt Dramatic Club" on invitation of Mrs. Pratt. About 75 spectators—very good amateur performance. Julian Hawthorne, Miss Louisa Alcott, and some other notables, are here.

July 18, 1882

Mr. Ricketson left a fine ambrotype of Thoreau for me to see—one taken only a year or two before his death. It reminded me, very clearly, despite the full beard, of the man I sat with, three times a day, for three months, while boarding with his mother in 1856–1857.

July 21, 1882

I tried in vain to seclude myself this forenoon for intense thought on my philosophy. The young people were reading aloud, talking, laughing,— and it was impossible not to hear. The cottage is so slightly built that its partitions do not divide: a word goes all over the house. After trying in vain on the piazza and then upstairs, in desperation I took my papers with me, and tried to find a silent spot on the bluffs. But the beach was full of bathers, and the bathers full of noise.

August 3, 1882

Katie and I quietly celebrate together our twenty-third anniversary to-day—twenty three years of mutual love unbroken by a quarrel or by decay of faithful attachment. Little of outward prosperity, much of sorrow, struggle, and sacrifice, no marring of home happiness except by death of our little infants. Ethel would be 22, Gertrude 15, Margaret 7: their little white crosses stand together in the Beverly cemetery, and the sweet memory of their babyhood lives in our hearts. Shall we not be welcomed by them by and by, as the end arrives? God only knows, but I dream of that, and love on.

1 8 8 3

January 3, 1883

I met Fanny returning from sewing-school with a little basket in her hands. "Why, what have you in that basket, little one?" said I, holding out my hand.

"Button-holes!" she replied demurely. She had been learning to make button-holes, and had her work with her. She took my hand and voluntarily joined me.

Mother was dressed and waiting to see me. The cheerful firelight rendered gas unnecessary, and we chatted in its beams—Mother overflowing with old anecdotes and humorous stories of her rich observation and experience. A dreaminess steals over me as I listen, and a wistful longing to prolong these blessed days when the world has not lost the precious light of a Mother's love.

"You have been just the best wife that ever was . . ."

———

February 2, 1883

Alone in my study, I sat down and wrote Evie a letter out of my heart. My eldest child has come to years of manhood, and the father's authority, long practically disused, has ceased forever. My son must be responsible, at least by human law, for his own fate now. But what does human law have to do with the human heart? A faithful, obedient, and loving son has my Everett been to me, and a pang goes deep at the bare thought of my separation, however formal. I am no longer a young man—I feel it now; and ere long the dear children will all have gone out from under the paternal roof. The thought is bitter pain—into how many hearts has that pain entered! Let me only be grateful that the hour of parting is still postponed—that my noble sons are still in the old home. What unutterable motions of longing and of love stir our human souls!

April 25, 1883

This afternoon Katie proposed to make some calls with me—the first time since last autumn.

May 6, 1883

At 5, I went to see Mother as usual. Rang the bell, and was going upstairs, when the girl asked me if I had not heard that Mother had an attack last night. My heart almost stopped beating. Emmie came down, and told me that Tilly Brown, the woman who waits on Mother, heard her saying something inarticulately at 12½ o'clock, and found she had suffered a stroke of paralysis.

May 7, 1883

Mother suffers more than at first—is restless, and uncomfortable, does not realize her condition, and shows that her memory is affected.

When I unexpectedly visited Mother, she rose from the lounge, where she was lying with a beaming face, and exclaimed, "My Frankie!" Shall I ever forget that greeting of the Mother?

May 8, 1883

At 5, I went, and silently opened the blind-door, and went up stairs. I heard the Doctor's voice in Mother's room, and I waited till he and Emmie came out. It was not best for me to see her. The Doctor fears her weakness now: she is a little stronger than in the morning, but has suffered much today; he advised wrapping her feet in flannel, which are cold. I went over to the next house and begged an old flannel petticoat to tear in strips, as Emmie had none. Aunt Annie and Emily Ezra gave me one: they were very sympathetic, but I saw in their eyes what they did not say, and my heart sank within me.

May 9, 1883

Mother asked for Katie and sent her her love.

May 13, 1883

Mother is slowly losing ground the past two days. The Doctor says I might see her one to two minutes but I must not read to her. I entered the chamber softly, and stepped to the bedside. The dear face lighted up, the feeble right hand stretched a little to clasp mine. I bent and gave her a long kiss. I spoke of the lovely Spring day, and tried to chat cheerily with her. She spoke lovingly of Katie and Evie, and I tore myself away. I could not finish my dinner, but went up to Evie's empty room, and wept.

May 29, 1883

"Dear Frank, Mother is very feeble—come earlier than you usually do. Emmie" Mother was fully in her right mind, but too feeble even to move. The light of love still shines in those dear eyes . . .

"You have been just the best wife that ever was . . ."

———

May 31, 1883

I sat beside Mother, and held one hand while Emmie held the other; and nothing could be more touching than the patience and gentleness with which she endured her pain. Emmie was not in the room all the time, and while I was alone with her, Mother said, "I have always tried to be faithful to my children."

"O Mother," I said, "they will bear you witness now."

"After you were born," she said again, in her feeble voice, "my whole life passed into you, and you have all been very, very precious to me. I have always wished that, when my hour should come, you all might be around me."

June 2, 1883

I found Mother sleeping under the effect of ether, from which she soon awakened. Edwin, Emmie, and I all sat close together, holding her two hands in ours, while she moaned in pain, but spoke to us feebly from time to time. She looked at each, and smiled as she looked despite the pain . . .

June 3, 1883

In the afternoon, I sat two or three hours by her bedside. Edwin and Mattie and Emmie were there most of the time. After a silence, she slowly and difficultly said:

"Longfellow's 'Summer Rain'?" We hastened to get the book, and Mother listened with shut eyes, and evidently enjoyed it much. I repeated:

"O Thou whose power over moving worlds presides," and this gave her satisfaction. The Doctor came at last, and we left the room.

June 7, 1883

I saw Mother a little while in the afternoon. She suffered much from restlessness and weariness, and the heat aggravates her pain. Still she listened with evident enjoyment while I read to her Bryant's "Inscription for the Entrance to a Wood." When I asked her if my reading tired her she said, "Such beautiful thoughts never tire me"—yet I saw that it was too great an effort for her to listen long.

June 14, 1883

Mother's 76th birthday. A lovely day. Right after lunch, I went to Coolidge's greenhouse, and got a bunch of white carnations, white roses, and heliotrope, which I carried to Mother, with one of my photographs. Fanny had left for her a bunch of daisies on going to school and Mother left these in full view.

Surely the peace of God is hers; "we cannot fall out of God's hands," she said to me today.

"Mother, I need you more than any of them, for I am the only one who has not been a success!"

"I consider you a success," she replied, "You have helped man in the highest object that is given them to do—you have showed them the truth—always love Emmie; she is the dearest child, too."

She said, "I was very glad to see Katie [she had called that morning]; and to see her looking so fresh and fair."

"She has been a good wife to me, Mother."

"And a good daughter to me."

I sat holding her hands—she was so weak that her voice was scarcely more than a whisper: every now and then she would say some tender word, and she looked so beautiful with her almost white hair and her serene, loving face. She called for Emmie, made her take a box out of the drawer, and sent to little Fanny her own engagement ring, garnets set in gold, and Father's wedding gift to her, a beautiful topaz pin set in pearls. She spoke of her own near end, so simply and trustfully, without a shadow of fear. As I kissed her goodbye, she said, "I shall be living tomorrow." This was a comfort to me.

June 15, 1883

Mother told me yesterday afternoon she had told Emmie where the box is that contains her diaries and other papers, that it may be given to me by and by. That is to be my legacy—the records of her soul.

"You have been just the best wife that ever was . . ."

June 19, 1883

Henry, Edwin, Willie, Emmie, and I all met this evening by Mother's bedside—exactly nine years since we last met there together, on Willie's Class Day [at Harvard], June 19, 1874. Four stalwart sons and the one dear daughter—all but Stanley; and he, the hero—was he not there too? God alone knows. We sat over half an hour in perfect stillness, waiting till the dying Mother should wake and see us, as she so longed to do, all together with her. At last she roused herself a little.

"Do you see we are all here, dear Mother—Henry, Edwin, Frank, Emily, Willie?"

"Yes," she said, half articulately, "I—must—leave—them—all."

We kissed her all—Henry, Edwin, Emmie, Willie, and I. I stooped to kiss her last, "And one for Katie?" I said, as well as I could.

"Yes, a good daughter she has been to me."

And one by one, with wet eyes, we left . . .

June 22, 1883

Abbot Vaughn called for Katie with a carriage at 9 A.M., because Mother had repeatedly asked for her, and was much brighter this morning. She at once went and I followed giving Walter two exam papers to write mean while. I found Mother asleep and Katie waiting till she should wake. I went into the sick room, and sat by Mother. When she saw me, she smiled lovingly. Katie was sent for, and Mother seemed delighted to see her: she drew her down, kissed her, and affectionately passed her hand slowly over Katie's face, with trembling fingers. Then she tried to say something: nobody but I understood it, and it thrilled me—"Did Henry meet Katie?" O loving, self-forgetful Mother! No one knows what a world of tender solicitude for Katie and me there was in that question, but it showed me how the great soul has lost none of its divine greatness of love. I read to her the 91st Psalm, at her wish. [There was] a rose, which lay on her pillow; she asked me to hold it to her nose, and she inhaled its fragrance with pleasure. When it had fallen on the floor afterwards, I again held it to her; she put up her trembling hand, took it, and laid it on her bosom. Emmie and Katie exchanged glances, and almost broke down . . . She could not speak plainly but some things, we understood.

June 26, 1883

At peace. It was noon before I finished hearing Walter, to whom I have been giving double time since Garrard left; and I at once went to Emmie's. Carrie and Ethel were just coming out, but returned on seeing me, and left the blind-door open. As I went up from the gate a sable crepe on the bell handle told me all—and the iron entered my soul. Emmie came into the hall and told me, as I leaned my head against the banisters, that Mother quietly ceased to breathe at a quarter before ten. She spoke of "thankfulness"—I could only ask if I could go upstairs.

"Alone?"

"Yes."

I went up—there was no need now to steal on tip-toe through the hall, as I always did—entered, drew the curtain close behind me. I was alone with Death. I drew the napkin from the face, and looked at the pale, moveless features, and sank on my knees by her side, and buried my face in my hands. O this agony of eternal parting—eternal for all we know of this life, though who shall say more? I need record no more here—I shall never forget it.

As I came from the room, the nurse looked at me with sympathy in the hall: had she looked in? I took my hat and left the house. Edwin hastily followed me outdoors, and offered his hand, which I pressed. But when he said—

"It was just like a gentle falling asleep."

I could only utter:

"I cannot talk, Edwin,"—and came away. I went up to Evie's empty room and sat alone, till I could command myself—then I went to Katie in her chamber. God bless her faithful, loving heart.

"You have been just the best wife that ever was . . ."

June 27, 1883

Mother will be laid to rest at Beverly, beside her dear ones; the services here will be at Emmie's on Thursday, at 10 A.M.

July 3, 1883

My dear wife is very tender towards me: I am boundlessly grateful to her. Her love is priceless—all the more because it enfolded Mother too.

July 16, 1883

Emmie sent up a valise full of letters Katie and I had written to Mother, which she had carefully preserved, neatly tied and labelled.

July 17, 1883

I went again to Emmie's and asked if she could let me have now the "box containing her diaries and papers" that Mother had told her she wished me to have. Emmie at first did not remember it, but did afterwards; and she at last found it in the closet. I told Mother long ago that I coveted these papers, many of which she has shown me, and some of which she wrote at my request. Stanley went with me, to help bring the precious trunk home.

September 10, 1883

It has been impossible [this summer] to carry out my plans to work on my philosophy. There is no place to get out my papers or books, and no chance to write in the evening. It has been a great disappointment to me. The few precious months of summer leisure have been ruined. Next year we intend to stay home, where I can work . . .

September 18, 1883

Our new house is full of carpenters, plumbers, etc.—no chance of getting into it this week, I fear.

September 26, 1883

Katie was a half a day at the house. I reserve the parlor for my book boxes, etc: they will about fill it, together with the parlor furniture. The boys are exceedingly fond of their mother, and eager to save her fatigue: it is beautiful to see my family all together—so united, so uniformly kind, so affectionate to each other. I am unspeakably grateful for my happy home, which atones for so many other troubles.

October 3, 1883

This noon we first broke bread together in our new home. May Heaven bless it!

October 16, 1883

Katie's 44th birthday. The two boys surprised her with a nice present, a hall-stand of black walnut, with marble top and two side stands for umbrellas. Fanny gave her some peanuts, and I (beside the basket for silver, which she asked be my present!) gave her a nice cut-glass inkstand.

Katie Abbot, Cambridge, Massachusetts, circa 1885.

"You have been just the best wife that ever was . . ."

209

December 13, 1883

Stanley's 20th birthday. My little, lovely, fascinating, darling baby has become a man indeed. I see the same exquisite nature in him still, and rejoice in his pure, sweet, truthful manliness . . .

December 25, 1883

Fanny got into our bed this morning early, and opened her stocking of presents. We had a pleasant breakfast together, and then exchanged our little gifts with merriment and love. Katie gave me a lovely jar to put the leaves I trim from plants into; Evie and Stanley gave me a pin-cushion, and Fanny a little court plaster case made by herself, with a verse of her own (the dear child shows genius, in poetry and in drawing).

1 8 8 4

August 3, 1884

Our silver wedding. At breakfast we all met in love, at 8½ o'clock. I was surprised by the present of a beautiful gold-watch, with a card "From Katie and the children," with this lovely message on the back: "Dear Frank, That the links of this chain may prove as strong and lasting as the links of the golden chain that has bound us together as long, is the wish of your loving wife and children. August 3, 1884."

At noon, we had a picnic in the boys' "snuggery." I first read my poem, "The Silver Wedding Song" my voice faltered a little, and Katie's eyes were wet.

> *The Silver Wedding Song*
> . . . Though to our five and twenty-years
> Trouble has been no stranger—
> Though we have known our share of fears,
> Of want and pain and danger,
> Though oft through sorrows, deep and great,

In tears our pathway treading,
With grateful hearts we celebrate
This day our Silver Wedding . . .

1 8 8 5

January 7, 1885

I called for Fanny at Miss Post's dancing class, at Lyceum Hall, about 5
P.M. She does not have a very good idea of keeping time to the music;
her musical sense is feeble, but her talent for drawing is marked, and I
am sending her to take lessons of her Aunt Emily in that. I hope to give
her the best education her health may permit, and cultivate her mind
just as faithfully as if she had been a boy.

January 17, 1885

I walked to Boston at noon. At 3, I visited Paul Philippotean's "Cyclo-
rama of Gettysburg," a marvelous piece of realistic painting of the great
battle; the spectator stands on Cemetery Ridge in the
centre, and looks around the whole horizon as if on the
spot. It is impossible to believe it is a painting, and not
the real scene. Little Round Top, where my dear brother
fell at the head of his company, was painfully interesting
to me.

February 11, 1885

I went for Fanny at dancing school at 5. I like to see her
dancing—watch the dear childish figure as the long yellow hair waves over her shoulders. Every now and then,
as she waltzes past me, she smiles at me as she catches
my eye. My little girl is very precious to me, all the more
because my Ethel, Gertrude, and Margaret fell like early
blossoms out of the reach of my earthly love. What joys
would these lost daughters be to me, if they were here

Fanny Abbot, circa 1885.

still to love their mother and father! Little Fanny is trebly precious to me for the name she bears. . . .

February 12, 1885

I called on Reverend Samuel Longfellow at 4:30, and passed a pleasant hour. He is writing his brother's life, and promised to call. Miss Alice Longfellow came into the room, and was introduced as "remembering me." She was one of my Sunday School scholars in 1858–1859 and I have not seen her since; but I told her I had a lock of her hair, with that of all her classmates, among my treasures. I do not know whether she cared much for me—I loved my little scholars much.

March 7, 1885

Katie is better. Our love is very deep and strong—as I told her, "my home life is the only part of my life that has not proved a failure."

June 19, 1885

Harvard's Class Day. I went with Katie to President Eliot's reception and then walked to Evie's room, through the illuminated yard, to listen to the Glee Club on the green. Home by nine or so, tired and rather sad—as crowds always make me feel.

June 29, 1885

Katie exhausted herself in caring for Mr. Rand, our neighbor, who came back last Sunday from Cottage City to his shut-up home, and has apparently had an ether-debauch—poor fellow. She got Mr. Lovering and Doctor Wyman to look after him—went in, carried hot coffee and gruel, bathed his head, and did all that her tender, womanly heart could think of, to recover him. God never has made anything so divine as a true woman's soul, and I see Him there whenever my faith grows dim.

June 30, 1885

To think I would refuse to go to Europe! Yet I have done it tonight. I went to Boston in the forenoon, on getting home, I found a royally generous letter from Edwin, urging me to go at once to Europe for 100 days, and offering me a letter of credit for £200!!! He thinks me ill—but my disease was aptly described as "consumed by the inward fires of suppressed energies." Tonight I went to Emily's and saw him—thanked him warmly, and declined. I am willing to postpone my duty to philosophy to obey the more pressing duty to my family, but not to take pleasure or yield to the luxury of foreign travel.

July 1, 1885

Today we all (except Stanley, now at Vermont) came down to Nonquitt Beach, and got the cottage we had in 1882. Katie got very tired, but now can rest.

July 19, 1885

It is very hard to write here at Nonquitt; though Katie tries to shield me all she can, I am tormented with interruptions. Still I persevere—what great work for man was ever done under difficulties? I am daily seeing my truth clearer and saying it better—than I know well. May it be a light to others when I am gone.

August 3, 1885

Our 26th wedding anniversary. At breakfast, I gave Katie a pearl lace-pin; after it, she gave me a gold scarf-pin in the shape of a horse-shoe.

"You have been just the best wife that ever was . . ."

August 5, 1885

I had a serious talk this morning with Katie about Everett and Stanley and I shall not forget it. We perfectly agreed, as we have always done about our children, who owe more than they ever know to this entire concord of their parents. It is the simple secret of our unbroken home harmony, and of the system of family government which has been intact from the beginning, with only some slight interruptions from Katie's impaired health during the last ten years.

August 16, 1885

At three, I walked over to Round Hill slowly, and joined a little party. I lay on the sand, with my head under Katie's umbrella, while Fanny and Emmie played, digging holes in the sand with glee and laughter. We all walked home about 5.

September 14, 1885

My book finished. I have just put down the last line of my *Scientific Theism* at 12:10 A.M.—273 pages freshly written in five weeks only—and may the work quicken the faith, bless the life, and lift the spiritual level of many and many a poor doubt-tortured fellow being! I shall be neglected still in my life, but when I am dead this book will be studied and felt. So be it!

September 15, 1885

We leave Nonquitt. Last night I wrote the "Dedication" of my book to Mother—six lines only—with wet eyes. We all took the 9:30 boat, and I got to Cambridge in the afternoon. I stopped in Boston and took my manuscript to Houghton and Mifflin.

September 24, 1885

My book rejected. Returning tonight, I saw on my desk a package which I instantly recognized as my manuscript. Not a word of explanation but the printed tag of the address "from Houghton, Mifflin, & Co." My heart became a lump of lead. I sat down wearily and thought. After all my labor, and after all its grand success, is this to be the end?

September 25, 1885

I find this morning a note from Houghton, Mifflin, & Co.: "We find it so exclusively addressed to close philosophic students that we are unable to see how we can publish it without any hope of securing ourselves against loss, to say nothing of making a profit. As we are obliged to look upon such books in a strictly commercial view, we feel compelled to return to you a negative answer to your request for publication."

September 28, 1885

My book accepted by Little & Brown.

October 18, 1885

Katie's 46th birthday. We all gave her little presents—for we all feel poor.

November 6, 1885

Today I am 49 years old.

November 15, 1885

My earnings are not enough to take me through the year—my savings are melting away—my profession as private tutor is itself vanishing—it is the last string to my bow—I am in despair at the thought of dependence. My book is the one ray of hope: will the world find it out, and enable me to do the rest of my work? But I cannot keep hold of hope now—I am too old to hope.

November 20, 1885

My book is printed, but will not be published till December 14th in London and December 15th in Boston.

"You have been just the best wife that ever was . . ."

November 25, 1885

I rack my brains in vain to discover some way of earning money honestly. To eke out the short income of this year. Minister, editor, professor, schoolteacher, tutor—all doors shut in my face: what can I do to provide for my family without dependence on Edwin?

November 26, 1885

Thanksgiving Day. It has been a terrible Northeast storm ever since Sunday, and today snow lay on the ground. Everett and Stanley went up with a party to Nahant to see the tremendous surf and breakers. They returned about 3 P.M. in time for dinner.

We dined all together cheerfully at 3. I tried to put away my inward sadness, and succeeded tolerably; but the old memories crowded thick and fast upon me. After dinner, Katie and the three children sat down with me to a game of cards, for I longed to do something together for the children's sake—that they may remember these days of their home life lovingly in after years.

Katie read aloud to me the "Christmas Carol" of Dickens, and I forgot myself in the glow of sympathy with Scrooge's life-lesson. And now, I am alone in my study with my thoughts.

December 1, 1885

Tonight I received the first bound copies of my book, 50 in all, I opened the package alone with Katie, and handed her the first I took out. She looked at it, and presently laid it on the desk.

"Don't mix that with the rest. Is this it?"

"Yes."

"My darling, I want to give you the first bound copy of my book."

The dear face looked at me with swimming eyes. I was deeply moved. I bent over her, and kissed her,—laid my face to hers and felt her tears.

"You do care a little for my book, don't you?"

"Indeed I do!"

Tonight, I have been writing an inscription in this book for her, out of my heart.

December 31, 1885

Farewell, 1885! Thou art a notable year to me, for thou hast brought to birth my first book. But I wish not to delay there . . .

1 8 8 6

March 13, 1886

Harvard makes an offer to me at last. President Eliot sent a note by hired man, early this morning, requesting me to meet him before 12 at his office, and I sent word I would go. I am ashamed to confess it for experience should have taught me better, yet true it is that the message caused a little flutter of hope that Harvard might at last wish the service of my best powers. Well—Harvard has made her offer: that I do subordinate cataloguing work in the Library, five hours a day, at $1500 a year. President Eliot made this offer in all kindness; he knows I need honest work, and he offers the best, I dare say, he has to tender. I listened silently, made a few inquiries, asked a little time to consider the matter, and retired. No one University in America would dare to appoint me with my religious record to any responsible position. I chose the path of self-respect and clear conscience, and I am still paying the price of that costly luxury. That is all. Yet I feel the cut of this bitter blow, in spite of all my pride of character— I cannot help seeing the irony of fate in such a proposition to a man who has at least proved capacity for higher service. Let me now be proud enough to turn away from all that, and direct my course by other thoughts—let me leave it to others to discover the slight, if it be one.

March 30, 1886

President Eliot's messenger brought a note this morning, saying I was yesterday appointed "assistant in the Library" at $1500 a year, five days a week, "four weeks vacation during the year." My heart sank at this last unexpected stroke: my stern and unrelenting destiny would, then, deprive me of my last hope—three months of life in the dreary year to fulfill my task

"You have been just the best wife that ever was . . ."

in philosophy. I did not dream that the Library "year" was two months more than the "academic year." I wrote in answer that, to avoid embarrassing Mr. Eliot himself, after this appointment by the Corporation and Overseers, I will go to work on these terms till July 1, and then resign the place; and asked to be informed if that is satisfactory. My wife and daughter must have three months at the seaside; the house must be shut; it would cost nearly all I should earn just to pay my board; it is too much.

March 31, 1886

Katie told me she would not leave me to work in Cambridge while she was at the seaside, so I was really relieved today when Mr. Eliot wrote me that it was not worth while for me to begin, if I could not go on, and he would consider my note as a "refusal" to accept the place.

May 21, 1886

I attended a reception at Mrs. Mosher's at 6 P.M., in honor of Frederick Douglass and his wife. A large gathering including Reverend Samuel Longfellow, Miss Elizabeth Peabody, John Orth, Joshua Kendall, Daniel Ricketson, and others. I had a few cordial words with Mr. Douglass.

June 30, 1886

Everett's Graduation. Katie and I went to Sanders Theatre at 10:45, and stayed till nearly 1, hearing all the parts and seeing the diplomas distributed. We were delighted to see that Everett is graduated "cum laude," getting honors in Latin, Greek, and English. I ought to be satisfied—I will be.

Life whirls me on, but my heart has been full of the past today . . .

September 11, 1886

This afternoon Fanny was singing in the room after our bath in the sea. I listened to the sweet, bird-like voice, fearful to stop it if I spoke. By and by, I went down from my tower, and kissed her, and told her I liked to hear my Canary finding her voice again, especially in singing the "Psalm of Life," and asked her if she knew it all.

"Yes, I did once," she said, "and, O Papa!" she put her arm round my neck and began to play with my beard— "I wish you would publish a book of your poems!"

"What made you think of that?"

"I heard Mamma say she wished you would—and I know she would be glad if you did."

"Should you really care to have me print my old poems?"

"Yes, indeed! Won't you, please?"

I kissed the dear child, more moved than I cared to show. Shall I? I never felt it so much like now.

1887

January 25, 1887

Thirty years ago today, my Katie and I owned our mutual love and plighted our lifelong faith. Well, has the pledge been redeemed? Through joy and sorrow, difficulty, trial, and hardship, we have been one in heart and soul; no quarrel has ever arisen between us, no deep alienation, no irritation longer than a few brief moments—for we are human, and it would be false to say there has never been even a momentary jar. But, because our love has been built upon the rock, no storm from within or without has ever, even for an instant, shaken its deep foundation; and today we love each other more than ever. Let me not forget what a priceless blessing has been mine in this faithful, devoted, loving wife!

December 20, 1887

Tonight . . . began Darwin's "Life and Letters" by his son. It gratifies me to see two of his letters to myself printed in part; I gave copies of his eight letters to me to his son W. E. Darwin, several years ago, when he called to request them. Nothing could be more beautiful than the character brought so simply and so touchingly: it revives and renews the personal attachment I felt for the man at the time. Darwin was the truest saint of science; truth glorified her faithful, unselfish, loving-hearted child.

"You have been just the best wife that ever was . . ."

———

1888

January 1, 1888

I have spent the first day of this New Year chiefly in writing. My little family are all well. For that I am grateful. Their love and happiness are precious to me, and I can still live for them.

February 8, 1888

Professor Palmer astonished me today. He called just before the end of Wayne's recitation, at 10, to say that Professor Royce is sick—that one of the "advanced courses in philosophy" must be put in other hands—that Palmer himself is authorized to find a substitute on his sole responsibility; that President Eliot himself, as well as Professor James suggest my name first of all—that they all agreed in preferring me—that three lectures a week on Monday, Wednesday, and Friday, at 12 o'clock are required, till the end of this half-year in June, for $500 . . . I was naturally astounded after Eliot's letters more than a year ago.

February 9, 1888

President Eliot is shrewd, is kind, too, but shrewd. My engagement for this half puts a stop to all suggestion that Harvard University is too timid or illiberal to employ me, since I now am employed; but neither the President, Corporation, nor Faculty is at all committed—Palmer does it all on his personal authority. If I succeed, the College gets the credit; if I fail it loses nothing, being uncommitted. I cannot but admire the shrewdness of all this. In case of a brilliant success (most improbable!), and above all in case of no outcry from the public, Eliot might see his President's "duty" no longer in the way of a more permanent engagement . . .

April 12, 1888

I received this morning from "Arthur G. Davis, Keeper of Corporation Records," an official notice dated "50 State Street, Boston, April 11,

1888," that "on the 27th day of February," I was "appointed by the President and Fellows Instructor in Philosophy for the year 1887–88," and this appointment was confirmed by the Board of Overseers yesterday.

October 19, 1888

My dear wife is 49 years old today. Our birthdays are getting more numerous nowadays, but our love is ever young.

1 8 8 9

April 5, 1889

Wilton. I went to Chestnut Glen this morning alone and sat on the old stone, and heard in fancy once more Katie's—"O, I will, I will be your wife!"

June 15, 1889

I rose early this morning in order to go to Beverly, and lay my white roses, now in full bloom, on Mother's grave . . . I got home at 6:15—no one knew where I had been. Katie perhaps guessed it—she kissed my eyes and pressed my hand when she went to bed—but I could not say a word, even to her. Darling, if you ever see this page, know that my heart said, "God bless my dear wife!" when you turned away.

June 25, 1889

I went to dinner at the Union Club on Park Street, 7 P.M. Twenty-four members of the Class of 1859 were present. These grizzled or bold men—are they the boys I knew so well 30 years ago? Am I the boy of 1859? Yes and no. What a mystery is life! Death I never feared, but life I fear more and more.

"You have been just the best wife that ever was . . ."

221

June 27, 1889

I went to the Phi Beta Kappa. In the procession, I saw Everett sitting at his window, 20 Stoughton Hall—I shall never see him sitting there again. But I shall never forget the smile and bow he gave me as I passed. I did long that he might have been in the procession too—poor old fool of a father that I am. God bless the boy!

August 3, 1889

We celebrated our "pearl wedding" today in quiet fashion. I gave Katie her diamond ring, which pleased her greatly, as she sat by the east window of the Tower. We sat and talked all the forenoon there.

August 27, 1889

At dinner together this evening, we were talking of Holmes and Lowell, Longfellow, Bryant, and Whittier. Fanny asked me if I had my own poems all ready to print in a book by and by.

1 8 9 0

January 1, 1890

A new decade begins now—what will it bring?

March 30, 1890

To my immense surprise, [my brother] Edwin [wishes to] send me and Stanley to Europe this summer! My first impulse was to say no, unqualifiedly—I would far rather go to Nonquitt and work on my great task. But he shrewdly baited his hook avowedly with Stanley's company, for my sake, as he told us both. Katie wants me to go, too; she and Fanny (I insist on her taking both the servants) will go to Nonquitt by preference, and I really suspect she will rest better so than if I were there. But I go only for Stanley's sake, dear boy—and I shall leave him in September for a year's study at my own expense.

April 27, 1890

Katie came down stairs this afternoon for the first time since Thanksgiving—over five months! She got down alone, but was very tired by it, and lay half an hour on the lounge in my study. I did not know she was thinking of such an attempt. Stanley and I carried her upstairs in our arms, making a "chair" for her by joining hands. It is cheering to us all to see her gaining strength, however slowly.

June 30, 1890

Bade goodbye to Katie and Fanny at Nonquitt, and Stanley drove me to New Bedford to catch the 10:55 train. I took the 1 P.M. train for New York from Providence Station by Shore Line, and got to New York at 7:30. [From July to September 1890, Frank and Stanley Abbot toured Europe.]

September 27, 1890

Land at Boston. Home. After a long and tiresome voyage, we landed at East Boston about 6:30–7 P.M. Stanley and I took a hack to Bowdoin Square, and a horse car to Mount Auburn, arriving at about 8:30. We found Katie just going to bed—she and Fanny were, well, not sorry to see us!

October 6, 1890

Stanley leaves home. Today my dear son Stanley left his parents' roof to begin the world for himself as junior intern at the McLean Asylum, Somerville, and assistant in histology at the Medical School. He would not say goodbye in the morning and said he might return at night—but he did not come. It is a pang to me—one more, and a deep one. Now both my sons have left us, never again to be other than visitors in the home of their childhood.

"You have been just the best wife that ever was . . ."

223

1 8 9 1

August 3, 1891

Our day—quietly spent together, none remembering it but ourselves, not even the children. Why should they, dear children? How little can others, even the dearest, enter into our lives? We live alone, and we die alone: only God is with us. O Mother, no one understood my lonely nature but you—and you have left me.

August 14, 1891

At Nonquitt. I have watched Everett depart—his dark blue form and Fanny's white form disappearing in the cedars of the winding path to the pier—then reappearing, as I looked from my Tower, and passing over the long pier to the moored Cyquet. Fanny remained—the boat is now receding over the Bay. God be with the boy, as He is, in his heart as well as all around! Evie and I had a most blessed communion last night, till nearly 2 o'clock—we never came nearer each other, and parted with a long embrace.

September 7, 1891

Evie has returned. Last night, about 11:30 o'clock, he came up to my Tower, and we talked till 1 A.M. We discussed our family affairs all round in loving confidence . . .

September 28, 1891

Cambridge. The burden of life must be taken up again—the rush of cares that cannot be shunned, the heat and the turmoil . . .

November 26, 1891

On this, Thanksgiving Day, I thank God most humbly and most grate-fully for my wife and my children, for the holy memories of my father, my mother, and my lost friends. These are my life-treasures . . . What I have most sought He has granted me, love and truth: let me forget the sorrow, the injustice, the cruel wrongs and disappointments of my life.

December 25, 1891

We all waited from 8½ to 10, hoping Evie would appear from New York, but gave him up then, and adjourned—Katie, Stanley, Fanny, and myself, to distribute our little gifts. About 11, Evie appeared, to our surprise and delight—his train had been delayed three hours. It has been long since we were all together.

1 8 9 2

August 3, 1892

Thirty-third anniversary of our marriage. It is sweet to see the light of love in those dear eyes, kindled by the thought of our past. The world knows nothing of it—never knew, and never will know. There are some things in life that never get revealed.

1 8 9 3

January 1, 1893

1893! I write the name of the New Year with a secret dread which I try to suppress in vain, unreasonable as it is. In 1863, my hero-brother died; in 1873, my beloved father; in 1883, my idolized mother, the divine joy and solace of my life. And now, I shudder at the possibilities of the future year I am beginning, lest other lives dear to me glide beyond my powerless hold.

Tonight, I stole very softly upstairs, and looked into Stanley's open door. It was raining—the dim moonlight, shining through the clouds, half-lighted up the room—he lay sleeping in his bed. The last time under my roof! I stood, and watched, and loved, and sorrowed. I went

"You have been just the best wife that ever was . . ."

225

downstairs as softly as I came. My son, years hence you may read these words—know then how your father's heart yearned over you as you slept!

January 2, 1893

At last! Stanley has just left us, at eight o'clock in the morning, to come back no more as an inmate of his father's house; and he left me rent with sorrow. In the parlor he clasped his mother and his sister in his arms, with parting kisses. I went into the hall. Soon he came, and then, alone, he embraced me with both his arms and I him. We looked into each other's wet eyes—I uttered my soul-felt blessing in a broken whisper— and he was gone! I watched his retiring figure down the street—and all alone, O how alone! That calm, cheerful, loving, generous presence, going out and coming in, always with an affectionate smile,—that dear communion of never failing love and tenderness shall no more be a part of my daily life. One more mighty change—one more step to death. I am growing old at last. God's blessing on my boy!

February 20, 1893

This afternoon I went to Parker's, to attend the annual dinner of the Boston Civil Service Reform Club and hear Theodore Roosevelt, of the U.S.C.S. Commission. Here I met Charley Sprague, my old pupil of 1878–1879, who was delighted to see me and I to see him. I sat by Joseph Knight, the art-publisher. We had a grand speech from Roosevelt . . . I met William Everett at the coat room. He grasped my hand warmly, and turning, said, "Lieutenant-Governor Wolcott, let me introduce you to Frank Abbot, my classmate. He ought to have $10,000 a year paid to him just to write poetry—he would have been the greatest poet of the nineteenth century!" Wolcott and I laughed at this spurt.

April 13, 1893

I went to Boston at 10 A.M. with Katie, in a coupe (she cannot ride in a street-car without too much fatigue), to John H. Pray's, and selected new carpets for the parlor and library. The old ones had gone seventeen years.

It was that day that we stopped at Doctor Dixon's, 232 Clarendon

Street, to consult him about Katie's eyes. I waited in the coupe. This was the first hint of Katie's troubles, and as Doctor Dixon, finding grave cause to suspect kidney trouble in her disturbed eyesight, advised her to consult her physicians. But Katie did not tell me anything at the time.

May 3, 1893

This afternoon, I went upstairs to see Katie, who was lying down on the bed. I asked her if she was very tired.

"Yes," she said gently, with a smile, "but that is not the worst of it."

Startled at this, I asked further, and she said that, when she went to Doctor Dixon about her eyes, she learned that she has symptoms of Bright's disease. My heart stood still. She says, however, that Doctor Wesselhoeft tells her it is fortunate that she discovered this so soon, for—he says—she will get over it. Ah, who knows? A secret terror has filled my soul. I dare not trust—I should go mad to despair.

May 4, 1893

When I left Katie yesterday afternoon, though I had dissembled my inward horror and fear, and spoken what words of cheer and hope I could sum-mon to my tongue, the thought of what may be completely unmanned me. I must not show anxiety to her. She is too feeble to bear it, or to feel that she must comfort me. Love bids me spare her this new burden! And I cried out in my soul to God for strength to show my love to my wife now by keeping up her courage and hope with the uttermost of my power . . .

May 11, 1893

Katie does not know, but guesses, at her own danger. Is it possible for me to lose this companionship and live?

"You have been just the best wife that ever was . . ."

May 13, 1893

Doctor Wesselhoeft came to see Katie this afternoon, and I waylaid him as he was going. I asked him to tell me the truth as it is—no matter how terrible. He told me that Katie has no "Bright's disease," as she thought, but diabetes—thank God, the "milder of the two forms." The more dangerous form means death in a year or two, but the milder, if not certainly curable, may last twenty or thirty years, with little pain. He spoke encouragingly—I believe, honestly. He thinks she should avoid a diet of starch or sugar, but expects her to gain this summer. Her eyes are affected, but she is to do as she likes, avoiding all strain or fatigue.

May 14, 1893

I told my darling what Dr. Wesselhoeft said, and we rejoiced together over the hopes he holds out. She does not want to leave me, dear, precious wife! Must I forego that old blessed hope of a peaceful old age together? It cannot, it must not be!

May 15, 1893

I bought tickets for Fanny to Detroit, to enable her to go from there to the World's Fair with me, if I go. It will be Fanny's only chance to attend the Columbian Exposition, I fear, and both Katie and I want her to not lose that. Katie will be left almost alone, but insists it will be good for her. O unselfish wife!

May 18, 1893

Fanny and I took the 10 A.M. streetcar for Boston. Katie stood at the door, watching us till the car came at the foot of the street—I shall never forget the patient figure with the white apron, as we waved our goodbye. Never did wifehood or motherhood find a higher illustration!

May 27, 1893

We have spent four solid days at the Fair with Fanny, walking all day long. It is absolutely impossible to make any record of what I have seen—it is infinitely too much! But the glory of the architecture, the exquisite beauty of the White City, is too great for words.

June 2, 1893

Katie is very weak—has lost 20 pounds in a short time. Poor wife, she suffers much from this weakness, but never complains. It wrings my soul to see her look so worn and feeble.

June 6, 1893

Katie went to Concord today, notwithstanding the heat (93°) by a coupe to Porter's Station. Soon after, Doctor Wesselhoeft called, and I had a talk with him. The disease is more threatening than he thought it at first.

June 22, 1893

The last book she ever gave me. I found in my tower-table this morning, Marvel's *Reveries of a Bachelor* and *Dream Life*—a present from Katie, in memory of our young love of 1857. A precious token it is to me.

That book I read just before I met Katie for the first-time at Concord, January, 1857. We often spoke of it, for she had read it, too, and it seemed so appropriate to our young, happy love, that to both of us it seemed a sweet coincidence to have been so prepared for each other. The gift of that book meant so much! She brought it from Boston to give to me here. O my darling!

June 28, 1893

Stanley takes the degree of M.D., for which I gave him the fee of $30.00, at Commencement today.

The burden of dreadful fear is mine, day and night: my little Katie is entering the Valley of the Shadow of Death, and I cannot go with her. The woe is too heavy for me. It would be cruelty to betray my terror to Katie. She has enough to bear, dear soul of womanhood! If I could but shield my wife—could but take her place!

"You have been just the best wife that ever was . . ."

229

July 23, 1893

I wrote all morning. In the afternoon I called Stanley up to the tower. Here I asked him to tell me, as a physician, his real opinion of his mother's case. He did so. The percentage of sugar Doctor Wesselhoeft found to be 2½ or 3—the worst cases are only 5 or 6. She gained nothing in Nonquitt—rather lost a little. In brief, he thinks the disease will terminate fatally in 2 years at the farthest, probably a year and half—and I am writing this down without going mad.

Stanley helped his mother to Sunset Rock, to watch the sunset from her favorite spot. Fanny and I followed her slow and uncertain steps. All were outwardly cheerful—she gentle and loving and serene. When was she not?

August 3, 1893

Our 34 years together. Katie has been much better in the past few days, for which I am thankful. In the last part of the afternoon, as I was writing in the tower, I heard Katie's feeble steps on the stairs. She came up to remember our 34th anniversary with a present—a Japanese silver salt-cellar in the shape of an egg. The dear wife sat down to rest, and gave me her dear gift with kisses of love. My own present to her, in advance, was the slab of petrified wood from Chicago, which I gave her in June on returning. O my beloved one!

August 9, 1893

Katie's face is so much thinner now that she seems to be many years older than she was last spring. The lines and wrinkles so surprisingly absent in the countenance of a woman of fifty-three begin to reveal themselves, and my heart sinks as I watch them coming. Dear face, how I love it!

August 25, 1893

A precious evening hour! Tonight, while Evie and Fanny went to the beach to join in a "corn-roasting" at the foot of Bare-Kneed Rock, with a crowd of many young people, I sat with Katie on the piazza watching the moon and its wondrous light on the bay towards the South, and talking, while I held her dear hand in mine, of the way we used to watch the moonlight from our little porch piazza at Meadville thirty-three years ago, as the beams stole through the leaves of the grape-vine that climbed all over it. Ah, how long will it be so?

August 28, 1893

Tonight, reading Stanley's loving letter to his mother, I could not help exclaiming. "He's as good as they make!" Later, as I carried her lamp upstairs to her room and set it down, she threw her arms about my neck, and said with a kiss,

"And you are as good as they make!"

August 29, 1893

Another wild and fierce tempest from the south-west, shaking the house to its foundations. My tower rocks enough to disturb my hand-writing. Seen from the window, the spray flies over Bridge Rock, half as high again. No less a storm seems to swamp over my life this year.

September 8, 1893

After supper, I was walking up and down on the piazza. Katie sat in the arm-chair at the north-east corner, watching the sunset, as I did. It was so beautiful that I paused at the north-west corner; and the dear wife got up, and slowly and feebly walked the length of the piazza, to take a seat on the piazza railing, just in front of the last pillar but one. How calm and serene she looked, yet how thin, and with what a far away look in her unutterable eyes, as the glow fell on the face I love better than my life! We spoke lightly and cheerily of the beauty of the sky—little things of no importance . . .

"You have been just the best wife that ever was . . ."

231

September 10, 1893

Doctor Bullard has been giving Katie eight one-quarter grains of codeia daily, and now wants to increase the amount to six one-half grains daily.

His aim is to eliminate the sugar altogether; if he succeeds; it will be re-covery, but will it leave no morphine-habit? I tremble at the alternative, success or failure.

Today, in the afternoon, I went to Katie in the parlor. She sat in the great arm-chair by the north window, where she loves most to sit when she sews, and I sat opposite by the fireplace.

October 18, 1893

A beautiful October day—my Katie's 54th birthday. We are alone in the house and breakfasted at 8:30. She has not been well in the past few days. At 3, I went to Gwynne's, got a horse and buggy, and took Katie to drive around Fresh Pond [Cambridge]. This she enjoyed, but got tired in an hour. I got her some hot roasted chestnuts at the Square, hoping to tempt her appetite. I ache all through to see how thin she has grown, and how feeble she is. It seems as if I were entering the rapids at Niagara—my darling is passing, passing, passing . . .

October 19, 1893

My dear wife is losing ground rapidly in the past few days. She is getting emaciated, and the lines in her beloved face are getting piteous to see. Her appetite fails, her mouth is painfully dry, and a drowsiness begins to appear which shows that the codeia no longer does its work as it should, but must be reduced in dose, as Dr. Bullard said. Dr. Wesselhoeft will not be back from Chicago till Saturday night. I wish I knew what to do about medical advice. But I fear none would be of much avail. The load of secret distress, which I must not show to her, is heavy on my soul. If it be Thy will may the cup pass from me, O thou eternal Love!

October 20, 1893

Tonight after tea, kneeling before her in her own arm-chair, I asked Katie if she loved me as well as she did in our first days of engagement and, throwing her arms around my back, she kissed me and said,

"Yes, better, far better."

"So I love you; and you have been just the best wife that ever was."

"And you," she replied with tears in her eyes, "have been as good and true as any mortal could be."

Then my own eyes ran over as I said,

"Thank you for that; I shall live in the strength of that meat many days. You did not really mean what you said last winter, that 'our marriage has been a failure'?"

I cannot leave unexplained to my children those seemingly awful words, "Our marriage has been a failure!"—as if it were my lost darling's verdict on our holy wedded love of thirty-four years. It would kill me to believe that she really thought that!

Some time last winter—I cannot now fix the day—Katie came into the study, where I was lying on the green lounge, in the evening after dinner. She looked sad and sorrowful (I could not guess why), and, standing by the register, she began to talk to me as if she were trying, poor thing, to throw off some load upon her heart. I was distressed, bewildered, confused. Suddenly, as I was struggling to make out her meaning, those dreadful words fell distinctly from her lips and burned into my soul like molten lead:

"Our marriage has been a failure."

"Oh my God, darling!" I gasped.

"I mean," she said, in a tone of hopeless misery that filled me with dismay, anguish, and measureless compassion for my somehow suffering darling, "I mean that, ever since your mother died, your depression—" those words, I clearly recall, but what more she said I did not then understand and do not now remember. The words I heard raised a whirlwind of emotions in my soul. My long, suppressed agony of ten years—my fierce struggle to consume my own smoke, keep my grief to myself, not poison my home's happiness with my own intolerable woe in Mother's death—my pity for my poor sick wife, who was too feeble to help me bear my pain without overtaxing her own already overtaxed nervous energy—my feeling that I could not, if I tried, utter my fathomless loss to living spirit less than infinite—all these things came rushing like a waterfall through my mind; and somehow, with my dear wife standing there, and seeming to find some dreadful sin against her precious love in the bare fact of my ten years misery, I was confounded with an incomprehensible sense of guilt towards her. I ought to have been happy all those years; I ought to have found her love enough to

"You have been just the best wife that ever was . . ."

233

extinguish even that sorrow; I ought not to have been wretched, even in my Mother's death, so long as my own dear wife was living at my side,—this seemed to be the burden of that awful accusation that "our marriage has been a failure."

What we said further, I hardly know; I remember saying,

"If ever a man made a solemn vow in all sincerity, or ever strove, his life through, to redeem it in his conduct, it was I when, on our marriage day, I inwardly vowed to do all I could to make you happy."

"Yes," she answered, "and so did I; yet you have not been happy."

And so I somehow got the notion that my unhappiness in Mother's death was my sin against my living wife. What could I do? I felt guilty of the charge—I had been unhappy when I ought to have been happy; I could not deny the fact, nor clear myself of the sin. No wonder that I was powerless to dispel my poor little darling's misery at finding her utmost efforts fail to make me happy. No wonder that, at last, I had to let her go upstairs to bed, with that piteous look of hopeless sorrow still on her face.

But, when she had gone, I could not bear it. I followed her up very soon. I took her in my arms, I rained kisses on her weeping eyes, I caressed her with every tendered endearment, I poured out my love in words of passionate tenderness, I fairly overwhelmed her doubt and grief with assurances that our marriage had been no failure, thank God! But all that the truest union of hearts and hands ever made could possibly have been. And so, in peace and love, at last, she sobbed herself to sleep in my arms, and was soothed into rest of body and soul.

But, all the while, those dreadful words she had let fall remained unrecalled. They oppressed me day and night ever after. I could not drive them from my mind. If she herself did not someday freely and fully unsay them, I knew I should have no peace, but hear them echoing and reechoing in tones of despair while I lived. How I longed to hear her say it was all a dreadful mistake—that so complex is our human lot, no one can ever "make" another "happy," beyond the power of outside sorrow to stab the heart! Again and again did I think to re-open that sad talk of ours, and lead her to see and say that our marriage, as indeed I knew it to be, was one of God's divinest successors in the world. Alas, I did not dare to!

What if she should reaffirm her despondent words, and utter them again? That would drive me to despair. So I let the months glide by, and still she had not laid this spectre to rest—had not unsaid the terrible words that so preyed upon me. Should I ever dare?

What it was that taught me, in that blessed twentieth of October, to seize this my last chance of winning my acquittal from her own dear lips, who shall say? I did not know how to bring that talk back to her memory without re-opening the old wound afresh, and drawing on myself, perhaps, a renewal of that awful verdict. I am not superstitious—believe in no special providence—believe only in the universal providence, equal and impartial to all. Yet I believe so reverently in this universal providence of God, that I believe He, in his infinite mercy, moved my suffering soul to improve this last possible chance of ever hearing my acquittal from her beloved lips, that I was taught how to speak aright. As I stood before the fire, looking at the thin, worn, placid face of her I loved better than my own soul, and knew I must someday, not far-distant, lose it out of my earthly sight forever (though I did not dream the agonizing parting was so near), the impulse seized me to speak then and there, and stake my all on the issue. A divine courage of love irradiated my soul. I stepped forward, kneeled before her as she sat in her dear father's chair, put my arms around her, and looked up appealingly into the dear, sweet, wonderful eyes into which I never looked for love in vain.

"Do you love me, my darling, as well as you loved me in the first days of our engagement?"

Quick as light, she threw her arms about my neck, leaned her dear hand on my shoulder, and said with unutterable love in every tone,

"O Frank, yes! Better, far better!"

"So do I love you! And you have been just the best wife that ever was!"

Then she raised her head with eyes full of tears, and kissed me, and uttered words that thrilled me with joy too deep for this world:

"And you have been as good as ever a mortal could be!"

There, thanks to the merciful Father of us all, I put my trembling question, hardly daring to trust my voice,

"Thank you for that! I shall live in the strength of that meat many days. You did not really mean what told me last winter, that 'our marriage has been a failure'?"

Nothing could express the tone of sweet contrition, of unfaltering assurance of deathless love, as she said emphatically and slowly,

"You have been just the best wife that ever was . . ."

"No—I didn't, I didn't!"

It was enough! The stone rolled away from the sepulchre, and Peace issued out of the tomb.

"I knew you didn't. You were only sick and tired. Never was a marriage more successful, for we love still—love just as we loved in those dear days when we gave ourselves to each other." And we kissed, O how long and tenderly!

Three days later, when I paced up and down in our chamber beside her austerely silent form, how I fell upon my knees in an agony before God, and thanked Him, with a gratitude even stronger than the agony, that He had inclined my heart to speak.

"She has said it! She has unsaid what it was the second death to believe!"

O my darling, lost to me forever while this life shall last, I bless you for granting me this boon of a divine memory in the very house of tears. You did not carry that crushing accusation to the judgment seat of God, but spoke me free from it with your mortal breath here below.

Not till I told this story to my beloved sons, did I learn the real meaning of that seeming accusation. She had confided to them her grief—had explained it to them as she failed to explain it to me. It was not, after all, that I was unhappy, but that I kept my unhappiness from her who longed to comfort me, and that I seemed to her poor yearning, loving spirit to be thus growing away from her—this was her grief. It was love's reason still—it was no accusation, but pure unselfish sorrow that I would not lean on her for the comfort she longed to give. O pathos of our human life, the limitation of our finite insight! I tried to suffer alone that I might spare her feeble form, her poor, exhausted, outworn nervous system; yet I failed to cheat her loving eyes, and she suffered because I would not make her suffer, too! O divine love of womanhood, anxious only to bless at all costs to itself!

October 21, 1893

Katie's attack. "I hate to leave you all alone, darling," I said to Katie as I left; but she smiled and said she should do very well.

Coming home at 8:30, I sat down to read. But I heard a noise upstairs before 10 that alarmed me. I rushed up to find Katie vomiting in the bathroom. In terror, I found this was the third time since her tea. She grew worse, and at last had great pain. I wanted to go for the Doctor and at last she consented. Dr. Swan was not at home, and I got Dr. Vaughn. Returning, Katie was in great distress—she said she had taken no codeia today at all. Dr. Vaughn gave her 1 gram, waited an hour, and gave her ½ gram more. At 3 o'clock in the morning he left, and I am sitting up to see if she needs more at 3:30 A.M. The end draws near.

October 22, 1893

The last sleep of coma. What a night of agony! I gave Katie the ½ gram at about 3:30 o'clock. Her distress was piteous to see—it wrung my very soul. The codeia did not all stop her pain . . . and I could afford no relief. At last, after 4, she began to struggle out of bed, declaring she wanted to lie on the sofa. So I helped her there; but she could not speak plain, she grew incoherent, her eyes opened like those of a hunted animal, she did not even recognize me. When she opened her eyes, sitting up on the sofa, she certainly knew she was dying—I shall never forget the look of love she gave me. Then she tried to speak—I put my ear close to her mouth, but could not understand. Then she raised herself a little, threw herself forward, and laid her dear head on my shoulder. It was her last good-bye. O my God! So restless, poor child, she became that I had to take her up bodily and carry her back to her own bed. Here she lay gently enough. I thought the codeia was working at last. She seemed pretty still until about 5 and breathed heavily and regularly. Thinking she was going to be better when she awoke, at 7 o'clock I laid down, my clothes on, by her side, and slept till 9, when Maggie roused me to announce Dr. Vaughn. He cast a glance at Katie.

"That is not codeia," he exclaimed, "that is coma; she will never come out of it."

I had got Maggie to go for Stanley at 6 A.M. Now I got Dr. Vaughn to telegraph for Everett. Emily came with Abbot [Vaughn, her husband]. Stanley brought Miss Gage, a nurse. I sat all day by Katie's unconscious form, holding her hands, in misery beyond words. At night, Stanley returned from the Hospital with Miss Penfold, a new nurse. Poor Stanley and I tried to comfort each other—but sorrow would not be comforted. We sat most of the time by Katie. To see her life ebbing away in unconsciousness—it was to weep in spite of ourselves.

"You have been just the best wife that ever was . . ."

———

I slept on a mattress, without undressing, so as to be ready at a moment's call, and lay down at midnight, charging the nurse to call me at the slightest change.

October 23, 1893

My darling dies. Miss Penfold roused me at 6 A.M. saying that "Mrs. Abbot was plainly feebler, and I had better come." I rose at once, and summoned Stanley, and we sat beside the dear unconscious one. She lay beautiful and peaceful, just breathing at regular intervals. Stanley went about from time to time on errands. Suddenly, as I sat holding my darling's passive fingers that had once done so much active work for me and mine, and pouring out my soul in agonized watching of the sweet face I love beyond all in the world, I saw the breathing had stopped. I called to Stanley—he rushed in to my side. I pointed—I could not speak. He assented. This was 7:40. Two or three times the mouth opened, as if to breathe; then all was motionless. This was death. My Katie is dead, and I am a wretched and desolate man.

Stanley and I went down to the parlor. We watched for Fanny and Evie at every car. Poor Evie came about 8:15—just too late to see his mother's last breath. Fanny is detained on her train, we hear, and will not be here until evening.

Dr. Vaughn and Dr. Wesselhoeft, the undertakers and the nurses, the comings and the goings and the writing of notes and so forth,—all those things have been before me in a dream. I am paralyzed. How can I live—how can I go on? O my heart's love, would God I could be buried with you in one grave.

What a sad homecoming poor Fanny has had! Stanley met her at the station in Boston with a coupe and gently broke the news to her on the way. About 9 o'clock, I heard the wails—the poor girl rushed in sobbing and quivering into my arms—it seemed as if her heart was breaking. I sat down in her dear Mother's chair, took her in my lap, and talked to her softly and lovingly (God knows how I did it), till in half an hour she was soothed and quieted and saw the merciful side to her mother and to us in this awfully sudden bereavement. My happiness ended with her life.

October 24, 1893

Yesterday, I went alone to my own room, where my motionless Katie lies, and had one sacred and secret hour of sorrow. O those cold lips, that never before omitted to return my loving kiss! The undertakers came and I had to go. Now the pale face is enclosed, oh so lovely to me! I took poor Maggie and Annie in, who loved their gentle mistress, and said so,

"She was always so kind to us," said Maggie, "how lovely she is!"

Ethel and May, Luly Nichols, Emery Brooks, Helen Bangs, came, besides Emily and Abbot; and poor Sue Loring, too. I am sick of faces—I want solitude—why am I made to talk so much? I locked myself in Katie's room for an hour. How peaceful, sweet, yet austerely unapproachable! How near—how infinitely far! O my gentle one, my faithful, tender one, this night I will keep my watch with thee alone!

Our old helper, Matilda Brown, returning with a niece from New Brunswick, came to the door to call on her old mistress, saw the crepe in dismay, and went to the rear to find her dead. I went down to see poor Matilda, and took her upstairs to see the calm sweet face.

"O you darling!" sobbed out Matilda, and she hid her tears in her handkerchief. The love she expressed was touching indeed. I gave her Katie's lovely picture of 1870. No one more deserves or better appreciates it.

And now begins the last night but one that my darling sleeps beneath the rooftree of her home—the home that she has made happy. The last night that she and I shall ever sleep in the same chamber, save one. I go to lay my tired head and aching heart beside her.

October 25, 1893

I slept last night in the chamber where Katie slept more soundly still. But I did not undress—I lay down on the bed as I was. At seven I rose. Emmie and Abbot came right after breakfast. Letters, messages, telegrams, cards with flowers, came all day—my darling had more friends than she and I knew. Annie Morrison came with white pinks and maiden hair; Lizzie Storer sent chrysanthemums; I cannot tell all.

"You have been just the best wife that ever was . . ."

. . . After lunch, I took Fanny to gaze with me on her blessed mother's face, and I pledged her my utmost efforts to be father and mother in one.

"Let us resolve here, by her side, to be all in all to each other, and not shut up our sorrow in silence, but love one another to the end of all."

"For her sake," said the dear daughter in a tearful whisper.

"Yes, for her sake, for her sake," I said with all my soul. And we kissed and embraced with tears.

Night—the last night forever with my own wedded wife of thirty-four years, the angel in my house and in my heart. Never more forever will that sweet face be with me beneath my roof by night or day. I must live and love her all alone. By God's eternal love, be still my guardian angel, O my Katie, even as you have always been. My heart is breaking till I taste your blessed love once more.

October 26, 1893

The Last Farewell. A most lovely, sunny day. I paced the room till midnight—lay down in my clothes—woke at 3 and gazed over the dear face once more—slept an hour or more, and rose at 6. Tasted breakfast. The study was overflowing with flowers sent by friends— Every vase in the house was more than filled. The casket was set in the bay window, amidst the potted plants she tended daily with loving care. Emmie and Fanny and Susie arranged the flowers in it—Fanny set lilies of the valley by the sweet head, and I laid a loose handful of violets on the dear bosom that never ceased till now to throb for me. She was lovely in her last repose, my own precious wife.

At 10 the house was filled with friends . . . I sat in Katie's chair at her feet, and the three children at my side in the green lounge; we had stood together before at her head and kissed the cold, white brow—I conquered my agony as I could for their dear sakes.

We took the train at 12:40, drove to the cemetery and alighted. The casket was laid on the sod, and the holy calm of that blessed face was once more then to be seen. All was still.

"Do you want one last kiss?" I whispered to Fanny at my side. She bent and touched her lips to the brow. I waited for the boys, but they did not stoop. Then, as the warm sunlight lay on the beloved form, I kneeled and kissed the forehead and the sweet, soft lips, cold as they were, in one long, lingering pressure, and all was over.

"Cover it up," I whispered to the sexton at my elbow and he did. We laid all our flowers in the closed casket. I took Fanny's arm, we four retired to our carriage. We had said farewell forever. The long ride home ended at last. We entered with tears the desolate house, where our good girls had brought perfect order.

November 5, 1893

Stanley and I sadly watched the lovely sunset in my upstairs study tonight, in memory of her who so loved to do it with us. It was an hour of tender communion in sorrow.

November 6, 1893

57 years old. For the first time in 37 years, I had no greeting of tender love from this wife of my bosom, and my heart is all tears. I went to my cabinet, took out the two rings I gave her years ago, which were always on the third finger of her dear hand, and hung them on my watch-chain, worn under my waist-coat. These shall be her present to me . . .

Night—as the sun was setting with a glorious glow in the west, I went up to our chamber alone, sat down in the little sewing-rocking chair she best loved and did so much patient work for me in, and watched with streaming eyes the beauty of a sunset which would have filled her gentle spirit with joy. Slowly it faded into the deeper darkness of the night—just as she faded in beauty out of my life. . . .

November 8, 1893

Katie's grave. I rose at 6, breakfasted at 6½, took the car at 7¼ & drove in a carriage to Commercial Wharf, where the *Cumberland* lay bound for St. John's, N.B., to bid farewell to dear old Matilda Brown. She was in the ladies' cabin. Here her face lighted up at seeing me! It evidently touched her deeply that I came to say goodbye.

"No other gentleman where I have served," she said, "has ever come to see me off."

She spoke most lovingly of Katie.

"You have been just the best wife that ever was . . ."

———

241

"She was always so kind! If a storm threatened, she would send me home before it broke, but other people always kept me to the last minute of my time."

I saw she had broken the handle of her traveler's bag, and taking a string out of my pocket, I carefully tied it up for her. This moved her greatly.

"I'll never take that string off," she declared.

The bell rang. I had to go. And so, I have said my last goodbye to this dear old soul, who loved my mother and my wife. She will never come again. I charged her again to let me know if she ever wanted money—she said she would, God be with her.

I walked through South Market Street, Quincy Market, and Faneuil Hall to Tremont Street, where I bought a beautiful wreath of white immortelles. Took the 10 train to Beverly, and went to the cemetery, and laid the wreath on my darling's grave. After a while, I walked to Salem; went to Frankland's marble works, and ordered a stone with the inscription:

"Katharine F. Loring, wife of Francis E. Abbot. Born at Concord, Mass., Oct. 18, 1839. Died at Cambridge, Mass., Oct. 23, 1893. She made home happy, and was all the world to her own."

November 9, 1893

I tried this forenoon to resume my work, but the dear face, with its wonderful, sweet, appealing eyes, shone between me and the papers, and melted my heart to tears. Again and again I sought to forget any sorrow and do my work; I could only throw down my pen and pace the room, while a whirlwind of agony swept over my soul.

December 30, 1893

With streaming tears I have been reading over Katie's letters since December, 1885. The last words she ever wrote to me were:

"Love and kisses to your heart's desire from Your loving Katie."

And I dare to live after such a loss! My heart is breaking.

PART VI

"I fly to memory . . ."

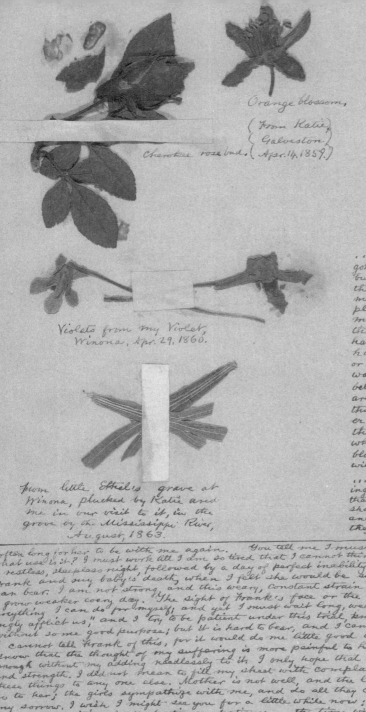

Orange blossom,

(From Katie,)
(Galveston)
(Apr. 14, 1859.)

Cherokee rose bud.

Violets from my Violet,
Winona, Apr. 29, 1860.

From little Ethel's grave at
Winona, plucked by Katie and
me in our visit to it, in the
grove by the Mississippi River,
August, 1863.

From Katie, Winona, Apr. 3, 186_

Galveston, March 2, 18__
... I went out to the cottage not long ago,
got a great many roses and other garden fl__
but I found some houstonias that pleased me
than all the rest. To be sure, the others laugh__
me for hunting for such flowers, when there__
plenty of others much handsomer; but those a__
more homelike. Besides, I love wild-flowers __
than those which are cultivated in gardens __
have always been my friends. Many times, w__
have felt lonely and sad, I have gone into th__
or woods and talked with them, and they h__
ways comforted me. To the wild-flowers I ow__
belief in God's love for me. Do you wonder __
are dear to me? I always feel as if they wer__
thing more than flowers, and never liked __
er any that I should throw away or pull to __
thoughtlessly... I got some orange buds too
when I was out walking. I couldn't reach __
blossoms, but I have the promise of some, an__
will send them to you... Your own Katie.

Galveston, April 14, 1859.
... The flowers I have pressed are hardly __
ing; I cannot press them well here, for some re__
that I cannot understand. They will not retain __
shape or color. However, I send an orange blo__
and a Cherokee rosebud, I wish you could __
them fresh... Goodby, darling. Katie. (Copied Mar__

I often long for her to be with me again. You tell me I must take care of myself, and I try to do so, __
what use is it? I must work till I am so tired that I cannot think of anything save bodily weariness, or else __
a restless, sleepless night, followed by a day of perfect inability for any regular work. The separation, __
Frank and my baby's death, when I felt she would be such a comfort to me, is almost more tha__
can bear. I am not strong, and this weary, constant strain upon my heart is wearing my very life a__
I grow weaker every day. The sight of Frank's face or the touch of his hand would do me more goo__
anything I can do for myself, and yet I must wait long, weary months for that. I know God does n__
ingly afflict us," and I try to be patient under this trial, knowing that it is his will, and that it is not __
without some good purpose; but it is hard to bear, and I cannot always say, "Thy will, not mine, be d__
I cannot tell Frank of this, for it would do me little good and only make his trouble harder to bear; __
know that the thought of my suffering is more painful to him than anything else, and his burden is __
enough without my adding needlessly to it. I only hope that with cooler weather will come renewed __
and strength. I did not mean to fill my sheet with complainings when I began, but I cannot sp__
these things to any one else. Mother is not well, and the least excitement makes her sick, so I da__
go to her; the girls sympathize with me, and do all they can for me, but they do not, cannot unde__
my sorrow. I wish I might see you for a little while now: I should feel so much better, if I could __
instead of writing. Well, patience, patience — the time will come when I can look back on all __
row and suffering, and read plainly the lesson God would teach. Till then, may He give me stren__
bear whatever He may send. Lovingly, Katie.

Cambridge, Sept. 16, 1860.
My dear little wife, ... As soon as I heard of our little Ethel's death, I was greatly distressed about __
knew your nature too well not to understand the inevitable results of such an overwhelming sorrow. Un__
come to you, I foresaw that you would suffer from your accumulated griefs so much as to injure yo__
health; and this fear was confirmed by a letter of yours to Mother which I almost insisted upon __
against her will. Fortunately, George Chaney, who has tried schemes of bringing us together which __
told you of on account of their impracticability, heard of a vacancy as teacher in the Meadville High S__
[Female Seminary], a place worth at least $1400 per annum. I applied for this situation several we__

1 8 9 4

January 1, 1894

The days become weeks and the weeks months already—the stretches of my life in which she has no part, no common knowledge, no mutual tender memories, are getting longer and longer . . .

January 2, 1894

Our New Year brought us all together, the children and the father, about the mother's vacant chair. Drifting away from me—drifting farther and farther into the past . . .

January 9, 1894

. . . I move as in a dream. Tears are my meat day and night. The lightnings of death have struck my dearest—why am I spared against my will? My work is all I have now.

January 11, 1894

At 10 o'clock, I sat down to read over in my college journal, the sweet story of my engagement to her who became my darling wife. It is years since I read it—I had thought of reading it over with Katie herself, but alas, neglected to do it till too late. It was half-past one o'clock before I finished.

January 25, 1894

Today—the thirty-seventh anniversary of the day when my lost darling and I first confessed to each other our mutual love—I took the pressed flowers laid by in memory of her, as she lay white, cold, and still in our own sunny bay-window, and fastened them in my College Journal at the end. O the agony of this silence, this absence, this emptiness of home and heart!

February 4, 1894

Walter Page came at 4 P.M. to stay the night by my invitation. I have given him a commission to paint a portrait of Katie for $100 reproducing the striking photograph of 1856, a side view, with a cloak hanging from the shoulders. He will put into his work, not only skill, but admiration and affection for one who was a sincere friend to him. It helps me in my gnawing sorrow to talk with an ingenious and unworldly young man like Walter, who is very sympathetic and full of good thoughts. We talked until midnight.

February 9, 1894

Katie wrote to me this exquisite passage in her letter from Galveston, Texas, March 2, 1859:

> *"I went out the cottage not long ago and got a great many roses and other garden flowers; but I found some little houstonias that pleased me more than all the rest. To be sure, the others laughed at me for hunting such flowers, when there were plenty of*

other much handsomer; but those were more home-like. Besides, I love wildflowers better than those that are cultivated in gardens; they have always been my friends.

Many times when I felt lonely and sad, I have gone into the fields or woods, and talked with them; and they have comforted me. To the wildflowers I owe my belief in God's love for me. Do you wonder why they are dear to me? I always feel as if they were something more than flowers and never liked to gather any that I should throw away or pull to pieces thoughtlessly."

That is the daguerreotype of my darling's innocent and beautiful soul. Such she always was, a sweet wildflower herself, from the day I first saw her dear face in the little brown hood to the night she laid her dear, dying head on my shoulder in speechless love and passed into the sleep that knows no waking. Her soul was the violet of my home, fragrant with heaven's own breezes, and lovely with a modest charm that kept me and keeps me her lover as in the days in yore.

Love has two sides! One is joy and the other is grief, and, because I have had the joy all my life, I blame not God because I shall have the grief till I meet her once more in the other life. But between that hour and this there is nothing but tears.

February 11, 1894

Stanley was here. After a while, I resolved to make an effort I had planned to make sometime, to break the reserve and silence which has prevailed about his dear mother—I cannot bear to have such a wall of separation between our inner lives. So I asked him if he would like to read the sweet story of our first love and engagement. He answered warmly, yes. So I gave him my college journal. My deepest regret is that I waited too long in showing it to Katie herself; I always meant to do so and I have punished myself terribly for not thinking to do it in that last sweet week we had alone together. Stanley came down, full of emotion, and we mingled our tears of love and grief. I took him to her chamber, opened the lid of her desk, and showed him, lying just as she left it, my old daguerreotype of 1857, in an open inner drawer, so that it is the first thing to see; and just above it in the purple velvet case, my miniature of 1872. These she had kept always in sight, treasuring up the memories of our beautiful love.

"I fly to memory . . ."

March 3, 1894

Page asked me to call and see his portrait of Katie again today. I did so, at 3 . . . I tremblingly hope he will give me that soul on canvas.

May 4, 1894

Walter Page brought out Katie's portrait this afternoon and now it hangs in my study. Ah, what I want is the divine soul itself . . .

May 7, 1894

Concord is the Mecca of my heart still, and I shall return to it in solitary pilgrimages of love and grief.

May 14, 1894

Thirty-four years ago, my Ethel was born at Winona. If she were but with me still, my whole life would have been different—probably Katie would be living at my side, for the trouble that crushed her began, perhaps, with her first baby's death.

June 22, 1894

Nonquitt once more . . . I went to Sunset Rock alone, where she went on July 23 for the very last time, supported by Stanley's arm, with feeble tottering steps; I sat on the very place where she sat then, with her dear serene face turned towards the West, watching the sunset glory she so loved to behold, and Stanley sitting at her feet.

July 8, 1894

After supper, as it is a cold day, Stanley built a fire in the fire-place. He put a piece of drift-wood on the fire, and it burned with exquisite colors. I thought how Katie used to do this, sitting on the floor and watching the colors with placid enjoyment. Stanley put out his hand to me—I held it silently.

August 27, 1894

. . . In sheer self-preservation of my being, I fly to memory, that the remembered love of the past may be still the life of the present. Nobody can understand this save those to whom love is life—those who are capable of great and overmastering spiritual passion. All my life long I lived and strove on that supreme love which ever ministered to the deepest and divinest cravings of my spirit; I loved in my beautiful wife the individual expression of the universal Eternal Love; and I live now in her and in it. All else is shadow—this life eternal.

October 8, 1894

Doctor [Oliver Wendell] Holmes died yesterday, last of the Titans of our early literature. Bryant, Emerson, Longfellow, Lowell, Whittier, Holmes—all gone, the poets that shone in my youth, and none is left to take their place.

October 22, 1894

I did not want to go to bed last night—but compelled myself to do so, lest poor Fanny should be distressed at finding me still dressed when she came to wake me in the morning. O the long, sad hours of this night, as my suffering darling bade farewell to life and pain together . . . in the darkening down of coma, her only relief! My whole soul is in tumultuous chaos of agony—but thank God, she is at rest!

Tonight, just before tea, this dear child came to me, alone in the study, and silently put her arm about me. It was her way of saying she remembers the day—and I strained her to my heart. My poor little motherless girl! Would God I be more to her!

"You love me, Fanny?" I whispered.

"Yes," she said, and kissed me with a long, tender kiss.

"And I love you!" I said, kissing her in return. It was the first sign of

"I fly to
memory . . ."

———

249

sympathy from her in these dreadful days, but I know her heart all the same . . . and now it is past midnight—it is already the 23rd, the day that my darling died. In less than eight hours, my loss will be one year old. O Katie, sweetest, and best gift of God, my soul is perishing for want of the love you gave me! The agony is bitterer than death. O my own, my own, shall we never kiss again?

November 4, 1894

Katie's heart-treasures found. It is afternoon—I am all alone—every one is gone out. I went to my own chamber—O so empty!—and walked up and down. Suddenly, I noticed a little black-walnut desk, standing on the table beside the bed where my darling used to lie. I had never happened to open it since she died—I did so now. How my heart and my eyes filled, to find the hiding place of my darling's heart-treasures! Here are the verses I gave her at Nonquitt, August 3, 1875—my letter of January 25, 1877—my letter at Fayal, August 3, 1879—the gift-presentation I wrote for her on her first coming down stairs, Christmas, 1876, after the birth of

Frank Abbot in his Cambridge, Massachusetts, study, circa 1897.

her poor little still-born baby— [and news clippings of poems entitled] "Weariness," "Tired Mothers," "Heart-Break," "Childless," "My Baby," "What were Home without the Baby?" and "After the Burial," that revealed to me, oh how movingly! the many tears she had shed in secret, poor bereaved mother weeping for her little lost babes out of sight, yet always wearing a loving smile for her husband—who was not deceived.

1 8 9 5

January 18, 1895

It was January 17, in 1857 . . . How exquisitely lovely she was, with her pale face, and the rich masses of her gold-brown hair falling about her shoulders, and those great, soft, liquid eyes, already beginning to glow with that light of love which never faded out of them.

January 24, 1895

Today, eight and thirty years ago, a lovely girl gave me a little slip of pine wood, a "piece of chip," and it meant that she gave her heart knowing well that I had given her mine in silence already. All the poetry, the romance, the love, that ever clung to my gift, clung to that poor "piece of chip"—I knew it, I felt it, I thrilled to the centre of my being.

   Tomorrow, soul of my soul, I purpose to go to the town, the house, the very room, where you and I first confessed to each other this love, this immortal love of ours. Thirty-eight years have passed, since I was in that room. Then we were young and happy, O so happy! Now I am old and alone, old and in such sorrow as fathoms, the capacity of a human heart for pain. But love is stronger than age or loneliness or sorrow or death—I love you, O my lost wife, with a love eternal.

"I fly to memory . . ."

251

January 25, 1895

At Concord. Here I sit at nearly 5 o'clock, in my room at the Thoreau House. It was about this hour that I told to Katie my "dream" of the "living flower," and when I asked if it would do any good to ask the gardener—could I then have the flower? How low and soft and sweet was her gentle "I hope so!" O the bliss of that hour—the first kiss from those soft, warm lips, the dearest mouth to kiss that ever was! God gave me then a blessing beyond all power to comprehend; but life, life, life for nearly 37 years of unbroken love and happiness in each other revealed to me its meaning. Father, in my tears, I forgot not to thank thee for it all.

[That night, Frank wrote the following poem]

The Living Flower January 25, 1857
Thick lay the mantle of the snow
Over the frozen stream below,
Over the hills and meadows bleak
And leafless woods and buried lake.
Icy and keen, the Arctic blast,
That up in the village swept so fast,
Rushed whistling through the elms and tossed
Their crackling branches, stiff with frost,
While, shrinking from its lusty stroke,
The traveler bent and hugged his cloak
Yet, blue and bright, the heavens above
Smiled on the natal day of love,
And, conscious of the joyous birth,
Poured seas of sunshine over the earth.

Ah, 'twas not January, but June,
That halcyon Sunday afternoon!
For who that love can ever forget
The hour when first their kisses met,
The hour when first, no more alone,
Two souls became forever one?
Though Winter roar in blustering mood
Over hill and valley, field and flood,
And like a furious demon rave
Above fair summer's frozen grave,
Forever in their hearts shall sing
The memory of eternal Spring!

A gentle girl, an ardent boy,
Innocent hearts of love and joy,
That never had learned the tricks of speech
The secret of their love to teach!
Though their young souls in love had met
Like rivulet with rivulet,
And in the rapture of a dream
Flowed into one commingling stream,
Yet never had their lips confessed
What made them each in each so blest.
Now the momentous hour had come,
Here in the plain New England room,
Where there was nought to catch the eye
Save forms of grave simplicity,
Silence to break, life to begin,
Love to reveal, and heaven to win.

Ay, the momentous hour had come
To breathe the word that builds a home!
Never was a lovelier vision seen!
Soft, pale-brown hair with golden sheen,
Falling to tiny shell-like ears
With curves as graceful as the sphere's,
Delicate cheeks and dainty chin,
Fit home for smiles to nestle in,
A mouth whose sweetness seemed to say,
"No word but love can pass this way!"
And eyes whose moving eloquence
Spoke truth and trust and innocence,
Whose depths unfathomed, pure, divine,
Held all of Heaven on earth may shine:
What brush, what pencil, ever could trace
The beauty of that angel face?
Fair as a lily of the vale,
As slight, as fragile, and as pale,
Save for a softly mantling flush,
The veriest phantom of a blush,

"I fly to memory . . ."

———

253

That touched her cheek as sunset's glow
Touches a bank of virgin snow,—
Sweet as a fragrant mignonette,
Or shyly nestling violet
That lifts its timorous eye of blue
To rival heaven with softer hue,—
So fair, so sweet, in girlhood's dawn,
That gentle figure sat withdrawn,
A childlike, winsome, fairy elf,
Lovely as Beatrice's self,—
A soul transparent, crystal-clear
As is the morning's dewy tear,
And pure as is the cloudless sky
Where Day, out-wearied, goes to die
In glorious depths, more felt than seen,
Of burning gold and palest green,—
A guileless spirit, true and free
From every trace of coquetry,
That knew to please no other art
Than the sweet magic of the heart,—
A form of frail and tender grace,
A pure and rapt Madonna face,
A vision from the upper skies,
A yearning angel in her eyes!

Dazzled, entranced, the boy was filled
With love that every fibre thrilled.
Not moved by every maiden's glance,
Nor touched by common charms, perchance,
In that slight girlish form he knew
The home of all things pure and true,
Of love and innocence the shrine,
The radiance of a soul divine
Whose spell of power is heavenly eyes,
And in divine expression lies.
How dared he lift his eyes to her,
Even as a mute, rapt worshipper?

What marvel, if with awe he felt
'Twas at God's altar he knelt?

Almost had sunk the westering sun,
Ere prisoned love its freedom won,
Or dared the fateful words to speak
That, even unuttered, burned the cheek.
With throbbing pulse and trembling tongue,
The boy, to life and love so young,
Heedless of arts or studied grace,
Bowed in his hands his feverish face
Before the homely wood-fire stove,
And faltered forth his dream of love:—

A youth there was who Nature loved,
And oft in her recesses roved.
Far from the wrangling of men,
He sought the peace of sylvan glen,
The silence of forgotten glades,
The mystery of ancient shades,
The templed calm of dark pine woods,
Where, safe in sheltering solitudes,
Though hunted by pursuing Day,
The shy nymph Twilight sleeping lay.
Oft by the river's banks he walked,
And with the flowers that graced them talked,
As one would talk to some fair child
That nestled in his arms, and smiled,
And listened pleased, yet never spoke
Or infancy's sweet silence broke.
Nature was beauty everywhere,
And beauty to his soul was dear—
So dear he to himself would say,
"The flowers I love should live for aye!"

Ah, in a world so bright and glad,
He scarce knew why, his heart was sad;
Something there was, he scarce knew why,

That dulled his joy and dimmed his eye,
And left a heart that should be gay
To melancholy thoughts a prey.
One summer evening, soft and cool,
As by the river beautiful
He mused alone and void of cheer,
His guardian angel, hovering near,
Accosted him with gentle mien:
"Shall peace pervade this lovely scene,
And yet be absent from thine eye?"
But the youth answered with a sigh—
Their beauty gone, their fragrance fled,
He pointed to his roses dead.
Then breathed once more that pitying voice:
"I blame thee not! Wouldst thou rejoice,
And know of blessedness the power,
Go thou, and seek the Living Flower!"

A thrill shot through the listener's breast—
Straightway he entered on his quest.
Long roamed he through the world in vain,
And nothing found but nameless pain.
Hillside and grove and meadow fair,
Restless he wandered everywhere;
No flower he found that did not fade,
No flower but withered while he stayed.
In vain he sought with tireless will—
The Living Flower was hidden still.

At last a garden he espied,
A modest garden by the side
Of ways that many passers trod,
And passed unheeding: yet its sod
Bloomed like an Eden aisles of eld—
His heart stood still as he beheld!
Here in a clustering group of three,
All lovely and most fair to see,

One loveliest flower unrivalled grew,
Such as no royal garden knew,
Such as in Paradise alone,
Fast by the Tree of Life, had grown,
The joy of that immortal bower,
The Amarant, the Fadeless Flower!

Spell-bound and rooted to the spot,
All other joys and hopes forgot,
The youth felt but one vast desire
Course through his throbbing veins like fire
No need of Gabriel to reveal
What Lucifer could not conceal:
Here was the blessedness, the power—
Untaught he knew his Living Flower!
Burst from his soul one mighty cry,
Grant this, O God, or let me die.
Yet, ere he stooped to pluck and plant
Deep in his heart the Amarant,
Fear gave him pause—he could not choose—
What if the garden's lord refuse?
O maiden, if the youth shall seek
The greatest boon that lips can speak,
If the good gardener shall bless
His pleading with a generous yes,
Oh, answer thou, in this still hour:
Can he then have the Living Flower?

Trembling, the boy had told the whole,
The inmost secret of his soul;
There is no more for lips to tell,
When love is told! A silence fell
That held the potency of time,
Ay, of eternity sublime,
A silence in whose mystic womb
Slept endless joy or endless gloom.
For him, in love alone was bliss—
For him, there was no love but this!

Bending with face concealed, until
Her answer should the silence fill,
He waited like a soul that waits
And trembles at the pearly gates.

At last, at last! A gentle breath
Came floating, as a misty wraith
Floats over some moon-lighted lawn
Or some dim stream at earliest dawn,—
Came soft, sweet, low, a tremulous tone
Such as the wind-harp yields alone:
"I hope so!" That was what she said!
The quivering boy upraised his head,
And gazed into those wondrous eyes
As martyrs gazed into the skies—
Those eyes that shone like mountain lakes
When the still summer morning breaks,
As fathomless as the heaven's deep glow
Reflected in the deeps below.
What worlds of tenderness divine
In those pure eyes appeared to shine!
Yet what was he—his eyes grew dim—
To dream that it should shine for him?
Fearful, with no exulting pride,
"And do you mean that?" low he cried.
In accent yearning, gentle, true,
She softly answered, "Yes—I do!"

Then over him in tumultuous flood
Broke a vast sea of gratitude,
A sea of love and joy and hope.
As if the firmament should open,
And at the pearly gates, with awe,
A cloud of welcoming arms he saw.
Low bent he at the maiden's knee,
Seized the small hand in ecstasy,
And covered it with kisses, while
She answered with a happy smile—

Then kissed, while trembled every limb,
The dear, sweet mouth upturned to him.
So love made two forever one!
Blushed with delight the setting sun,
Over their first rapturous kiss to throw
The halo of Heaven's roseate glow,
And seal it what their fate decrees—
"Kiss of Eternity" for these.

Then through his echoing soul there pealed
A deep-toned bell! He heard, he kneeled
Low at her feet, and reverent laid
Upon her lap his humble head:
"O God, I thank thee!" gasped in joy—
"O God, I thank thee!" gasped the boy.
"And now that little hand is mine,
And the heart, too!" In words divine,
Rich with love's sacred promises,
She whispered low, "Indeed it is!"
Whispered with sweet, unconscious art,
"And both the hands and all the heart!"
So fell that holy evening hour,
And so—I won my Living Flower!

April 2, 1895

Last night I read over some of her old letters of 1867 and 1868, so tender, so affectionate, as divinely eloquent of her unbounded love—
"Goodnight, with loving kisses from the little wife who loves you more than all the world beside—" . . . I know I am one of millions, no worse off than they; but have they the same power to feel? I know not, but I hope they do not suffer like this.

"I fly to memory . . ."

259

April 3, 1895

A little bottle stands before me—"Morphia Pills (Morphia Sulp.) 100. 1-8 grams each." It has been in my desk drawer some ten years . . . I live on now for the sake of Everett, Stanley, and Fanny . . . no words can express the intensity of my longing to die, to be at rest by your mother's side, to start once more in the quest for my "living flower."

August 3, 1895

Katie darling—darling of my youth, my manhood, my darkening age! This is what we used to call fondly "our day," the one day of all the year sacred to us alone. Your little wedding ring, a slender circlet of gold with one tiny diamond (for I was very poor), lies before me. I wear it on my watch-chain now, out of sight of all eyes, and it speaks to me of "that bright August morning" when I put it on your little hand and kissed it, in token of my heart's pledge of fidelity to you . . .

October 18, 1895

Katie's 56th birthday. I waked up at 6:15,—to kiss the empty pillow with tears. I took the 9:02 train to Beverly. I laid my poor little wreath of white immortelles on the beloved grave, sat under my favorite hemlocks and wrote some verses in sorrow and bade farewell to the spot where I will one day lay at rest myself.

November 6, 1895

Today I begin my sixtieth year, darling, but with no kisses of love from you. Before me lies your exquisite miniature of 1870, with which you surprised and delighted me on my birthday of that year twenty-five years ago . . . you had conspired with your own loving heart to bring to your husband what you knew he would prize the most, a dainty, soft, delicate photograph on porcelain, very slightly tinted, of the sweet angel-face that found its Heaven on my own bosom, and made that truly a Heaven. To me, the beauty of that dear face never faded—the eyes told me still the same story of inward loveliness undimmed, even when sorrow and disease had stolen away the girlish charms. It was the soul-beauty I had loved always the best . . .

O Katie, your old husband is still the young lover, adoring you as the quintessence of all the beauty of this world. Blessed be the day, when I go to you once more, my own living flower!

1 8 9 6

January 2, 1896

I shall leave at my death a collection of poems which have been at least one merit—truth to life. I shall never publish it. Yet I will build a monument to the sweetest and divinest love I ever heard or dreamed of. If the world wants it, it may have it when I am dead.

January 7, 1896

Thirty-nine years ago this evening, Katie dearest, I was introduced to you at Mrs. Dana's, by Henry Dalton. Was there ever anything so sweet and fair as you were then? It was love at first sight, but for all eternity. We danced two or three cotillions together—we spoke of music and poetry—your eyes were simply wonderful to me—you were lovelier than any wildflower that any wildflowers ever grew. I did not sleep all that night. And you, my darling, cherished the memories of that blessed time just as I did—witness that boyish daguerreotype of your lover, lying ever visible in the drawer of your writing desk.

April 30, 1896

This afternoon, Katie darling, [we found] what I have longed for in vain ever since you left me in this wilderness of sorrow—what Stanley and I have in vain sought for together—your little brown silk hood and your little blue silk skating-cap. These precious mementos at last [are] discovered . . . The bewitching little hood you wore when I saw you for the very first time, in December, 1856, only two or three weeks before I was introduced to you on January 7. It was at recess, as I sat at my desk in the little schoolhouse, now a part of the Concord Library. You came in at the door, one bright frosty day in winter, smiling and laughing with glee

"I fly to memory . . ."

———

to meet your old schoolmates. They crowded about you with shout of welcome and eager questions, and that wonderful silvery little laugh of yours, unlike any other's I have ever heard, rings still in my memory as a bit of a divinest melody.

But what dazzled me and bewildered me was the beauty of this wintry hummingbird, that darted into the prosy schoolroom like a flash of light. And the tiny blue silk cap . . . What a picture of the lovely little wife it revives, skating merrily over the ice that first winter at Meadville! How the divinity students admired you and envied me!

August 3, 1896

"Our day!" I hear her dear voice still—but only in memory.

November 6, 1896

Sixty years old today—and yet mad with love as a boy of twenty, ay, as the boy of twenty I was, when I fell so madly in love with you, sweet Living Flower! I love you still as in the dear days of Meadville, Beverly, Dover, Toledo, Cambridge—I have no love but yours to live by, to work by, to die by, and it is yours to the end of this tumultuous but loving life of mine . . . Love—love—love! For you I am still all love!

Later. In tonight's mail, Katie darling, comes to me what may be a veritable message from you—who can say it is not? Anonymously sent, without day or signature, these yearning verses have brought tears to my eyes in streams:

His Wife

I cannot touch his cheek,
Nor ruffle with a loving breath his hair;
I look into his eyes, and hear him speak—
He never knows that I am there!
Oh, if my darling would but only know
That day and night, through all his weary life,
I, whom he loved in years long ago,
Am with him still—his wife!
I watch him at his task,

Katie's empty chair, circa 1897.

Where the broad sunbeams first light up his room;
I watch him till the Evening lays her mask
Upon the face of Day, and in the gloom
He lays his pencil down, and silent sits,
And leans his chin upon his hand, and sighs.
How well I know what memory round him flits!
      I read it in his eyes!
. . . Oh, if my darling then could only guess
      That she is near who died! . . .

    Whoever wrote these blessed words, this thrice sacred message to me
on my sixtieth birthday, God himself inspired them, and I take them
with a reverent gratitude I cannot utter. Only one heart still beating on
this earth could have been the fountain of this merciful gush of water to
my parched and perishing soul. It must have been Annie Hazlewood.
Forgetting her own equal sorrow in the loss of her husband, she has
found leisure to breathe these words of tenderness and pity for me. And

"I fly to
memory . . ."

———

263

you, Katie, if the dream is not all a dream, will shower your blessings on her for so remembering your Frank.

1 8 9 7

January 1, 1897

A new year begins. I am homeless in my own home. She who was my home left me alone in it three years ago. Everett lives in New York, and writes very seldom; Stanley lives in Waverly, and comes back every other Sunday; Fanny is in Tacoma for the winter . . . Of all men in the world, I once had the happiest home I ever knew, and Katie made it so.

January 7, 1897

This day I tore out and burned some pages in my college journal—let my secret perish with me. It was the explanation of my marriage—the world never understood it, and now never shall. In God's heart and mine I bury it forever. O my darling, how I love you! Yes, love and revere! Forty years of love, since I first spoke to her.

January 12, 1897

Tonight I [went] to the Twentieth Century Club to hear Edward Emerson lecture on his father's correspondence with John Sterling. It was extremely interesting.

After the lecture I spoke to Edward. He said on taking my hand, "Why, Mr. Abbot!"

"Yes," said I, "I came to hear you because I have such pleasant memories of you at school."

"And we," he exclaimed, meaning [his sister] Edith and himself, "we have the same of our old teacher, and often speak of you."

His face showed the pleasure of seeing me. What blessed memories of that winter of 1856–7 came up in seeing him and Sanborn! I was very fond of Edith and Edward—they were my sweetest scholars. And the glory of Katie's beauty and love is over it all!

40th anniversary of our engagement, Antiquarian House, Concord. At half past nine, I wrote here in the very room where Katie and I were engaged, forty years ago this day.

I have returned to my room in the Thoreau House. This mercury is down to zero—the wind roars loudly through the mighty elms—the sunshine floods the world—just as it was that blessed day, but oh, what a difference! I sat just where I sat then, before the stove, or where the stove then was, and read over in my college journal the boy's record of that happy, happy day—read it as well as I could for tears. Then I tried to write here, but it was too bitterly cold in the empty house, without a fire, and my fingers ached too much to hold the pen. But I have had my wish,

**Reuben Brown House, Concord, Massachusetts, where
Frank Abbot and Katie Loring met and fell in love, 1857.**

*"I fly to
memory . . ."*

———

darling! I have kept this holy day as best I could in memory of our holy love, in memory of you, the holiest and sweetest soul God ever made. My whole being is a whirlwind of love and grief for you—where can I go to you once more?

11 P.M.—I could not help it—I went again to that lost Paradise, and, at the very hour of our first kiss, I watched once more the sunset from our window, alone. Then I was a boy; now I am an old man. But the love then is the love now as ice to flame. Why am I here? I cannot help myself. This is forty years, this very day, since I told you my dream, heard your soft and blessed "I hope so!" and for the first time touched your dear lips with mine.

I read over my college journal the oft-read story of that first kiss— read it more by heart than by sight, for the tears came pouring from these old eyes and I could scarcely see the words.

. . . I would give the world and all it holds for one more kiss from you! I would not ask you to go back to that exquisite girlish beauty— your face as I last saw it was just as beautiful to me. It is the living love I want, the living and breathing love. That was your unfading beauty! No blight ever feel upon it—it was your life, your soul, your unquenchable spark of God in human form.

. . . If your love could be quenched by death, there is nothing eternal in all this universe. The fierce wind blows cold as a breath from Arctic seas today, just as it blew forty years ago, but what could chill your love or mine? The cold might freeze my fingers till I could not turn the pages, but my soul was hot as Kilauea at the core. I love—you love—we love each other till the sun freezes into an icicle. God is our pledge for that—or there is no God at all. Call me to yourself again!

Well—I have had my way—carried out my purpose—baptized my love afresh in its very cradle with tears of despair—knelt and kissed the very floor where you sat. A fool? Yes—in all eyes but yours! Love was once the blessed daily reality of my life . . .

February 3, 1897

Thirty-five years ago today, Everett was born at Meadville. How well I remember that anxiety, the terror, and joy! I had to go hurriedly for Doctor Cotton, and hunt up the nurse, Miss Hamilton. My sister Emily and

I waited in suspense in the library, till the baby's first wail told us the awful ordeal was over, when we sank on our knees side by side to thank God.

Later, I went up and took a child of my own in my arms for the first time with awe and gratitude. The dear, tender, brave little wife! She had uttered no cry in her agony! So it was all through her sweet and patient life.

May 5, 1897

Pressed flowers of love—all I have.

June 24, 1897

I have been reading Katie's letters to Mother in 1858, 1859, 1860. To one, dated March 18, 1860, was added—separate sheet, beginning,

"Now, dear Mamma, for a letter all to yourself, for no one else to see . . ."

For years I have put off destroying this precious letter, which gives a glimpse into the sweetest, loveliest, most child-like and innocent heart that God ever made. But I must delay no longer. Never yet have I destroyed a written word of hers, for every line she ever wrote to me is the holy scripture of Eternal Love. This letter is infinitely sacred in its guilelessness and purity and white unconscious dignity of girlish truth and love. It is only written with tears of blood that I can burn it—but she would have wished me to burn it, and for that reason I must. Out of love for her, on January 7, I destroyed some pages of my college journal, too sacred for any other eyes—now I bury in oblivion for others, in holiest remembrance for these divine words of a soul that was indeed "God's masterpiece."

"I fly to memory . . ."

———

267

August 3, 1897

"Our Day" . . . I stood tonight on Sunset Rock until the shades grew black about me . . .

September 1, 1897

Last night, Evie and I talked till two o'clock in the morning, up in my tower. The talk grew out of our letters of late and many other talks. He thinks I am "not brave and cheerful"—that I ought to conquer my grief in the presence of others. He says that Stanley and Fanny share his opinion, and that, much as they love me, they and he are obliged to condemn me in this respect.

September 6, 1897

Everett has gone back to New York . . . he does not understand. How could he understand?

January 7, 1898

Memory alone is alive. My world of love is gone, but no other world is real to me. O frail little figure in the past, I am nowhere but with you now.

IF EVER
TWO WERE
ONE

———

268

[Frank transcribed the following poem by the seventeenth-century poet Anne Bradstreet into his diary.]

To My dear and loving Husband
If ever two were one, then surely we;
If ever man were loved by wife, then thee;
If ever wife was happy in a man,
Compare with me, ye women, if you can.
I prize thy love more than whole mines of gold,

Or all the riches that the East doth hold.
My love is such that riches cannot quench,
Nor aught but love from thee give recompense.
Thy love is such I can no way repay,
The heavens reward the manifold, I pray!
Then, while we live, in love let's so persevere
That, where we live no more, we may live ever!

My little wife believed herself a descendant of Governor [Simon] Bradstreet. I know not if this is true; but the spirit of these lines by her supposed ancestors was what made my happiness for nearly thirty-seven years. It was the spirit of her whole life with me.

August 3, 1899

This is our Ruby Wedding. It is forty years today since you and I stood side by side in the minister's little parlor in Nashua . . . each of us vowed a life-devotion to the happiness of the other; but neither of us told this to the other till that night of your last year, in the Cambridge study, when we tried to understand each other's ill-concealed sorrow . . . our love burned brighter year by year.

How bright shone "our day," as it came to us with ever fresh renewal of our love! It glows in memory now with a splendor not of this earth. Your precious letter on our "Tin Wedding" of 1869—your precious words, "You have made my whole life very happy" on our "Crystal Wedding" of 1879—your blessed card-message with my watch-chain on our "Silver Wedding" of 1884—how holy to my heart are their memories now! And now this "Ruby Wedding" of 1899, in solitude and sorrow, all alone!

Love grows mightier than ever in the grasp of Death, but its name is now Grief. Shall Death's grasp relax when I go to sleep on your grave, and release this prisoner as Joy? Alas, I know not. All I know is that I love you now, Katie darling, with greater vehemence and tenacity and truth than ever before; I can no longer distinguish between my love for you and my love of God, for it was God in you that taught me to love, and it is love of you in God that keeps me loving still. It cannot be that such love as ours can perish, if the very idea of God is not an idle fiction.

"I fly to memory . . ."

———

269

1 9 0 0

August 3, 1900

"Our day"! Once more it comes, and a gulf of seven years lies between me and that afternoon when she came so feebly to my tower to give me the little Japanese salt-cellar in token of her priceless love. It stands on my table now—oh that she were here to give me one more kiss! I cannot get away from your memory, my own—you are with me always, go where I may, do what I will—I starve for you worse than ever, and can only go on doggedly with my work by sheer force of will. All joy went with you, darling—I shall not know more till I know I am going to you.

1 9 0 1

January 22, 1901

Victoria, the Good Queen, has died today. With all the world, I pay my deepest tribute of honor and veneration. True woman—true wife—true mother. She has gone to her reward, re-union with him whom she has mourned for forty years.

January 25, 1901

Eden. I stole away this afternoon to Concord, and went to the house hallowed for me by that first kiss of four and forty years ago. Shut up it stands all winter—one of the two great elms before it is gone—did it break from age? It seems a million years since that exquisite little creature nested in that old house. This day shines so in my past that it lights me still on the path to the grave. Those eyes of unmatched loveliness and depth—there were never such eyes. It was no intoxication of youth, romance, passion— no dream but soberest reality, lasting till I lost her. The beauty of her soul outlived the earliest blossom of her girlhood. It was never greater or diviner than on that Friday evening, the day before she was stricken down.

February 2, 1901

Today the good Queen has been buried—not in the grave, but in the heart of the world. Never was a throne so honored by all mankind as hers, simply because she was a true woman—true as daughter, as wife, as mother, as custodian of the home. She has done more for the ideal of home than any other single woman in all of history, and for that she will be loved to the end of time. In a corner, out of sight, unknown save by her own, my little Katie was no less a Queen, in my eyes and in God's eyes every whit as good as Victoria the Good. O that I could say in words what I knew her to be! If I could only say it, in verse or prose, all the world would weep for her.

October 18, 1901

Beverly. Dear, I have been to your grave today, the birthday I never yet forgot, and laid a lovely bunch of fragrant violets there, to breathe out their soul of perfume in homage to their sister violet, and so to die where I yet hope to follow their example. But my hour is not yet come. My great work is nearing its end. I remember how you yearned to see me finish my philosophy, and your wish is still my law—though more and more I see how utterly wild is any hope that my thought will be heeded or even heard. My children need me not—there is none living who needs me really now. Our love was all my world.

December 25, 1901

Dinner at 3 with Everett and Fanny. At 4½ o'clock, Stanley came, and having waited for him, Fanny then got the presents. What touched me most was a tiny copy of four poems by William Cullen Bryant with a card from Stanley:

"To Papa, in memory of boyhood days when he read and explained the beauties of 'Thanatopsis' and 'Lines to a Waterfowl' to an opening mind."

Bryant hallowed by me by the love of three generations, my Mother, my Wife, my Son!

"I fly to memory . . ."

1 9 0 2

"For us—we turn life's diary o'er
To find but one word: nevermore"

James Russell Lowell, "Eurydice"

January 3, 1902

Edward Emerson dined with us tonight—he was full of reminiscences of
his scholarship under me in 1856–57 and he said I "won the hearts of all
the scholars in two minutes" the first morning because, as I entered the
gate and found them snowballing, I joined at once in the sport for a few
minutes. I had wholly forgotten this. He and Edith Emerson were my
only Greek pupils, in Felton's Greek Reader. Simple, sincere, courteous
as his great father, I have always kept a warm feeling for him, and was
delighted to find that he held the same for me. The visit was a most rare
pleasure in my isolation. There is in him the same guilelessness that
made his father truly great . . .

January 7, 1902

Forty-fifth anniversary of my introduction to Miss Katie Loring . . . The
snow is falling fast. Are the years only snowflakes, too? Ah, what they
hold, the eternal love of two in one—that is no snowflake!

May 13, 1902

I wrote a letter to Stanley, asking him to see that I am at last cremated
and the casket of ashes rested on his mother's coffin at the lower end,
that all of me left on this earth may lie at her feet—where my heart has
lain for forty-five years. We must sleep in one grave, as my will directs,
and her ashes must not be disturbed. Everything is now arranged—may
the close not be long postponed. This year is the home stretch—I think it
will see the great task done—then I am free . . .

August 4, 1902

"The Obscure Recluse"—a *Transcript* cutting sent to me on July 31 by Mary C. Crawford, of Charlestown. Was this written by Reverend Edward Abbott? He called on me in June in a very friendly manner . . . he was, maybe is, editor of the *Literary World*:

"On a sequestered street on a retired corner of Cambridge, Massachusetts, aside from currents of conventional activity, surrounded by his books and papers, studious, reflective, industrious, and serene, Dr. Francis Ellingwood Abbot, who a generation ago stood in the forefront of religious controversies of that time, is carrying steadily forward with the philosophical structure upon which he began work as much as forty years ago, and which of late years has come to engross his attention to the exclusion of almost every other interest. To fundamental defects in the dominant system of the age, Dr. Abbot traced that gradual decadence in the moral tone, that social degeneracy, the evidences of which are noticeable to thoughtful observers on every hand. How far this profound and radical thinker will succeed in uncovering the defects, in pointing out the remedies, and directing the race into larger and apter conceptions of the truth, remains, of course, to be seen; but it is comforting to know that one consummate and devoted alchemist has shut himself up in his laboratory, determined to present the elixir of life in manageable solution, if such a feat be possible.

At any rate, while other men are busy in the public, he is just as busy in his seclusion, and some day the world will have an opportunity to consider the result of his labors. For the time being an inhabitant of another world than the materialistic which absorbs so many of us, his return may be looked for no distant day bearing fruits of a severe toil which may well prove to have been worth waiting for."

October 23, 1902

Can it be nine years that I have lived without you, my darling? How have I done it? I have learned what love is, and you taught me.

1 9 0 3

January 1, 1903

1863-1873-1883-1893-1903—how does it stand with me at the opening of
this fateful year? . . . Plainer and plainer does it become to me, as I study
my duty, that with the ending of my book my life's task will be done.
That book—it is the last duty to do.

January 17, 1903

Emerson's Little Pet

My living flower I named you, when I found
Maiden, so fragile-fair could bloom for me,
With childhood's heavenliest graces still so crowned
That earth and heaven appeared one to be.
Yet covet I those years veiled from my eyes,
When you, sweet child, to peerless Emerson
Dear as are ever the innocent to the wise,
Joyed to be made his pet-companion.
Wisdom and Innocence, with equal grace,
Met when the Seer saw no flower so fair
As God's own masterpiece in your sweet face,
And loved you in his workmanship most rare—
Through Walden's Wood, through Concord's Fairyland,
Roamed with his own Rhodora hand in hand.

March 5, 1903

I went with Mrs. Mosher, at her urgent wish, to a "psychic" this afternoon—a Mrs. Hand, 750 Huntington Avenue. She had an hour's session
alone—then I. The woman seemed simple enough, but I doubt her being in a "trance" at all. Nothing did she say to me that was not in my
own mind, so far as it was true. But she did hit some truths. She said
some true things I could fit to Stanley, Father, Mother, Katie. She said

(with no names) that my "wife" died in unconsciousness—had very "bad head trouble" that had long continued, and now impeded her communication—that a very near and close— "spirit Charles" was trying to help her—that she was very conscious to reach two others besides me, one "very far away." It was all of the truth except "Charles"—she had no such friend. I said nothing, paid my dollar, and left.

August 3, 1903

Can it be ten years since you gave me your last little gift on "our day"? A little longer—courage, weak heart.

August 15, 1903

What is life? The wild dream is nearly over . . .

September 29, 1903

A Life Task Done. At a quarter past twelve, midnight, I finished the last page of *The Syllogistic Philosophy*—the end of my life work. Begun in 1859, postponed till 1879, and steadfastly pursued ever since with all my powers—I now behold it done, this long weary task of 44 years. Thank God, only thank God! I have fought the good fight.

October 1, 1903

Cambridge. Fanny and I returned quietly to Larch Road today, after two desolate days of packing. I went to Harvard Square at 4, and got John Ames to affix his notarial seat to my deed of sale to Everett of the Nonquitt Cottage, and got my hair cut, besides getting from the Safety Vault some papers I wanted.

"I fly to memory . . ."

October 2, 1903

Tonight, after her reading *Daniel Deronda,* Fanny came and took her seat by me and told me that she and Ralph had come to an understanding and are practically engaged. I was surprised, for I had thought of this only to dismiss the thought; I had instead feared a little lest she become attached without return. But it seems otherwise. I have conceived the highest opinion of Ralph in the past years, and his successful entrance of the Law School showed me he had ability as well as grit. I told her I was happy for her if Ralph loved her as she deserves to be loved. She was happy in the approval and affection I showed her, called Ralph down, and I spoke to them both out of my heart. There will be no special announcement of an engagement, but a quiet understanding with a few friends. Ralph is 24, and Fanny is 31—differences on the wrong side, but that need be no bar to happiness. God bless them both. O my wife, my wife, why are you away?

October 3, 1903

I stopped at Notman's, 3 Park Street, and had my photograph taken. I know my children will want it, and I shall leave them this likeness as I now am, though I should prefer to omit it. The photograph I had taken in 1880 for Katie is the only one I should wish perpetuated. I want my children to know I remembered them lovingly to the last, and provided in season a last likeness of their father.

October 5, 1903

I am getting the manuscript of my book ready for the press, to leave it in form to print if ever it is called for, and make the least possible trouble for Stanley, dearest of sons. I grieve to leave such a chaos of papers and letters and things to vex my children, but this work is unnecessary.

October 11, 1903

My dear son Stanley came out to spend the afternoon with his old father—how faithful he is! We talked long of the finished book. He said he could not come out next Sunday, as it is not his turn for leave of absence, but would come Saturday. I said I was sorry, as I had hoped he could go to Beverly with me on Mamma's birthday (I had wanted specially that he go with me there once more). I saw he saw how I wished it—and at once said he would see if he could arrange it yet, and he would send me word.

I hope he can—I am sure he will be glad by and by to have gone with me there on that day. "The Bird is on the Wing!"

October 12, 1903

I am struggling to finish up every duty before the last great deed of all, now so near. Fate—or is it Providence that would grant me freedom from my burden at last?—has driven me into a corner. I am at bay. I cannot live on without sacrifice of honor and love.

My life work is done—no one really needs me more—the path of honor is plain, and love bids me to tread it. I will.

October 14, 1903

Fanny tells me that friends will come here for a visit on the 22nd, at 4 o'clock! I was startled—at first thought I had better have the visit postponed. Then it flashed through my mind that it would be well for my dear daughter to have friends she loves around her that day and the next. I let it stand.

October 18, 1903

The Birthday. Stanley did arrange to go with me to Beverly. We spent the afternoon together, chiefly conversing of my book and his future care for it. After supper, we talked awhile in the study—I read to him some immortal words of Lincoln. We had a sacred parting—I blessed him with tears. If he had known! I could not tell him—how could I? Would to God I could spare my children the pang that awaits them. By and by, they will see it is love for them that fills my heart all the while.

October 22, 1903

Goodbye, dear, most dear children! I have tried to think of everything to save you trouble in my departure, and made all the arrangements possible to break the blow. I sorrow in your sorrow, which for a time will weigh upon you. But you will soon, I trust, outgrow it. You have risen above that for Mamma—if for her, much easier for me.

"I fly to memory . . ."

Remember my ten long years of unending agony for your sakes and for my work, bravely born for conscience's sake and for love's sake! God bless you, all three!

"Francis Ellingwood Abbot
To Whom it May Concern
Pay every debt as if God wrote the bill.

Though love repine, and reason chafe,
Here came a voice without reply:
"Tis man's perdition to be safe,
When for the truth he ought to die

"Approach thy grave
Like one who wraps the drapery of his couch
About him, and lies down to pleasant dreams."*

Goodby, proud world! I'm going Home.

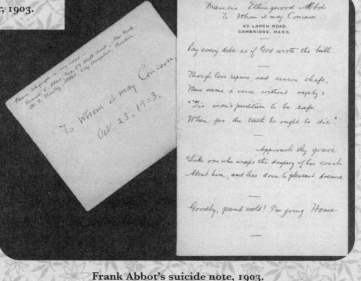

Frank Abbot, October, 1903.

Frank Abbot's suicide note, 1903.

*From "Thanatopsis" by William Cullen Bryant.

I do not fall out of this world by accident as a lunatic. I do not sneak out of it as a coward. I go out of it as a free and proud soul, with open eyes, at the command of honor and love. I have lived through ten terrible years that I might not desert my post. Now the discharge of my Commander has come, and I obey with joy.

The great work on philosophy I was born to write is at last written—not as well as I could wish, but as well as I could write it with all academic helps withheld; and I bequeath it to my fellow men with the hope that it may help them to know God better, and to make this world more noble, pure, and just. The toil of forty-four laborious years is over; I have fought a good fight and my course is finished; I am glad to die.

My dear children will not now understand that this is the wisest and tenderest way for them, but by and by they will. The infirmities of age would soon make me a burden too heavy to lay on their devotion eager and loving and boundless as it is and always has been. But, be that as it may, my decisive reason is honor and love.

My income has shrunk until, though enough perhaps for one, it is not enough for two. For this there is no help. I am past earning; begging is dishonor worse than death; living on my sons is unthinkable. It is impossible for me to go on without consuming and wasting the little I have to leave; and unfatherliness, too, is worse than death.

Nothing stands in the way of my clear duty but a blind instinct of life for life's sake, or in blinder superstitions in which I have no share. The law of my life is reason. I exercise the same right to die which justifies him who, clinging in the sea with a weaker companion to an insufficient plank, lets go of his hold of his own free will. None but the craven, the Pharisee, or the fool, dare question that right.

I thank the Master of Life that at last He calls me home to my wife and to my mother."

"I fly to memory . . ."

279

(Extract from Katie's letter at Crawfordsville, Indiana, March 1, 1857.)

" You ask me when I first _suspected_ that I loved you. I will tell you when I first _knew_ that I loved you. Do you remember the night we sat by the stove, playing with chips, and I gave you one and told you that, when I found the ebony, I would give it to you? I knew then that I loved you as I could never love another, and I knew, too, that you would think me that piece of ebony. God grant that I may prove _true_ ebony! Perhaps you think it strange that, knowing what I did, I should have told you so. But I could not help it — something seemed to say to me, 'tell him so', and I could not resist it. "

[Copied Jan. 25, 1894.]

(Extract from her letter at Beverly, Jan. 11, 1858.)

" I was afraid that you sometimes thought me rather bold, particularly that night when I gave you that piece of chip, but I could not help saying what I did. What have you done with that piece of chip? I know you kept it for some time. "

[Copied Feb. 8, 1894.]

(Extract from my letter at Cambridge, Jan. 12, 1858.)

" You say you feared I should think you bold, when you gave me that little slip of wood. If I had loved you less, I should have thought you so. But I had read your heart well enough to know that you would not show your feelings they were very strong. If you had been a coquette, you would never have done it; if I had been flirting with you, I would not have been pleased with it. You were too honest to do such a thing for effect, and I was too deeply earnest to your love to pout at my own success. It certainly was a strange thing; but, as Kingsley says in 'Two Years Ago,' it is the strange things that keep the world alive. At first I was too diffident to believe you meant all you mean; but, after I got home, I saw you could mean nothing else. You have that little bit of worthless pine to this that I did not keep silence when to have kept silence might have changed the destiny of both of us. And you imagine I could lose it? Do you pretend to wonder if I have it still? You know as well as I do that it cherished among a few tokens of my real life, of no value in themselves, but speaking whole volumes to me, whereas look at them. Only think, Mignonette, one year has gone already! How quick in passing will the rest seem, when they are passed! Today a mere boy and girl, tomorrow a husband and wife, then two graves, lying side by side, I trust. Oh dear my own, own darling, may that dark curtain of death, which must sooner or later fall on us both, when it rises, open the view of some happy realm, where grief and fear are strangers; and where truth and love shall dwell together forever! of us must in all human probability go first to that unknown land; but if we act towards each other as lovingly and faith fully as we now both mean to do, that dreadful separation shall be robbed of its bitterest sting. Hope shall spring for ashes of earthly happiness, and cheer the lonely heart of the one still destined to toil and suffer below. Dearest, let us never have to reproach ourselves with harsh words towards one another, for they bring untold suffering both to the speaker and the spoken to." [Copied Mar. 2, 1894.]

The _first_ letter from my darling, written as she was starting for Crawfords- ville, Indiana, Feb. 2, 1857, and handed to me by Jennie Loring on the same day.

"Dear Frank, please direct your letters to the care of Jacob Winn. The reason why I sent you off so quick was because I did not want you to see Mrs Dorr again. I could not forget what she said to you.
Kate

Dear Frank, you must be satisfied with this without a letter this time I hope it will say to you as much as any of my letters have, and tell you how much I love you. Your own Katie.

(Received Mar. 17, 1857.)

Epilogue

"Love called him . . ."

Two days after Frank Abbot wrote his last diary entry and boarded the train to Beverly, on October 24, 1903, the *Beverly Evening Times*, with the headline "Sought Death on Wife's Grave," breathlessly reported the story of his death:

". . . they found Doctor Abbot cold in death, stretched out, face downward on the grave of his wife. His hat, a derby, was pulled down hard over his face, and a handkerchief grasped in his fingers. Just in front of the marble headstone dedicated to the memory of Mrs. Abbot and inscribed: 'She made home happy and was the world to her own' was a bunch of pink and white carnations, tied with a bit of white twine and which were placed as a tender offering to one whom he loved so well."

Days after their father was laid to rest, Stanley Abbot sent his thoughts to the Harvard College Class of 1859 Class Secretary, Professor Charles Joyce White:

Boston City Hospital, October 28, 1903

My dear Mr. White,

My father's death leaves a void in the hearts of many friends . . . In justice to my father's memory I wish to say that his final act was not a morbid one, nor a *cowardly one. For the last ten years, that is since his wife's death, the life beyond this one had held far more for him than this one has. No one knows the intensity of his longing to rejoin her. But he felt that until his book was written he owed it to himself, his fellow-men, and his God to write it out if he could. That finished, he felt that he had a right to die. Had he felt it still his duty to live, he would have lived, for he never flinched from doing his duty, no matter what the consequences might be. Through the accomplishment of his life work he had earned the right to die. Further-more, in order not to become dependent on his children, thus imposing burdens on them which would interfere with their own proper life-work, it was his duty to die—so he felt. Still further, Love called him. Thus he ended his life at the behest of Love and Honor, having earned the right. We, his children, who gladly would have borne whatever burdens the infirmities of age and other conditions might have compelled him to lay upon us, and who loved him deeply, and who honored him in our hearts, we cannot say he was wrong, nor can we find in our hearts any blame for him. Many will condemn his act. We who knew him best and loved him would not. I hope the world will learn to take our view.**

On April 6, 2003, I traveled to Central Cemetery in Beverly to find the burial place of Frank and Katie. Although the sky was bright, a cold wind whipped over the acres of marble and granite headstones, many of which had been toppled by vandals. I did not know the specific location of the graves, but armed with details from Frank's diaries, I knew that he often sat writing verse in the Floyde lot which allowed him a view of the Abbot family lot. After nearly an hour of wandering among the stones, my pulse quickened when I saw, on a small ridge, the worn stones of the Floyde lot. Across a small ravine was another cluster of stones, some of which had been toppled over. Moments later, I was standing over Katie Abbot's headstone, knocked off its base by vandals but facing up. At the base of her plot was another stone base—which, as he wished to be buried at her feet—I knew to be Frank's. The head-stone, however, was missing, and my heart sank to realize that the monument dedicated to a man who sought to record every waking moment might be lost forever. Then, down the knoll, I noticed a stone that matched Katie's in size, facedown in the snow—I knew this had to be Frank's grave marker. Sensing that Frank would have approved, I turned

*Harvard College Class of 1859 Class Book. Harvard University Archives.

the stone over, and determined that it was indeed his. After a couple of gentle rolls uphill, the monument was adjacent to its original base. Within moments, the late winter sun began to melt the thin coating of ice to reveal the stone at right.

Although vandals may defile the unprotected stones that were meant to mark the existence of these remarkable people for eternity, it is comforting that, preserved in an archive several miles to the south, is the seemingly ephemeral evidence of the lives of Frank and Katie: his diary pages; their letters; the pressed flowers; the photographs created and exchanged more than a century ago— somehow more permanent than marble.

A happy note: the descendants of Frank and Katie were notified of the condition of the gravestones and they have since been restored to their original location: Frank's at the foot of Katie's, just as he specified.

—Brian A. Sullivan
Boston, Massachusetts
September 2003

"Love called
him . . ."

283

Notes on Sources

An almost eerie confluence of sources made this compilation—this one "diary" from thirty odd diaries and hundreds of letters—possible. Whenever a missing piece of the "puzzle" was needed to piece together the story of Frank and Katie Abbot, the source appeared either in the holdings of the Harvard University Archives, the Andover-Harvard Theological Library Special Collections, or from the personal archives of the descendants of Frank and Katie Abbot. The entries that comprise this book were selected and transcribed from the following sources; unless otherwise noted, all items were created by Francis Ellingwood Abbot:

- College Journal, 1855–1860; 1894, one volume, approximately 235 pages, consisting of daily entries relating to student life, 1855–1860; includes lock of hair, pressed flowers; transcriptions of Katie's letters to Frank, and a photograph of Katie. Harvard University Archives.

- Manuscript book of Poems, 1857, one volume, approximately 100 pages. Harvard University Archives.

- Letters of Francis Ellingwood Abbot, Katharine Fearing Loring Abbot, and the Abbot and Loring families, 1855–1903. Harvard University Archives.

- "Glimpses of Katie," 1902, one volume, consists of excerpts of Frank's letters to his mother, Fanny Larcom Abbot, 1857–1883. Betsey Farber.

- "Journey to Fayal, Azores, 1879"/Record of Katie Abbot's medical history, one volume, approximately 100 pages. Harvard University Archives.

- Diaries, 1877–1903, twenty-six volumes, consist of daily entries and news clippings. Harvard University Archives.

- "Canticles of Love and Woe," 1893–1903, three volumes, approximately 250 pages, consists of verse, diary entries, transcriptions of correspondence, and photographs of Katie. Harvard University Archives.

- "My Breviary," 1893–1903, one volume, approximately 80 pages, consists of verse, photographs, quotes, transcriptions of correspondence. Harvard University Archives.

Acknowledgments

The inspiration for this project was provided by the following individuals, in ways that defy description: Mark Levin, Maureen Minton, Erich Rhynhart, Virginia Smyers, Martha Stone, Mary Lovely O'Connor, Terri Messina, Kim Holden, Vincent Cragin, Chris Demakis, Gregory and Elizabeth Buchanan, Peter Fletcher, Steven Safren, William Pirl, Daniel Ovitt, Mark Weber, and Jim McKellar.

My colleagues at the Harvard University Archives: Harley Holden, Robin McElheny, Andrea Goldstein, Kyle DeCicco-Carey, Helene Fox, Patrice Donoghue, Andrea Gillis, Barbara Meloni, Robin Carlow, Colin Lukens, Amy Gray, and the rest of the staff for not only granting me permission to publish the Abbot papers, but for their dedication to preserving our cultural heritage.

Betsey Farber and Sue Kriegsman, descendants of Francis Ellingwood Abbot, for their permission to publish the Abbot papers, the generous loan of their family photographic treasures for use in this book, and their unbridled enthusiasm for this project; Quincy Sewall Abbot; Sydney Ahlstrom, Robert Bruce Mullin, and W. Creighton Peden, for their biographies of Francis Ellingwood Abbot, which were invaluable guides for the editing of his private writings; Stephen Sylvester and the staff of the Harvard College Library Digital Imaging Group for their expert digital photography of the Abbot materials; Fran O'Donnell of Harvard Divinity School Special Collections; Leslie Morris of Houghton Library; Joyce Woodman of the Concord Free Library; Kit Reed of Harvard Magazine; *and Elizabeth Marzuoli of the Massachusetts State Archives. And especially, Aliza Fogelson, my editor at ReganBooks, for initiating the project as well as for her editorial expertise.*

Chronology

1836	November 6, Francis Ellingwood Abbot is born in Boston to Joseph Hale Abbot and Fanny Larcom Abbot
1839	October 18, Katharine "Katie" Fearing Loring born in Concord, Massachusetts
1855	September 30, Frank enters Harvard College; begins his "College Journal"
1856	December, Frank, begins serving as instructor at F. B. Sanborn's school in Concord
1857	January 7, Frank Abbot is introduced to Katie Loring
	January 25, Frank and Katie are engaged
	June, Katie briefly returns Frank's engagement ring
	September, Frank enters his junior year at Harvard College
1858	September, Frank enters his senior year at Harvard College
1859	June, on Class Day, the Harvard College Class of 1859 Ode, written by Frank, is sung by the members of the class
	July, Frank awarded a bachelor of arts degree by Harvard University
	August, Frank and Katie are secretly married in Nashua, New Hampshire
	October, Frank enters Harvard Divinity School
1860	May, Katie gives birth to Ethel Abbot at Winona, Minnesota
	July, Ethel Abbot dies of cholera

September, Frank enrolls in Meadville Theological Seminary, Pennsylvania

October, Frank and Katie reunited at Meadville, Pennsylvania

1862   February, Everett Abbot born at Meadville, Pennsylvania

1863   July, Edward Stanley Abbot, Frank's brother, dies at the Battle of Gettysburg

June, Frank is awarded a degree in theology from Meadville Seminary

August, Frank and Katie visit Ethel's grave at Winona

December, Katie gives birth to Stanley Abbot at Beverly, Massachusetts

1864   August, Frank appointed minister of the First Unitarian Society of Christians, at Dover, New Hampshire

1866   April, Katie gives birth to a daughter who dies a day later

1867   April, Katie gives birth to Gertrude Abbot

August, Gertrude Abbot dies

1868   March, Frank Abbot delivers his final sermon at Dover and resigns from the Unitarian ministry

1869   June, Frank and Katie relocate to Toledo, Ohio

1872   June, Fanny Abbot born

1873   Autumn, Frank and Katie leave Toledo, Ohio, for Cambridge, Massachusetts

1874   August, Katie gives birth to Margaret Abbot

November, Margaret Abbot dies

1876   October, Katie gives birth to a still-born child

1879   July through September, Frank and Katie's trip to the Azores "Wedding Journey Twenty Years Belated"

1880   October, Frank opens a classical school at 63 Madison Avenue, New York, New York

1881   June, Frank awarded the Ph.D. degree from Harvard University

September, Frank closes his New York school and returns to Cambridge

1883   June, Fanny Larcom Abbot dies in Cambridge, Massachusetts

1886   June, Everett Abbot graduates from Harvard College

1887   June, Stanley Abbot graduates from Harvard College

1893   October, Katie Abbot dies

1897   January, on the 40th anniversary of his engagement to Katie, Frank travels, alone, to Concord

1903   October, Frank Abbot commits suicide on Katie Abbot's grave at Central Cemetery, Beverly, Massachusetts

Abbot Family Tree

THIRD GENERATION,
CHILDREN OF FRANCIS ELLINGWOOD ABBOT AND
KATHARINE FEARING LORING

Ethel Abbot
1860–1860

Everett Vergnies Abbot "Evie"
1862–1925

Edward Stanley Abbot
1863–1957

Gertrude Abbot
1867–1867

Fanny Larcom Abbot
1872–1964

Margaret Abbot
1874–1874

SOURCES
History of the Town of Wilton, Hillsborough County,
New Hampshire, by Abiel Abbot Livermore and Sewell Putnam,
Lowell, Massachusetts; Abbot descendants.

Francis Ellingwood Abbot was born in Boston in 1836. He served as class poet at Harvard and graduated in 1859. Abbot exchanged ideas with some of the major thinkers of his time, including Henry David Thoreau, Ralph Waldo Emerson, and Charles Darwin. A philosopher, teacher, author, and proponent of Free Religion, he died in 1903.

Brian A. Sullivan is senior reference archivist at the Harvard University Archives and the recipient of the Harvard University Douglas Bryant Fellowship in 2000. He has spent the past several years transcribing the journals of Francis Ellingwood Abbot and of Harvard College librarian John Langdon Sibley. He lives in Boston, Massachusetts.